SURVÍVOR

TRUST NO ONE

The official inside story of TV's toughest challenge

Dan Waddell

CARLTON
BOOKS

THIS IS A CARLTON BOOK

Text copyright © Carlton Books Limited 2001
Pictures © John Rogers/Carlton Television 2001
Design copyright © Carlton Books Limited 2001

This edition published in 2001 by Carlton Books
An imprint of the Carlton Publishing Group
20 Mortimer Street
London
W1N 7RD

A CIP catalogue record for this book is available from
the British Library.

ISBN 1 84222 374 7

Cover design: Alison Tutton
Design: Ann Salisbury
Production: Garry Lewis

Contents

Acknowledgements

FIRST AND FOREMOST, I would like to offer my sincere thanks to each of the sixteen survivors who kindly gave up their time to be interviewed for this book. To Mary Durkan at Planet 24 I extend my thanks for allowing me to fly out to the island – under a cloak of secrecy – to see it for myself and then hang around the offices of Planet 24 gathering information, viewing video-tapes and generally getting in everyone's way; thanks also to Nigel Lythgoe who offered me such a friendly welcome on Pulau Tiga. Ed Forsdick proved invaluable in answering a string of queries about the programme without losing his patience and corrected the factual errors that crept into the manuscript. Stephen Flett generously provided the psychological portraits of the contestants for this book and was an invaluable source of information throughout. Ian "Butch" Stuttard was always a will-ing, unfailingly jovial source of information, as were the other reality producers who worked with him: Michele Carlisle, Meredith Chambers, Caz Stuart and Simon Tucker. I would also like to pay tribute to the organisational skills of Kevin Reid and

Alice Bartley, without whom this book would have taken twice as long to complete. Dawn Hamilton and Catherine Bradbury were more than helpful in setting up the interviews with the contestants. I must also praise the skills of Jo Wallett, Reshmin Chowdhury, Cara Jennings and Suzi Nealson, whose transcriptions were excellently done and absolutely essential to completing this project.

I would also like to thank, in no particular order: Mark Austin, Christina Sayers, Peter Johnston, Debbie Stammers, Naomi Carter, Laura Vallis, Emma Curtis, Jane Macaulay, Silvana Job, Annie Gillott, Sue Lomas, Chris Barker, Matt Cummins, James Mullett, Drew Zoeller, Nick O'Dell and Jacqui Rutherford. Special mention goes to Mike Arnell for lending me that £20 in Kota Kinabalu. I must add that everyone working on the programme welcomed me to the island warmly and I thank you all for that. If I have forgotten anyone then I apologise profusely. On behalf of everyone involved with *Survivor* I take the opportunity to thank Datuk Douglas C. Primus, the island's owner, and The Honourable Datuk Chong Kah Kiat, Chief Minister of Sabah and Minister of Tourism, Environment, Science and Technology, Sabah, Malaysia.

At Carlton Publishing Group, I would like to thank all those who put in a great deal of effort, most of all my editor, Penny Simpson, for her enthusiasm and kind encouragement, which was always gratefully received. Others who have proved indispensable include Nick Lockett, Head of Pictures at Carlton, John Manthorpe and stills photographer "Jungle" John Rogers. I would like to thank my agent Araminta Whitley and her assistant Celia Hayley for landing me this project and being so supportive. Lastly, I would like to pay tribute to my wife Emma, who put up with wall-to-wall *Survivor* and all the secrecy for three months with patience and grace. Even when I started dreaming about it.

Timeline

DAY 1   Arrive on Pulau Tiga

DAY 2   Reward Challenge: Plant Survival

DAY 3   Immunity Challenge: Fire Spirits

DAY 4   Nick (Ular) voted off

DAY 5   Reward Challenge: Kota Cuisine

DAY 6   Immunity Challenge: Parachute Rescue

DAY 7   JJ (Helang) voted off

DAY 8   Reward Challenge: T-shirts on a Log

DAY 9   Immunity Challenge: Treasure Chest

DAY 10   Uzma (Helang) voted off

DAY 11   Reward Challenge: Wobbly Maze

DAY 12   Immunity Challenge: Mangrove Scurry

DAY 13   Sarah (Ular) voted off

DAY 14   Reward Challenge: ABC of Survival

DAY 15   Immunity Challenge: Assault Course

DAY 16	Jayne (Helang) voted off
DAY 17	Reward Challenge: SOS Signal
DAY 18	Immunity Challenge: Treasure Hunt Relay
DAY 19	Adrian (Helang) voted off
DAY 20	Tribes merge to form Sekutu
DAY 21	Immunity Challenge: Long Stand
DAY 22	Simon voted off
DAY 23	Reward Challenge: Breath Holding
DAY 24	Immunity Challenge: Island Quiz
DAY 25	Andy voted off
DAY 26	Reward Challenge: Archery Auction
DAY 27	Immunity Challenge: Fast Fire
DAY 28	James voted off
DAY 29	Reward Challenge: Bamboozled
DAY 30	Immunity Challenge: Underwater Scavenge
DAY 31	Pete voted off
DAY 32	Reward Challenge: 30-Second Assault
DAY 33	Immunity Challenge: Survivor Rescue
DAY 34	Zoe voted off
DAY 35	Reward Challenge: Mirror
DAY 36	Immunity Challenge: Hands On
DAY 37	Eve voted off
DAY 38	Immunity Challenge: Orienteering: Mick voted off.
DAY 39	Immunity Challenge: Fallen Comrades. Richard voted off.
DAY 40	Final Tribal Council

Personality Profiles

Eve Holding

Home: East Hanney, Oxon
Age: 30
Marital status: Divorced; lives with partner and his two children
Occupation: New Business Project Manager
Luxury item: Toothbrush

PSYCHOLOGIST'S PROFILE: Very gregarious but wary of new people; not likely to give much away about herself; energetic, impulsive, passionate and competitive; assertive, tough and uncompromising; prepared to speak up against the majority view if she disagrees strongly with something.

PSYCHOLOGIST'S PERFORMANCE COMMENTARY: After losing a friend and ally in Sarah, Eve did well to re-establish herself in the Ular tribe and to last another seven rounds; she managed to channel her considerable energy and passion into the challenges while competing against Helang; after the merger, Eve found it more difficult to restrain her opinions and frustrations – a fact which was noticed by the increasing number of ex-Helang jury members.

Jackie Carey

Home: Woking, Surrey
Age: 31
Occupation: Purchaser
Marital status: Boyfriend, Martin
Luxury item: Nelson Mandela autobiography

PSYCHOLOGIST'S PROFILE: Few extreme scores compared to other contestants; more able to blend in and adjust to changing circumstances; still capable of being outspoken at times; more likely to use short-term reactive tactics than an overall strategy; more guarded and wary of others than her smiling approach might suggest.

PSYCHOLOGIST'S PERFORMANCE COMMENTARY: Struggled physically at first; confidence increased with every vote she survived; what she lacked in fitness she made up for in staying power, observation, guile and adaptability; underestimated by others.

Mick Easton

Home: Betsham, Kent
Age: 55
Occupation: Civilian Field Technical Officer with Police
Marital Status: Married, wife Jean
Luxury item: Toothbrush

PSYCHOLOGIST'S PROFILE: Just as gregarious as most contestants but less assertive and dominant; more accommodating and tolerant; usually very responsible and dependable but willing to take on different roles and break rules for the sake of the game; also more tactical and creative in his thinking than people might realise.

PSYCHOLOGIST'S PERFORMANCE COMMENTARY: Voted off thirteenth – a credit to his scheming and acting ability; after considering various options he decided to exaggerate his age and behave in a confused and clumsy manner so as not to threaten or offend anyone; even so he still made sure he contributed to important activities such as fishing and challenges; it worked well, he was only three votes away from £1,000,000.

Nick Carter

Home: Nottingham
Age: 38
Occupation: Pharmaceutical Sales Manager
Marital status: Partner Vanessa, two children
Luxury item: Razor

PSYCHOLOGIST'S PROFILE: Clear sense of duty and fair play combined with a lot of energy and a need for adventure and excitement; reasonably sociable and assertive in groups, but no more than average for his tribe; more trusting and open than most contestants; less emotional, more stoical than others on the island.

PSYCHOLOGIST'S PERFORMANCE COMMENTARY: Nick allowed his physical energy and adventurous spirit to take over; despite his plan to be the "grey man"; he couldn't stop himself from taking charge because of the chaos, urgency and physicality of the first few hours of the game; his knowledge and skills benefited Ular but he paid the price because he came across as too bossy; he played the physical game and forgot the social politics of *Survivor.*

Pete Farrar
Home: Stockport
Age: 30
Occupation: Model/Actor
Marital status: Single
Luxury item: Bible

PSYCHOLOGIST'S PROFILE: Very straight, trusting and accommodating – a combination which may make him vulnerable to manipulation or exploitation; he is just as sociable as most contestants but less assertive and dominant; he has a stronger sense of duty and propriety than most – he is more likely to follow the rules; despite his obvious fitness and strength, the profile suggests Pete likes to conserve and manage his energy carefully.

PSYCHOLOGIST'S PERFORMANCE COMMENTARY: Unlike some contestants, Pete was unable to put on weight before the start of *Survivor* because of a modelling assignment; this and his large physical frame meant that he suffered more than most with hunger and obsession with food; despite this his performances in the challenges were impressive; he struggled with the political side of the game at times when promises were broken or he had to vote off people he respected.

Richard Owen

Home: Cardiff
Age: 33
Occupation: Clinical Research Fellow in Psychiatry; was a GP
Marital status: Separated
Luxury item: Nail clipper

PSYCHOLOGIST'S PROFILE: Physically and mentally strong, well-prepared; assertive, gregarious, very energetic and ultra-competitive; underneath there lurks a more emotional, romantic and idealistic person, seeking adventure and fighting for deserving causes; very close to the average contestant profile except for higher scores on dominance, original thinking and vigour – all three of which are correlated with success in military and management settings.

PSYCHOLOGIST'S PERFORMANCE COMMENTARY: Often came across as serious and intense, as if he didn't want anything to distract him from his goal of winning; when he did break into humour or song it was often carefully aimed at unsettling the opposition; his combination of physical prowess, political influencing skills and chess-like strategy ensured that he reached the final three.

Sarah Odell

Home: London
Age: 33
Occupation: Model
Marital status: Single
Luxury item: Liquid soap

PSYCHOLOGIST'S PROFILE: Less assertive and much less gregarious than most contestants – very selective about whom she spends time with and opens up to; comfortable with being filmed and photographed, but more difficult to draw out verbally and emotionally; mentally and emotionally tough and self-contained – can cope with a lot of pressure; enjoys physical adventure and challenge where her fitness and endurance will show.

PSYCHOLOGIST'S PERFORMANCE COMMENTARY: Sarah was in her element on the island and during the challenges but she struggled with the social and political side of *Survivor*; she was voted off to her great surprise, because she was on the fringe of her tribe; others can perceive introverted behaviour as aloof and uncaring even though that is not the intention.

Zoe Lyons

Home: London
Age: 29
Occupation: Bartender and freelance actress for various corporate training companies
Marital status: Lives with partner, Sindy.
Luxury item: Toothbrush

PSYCHOLOGIST'S PROFILE: Assertive, gregarious, witty and expressive; what she lacks in fitness and survival experience she will make up for as tribe comedian and catalyst; underneath, she is rather more guarded and nervous than her social behaviour might suggest; unlikely to reveal much about herself in this setting.

PSYCHOLOGIST'S PERFORMANCE COMMENTARY: Very pleased with her performance; described day 10 as her turning point when she deflected the votes from herself to Sarah; after that she grew in confidence and influence with each vote; although she was surprised when voted off, she was full of admiration for those who beat her at her own political game.

HELANG TRIBE

Adrian Bauckham

Home: Gravesend, Kent
Age: 22
Occupation: Barrister's Clerk
Marital status: Single
Luxury item: Soap

PSYCHOLOGIST'S PROFILE: Gregarious and humorous when there is not much pressure; impulsive and excitement-seeking but much lower energy levels than most; competitive in small doses when it is important to him, but otherwise rebellious; strong views with little room for compromise; wary and critical of others and likely to take offence easily if criticism is directed towards him.

PSYCHOLOGIST'S PERFORMANCE COMMENTARY: Adrian's inexperience and discomfort with island life in the early stages was evident; this gave way to increasing confidence, perhaps over-confidence with each vote he survived; he claims he was saving his energy for the individual challenges; he didn't get the chance to show what he could do, as the growing irritation of his tribe members over his attitude and lack of effort around the camp emerged in the vote.

Andy Fairfield

Home: Brackley, Oxon
Age: 40
Occupation: Airline Pilot
Marital Status: Married, wife Liz, three children
Luxury item: Toothbrush

PSYCHOLOGIST'S PROFILE: Very cool, calm and collected; a thinker and planner with principles – hasn't entered *Survivor* on impulse; less gregarious than most on the island but confident enough to influence others; capable of leading but likely to be more tactical; physically, mentally and emotionally tough.

PSYCHOLOGIST'S PERFORMANCE COMMENTARY: Became the first jury member – a role that was very important to him; if he couldn't win, he was keen to influence the final outcome; Andy put in effort when it was needed (fishing, building, challenges, etc.) and was very laid back at other times, keeping out of tribal conflicts but doing enough to get to the merger. If Helang had been in the majority, he might have won.

Charlotte Hobrough

Home: Rhoose, South Wales
Age: 24
Occupation: Detective Constable
Marital status: Married, husband Mark
Luxury item: Game of Twister

PSYCHOLOGIST'S PROFILE: A very assertive and dominant young woman with a track record of high achievement; gregarious and impulsive, she loves attention, gets bored easily and hates to be alone; underneath the fun and froth, she is more sceptical, more strategic and more emotional than she lets on.

PSYCHOLOGIST'S PERFORMANCE COMMENTARY: A curious mixture of spontaneous, impulsive, sometimes reckless behaviour combined with clever manipulation of the alliances and the voting; struggled after the merger when she lost some of the attention she had enjoyed previously, and family reminders came thick and fast (her own birthday, Mothering Sunday and family videotapes as part of one of the challenges); recovered well and began to influence the voting in the new tribe just as she had in Helang.

James Stroud

Home: London
Age: 40
Occupation: Runs a property developing company
Marital status: Married, wife Caroline, five children
Luxury item: Mirror

PSYCHOLOGIST'S PROFILE: Enjoys adventure and challenge; mentally tough and very resourceful – a real thinker and philosopher who enjoys debate and the pursuit of knowledge and wisdom; values integrity and principles; more private than most on the island; likely to experience some worry and nervousness among strangers.

PSYCHOLOGIST'S PERFORMANCE COMMENTARY: James integrated with his tribe better than he expected despite the fact that he slept separately outside the shelter; enjoyed the island and pushed himself hard in the challenges, but commented frequently that it was only a game show and he would refuse to do anything that he felt was inappropriate.

Jayne Meyler

Home: Steyning, Sussex
Age: 47
Occupation: Fitness and Reiki Instructor
Marital status: Married, one son
Luxury item: Book on healing

PSYCHOLOGIST'S PROFILE: Jayne is less dominant and more cautious than most of her fellow finalists; she is more likely to comply with the rules; she is likely to be more planned and structured in her approach to island life; not very tolerant or patient with others whose approach is different to hers; her survival will depend on how well she fits into her tribe and how well she puts up with behaviour which doesn't meet her standards and expectations.

PSYCHOLOGIST'S PERFORMANCE COMMENTARY: Jayne's fitness and experience of competitive sport were evident in the challenges but this was not enough; she was voted off because she voiced her frustrations with the young rebels in Helang; also, once it was clear that Ular would have the majority in the merged tribe, she made it known she would rather be at home with her seven-year-old son than serve as a *Survivor* jury member.

Jennifer "JJ" Adams

Home: Barry, South Wales
Age: 37
Occupation: PA to Managing Director
Marital status: Single
Luxury Item: Razor

PSYCHOLOGIST'S PROFILE: Very sociable and assertive in group situations; excitable, impulsive and impatient; more of a hands-on leader than a tactical thinker and planner; passionate and committed in everything she does; strong in her opinions and relationships – both positive and negative; the price of passion is more worry and frustration than most.

PSYCHOLOGIST'S PERFORMANCE COMMENTARY: Like Nick in the other tribe, JJ saw the need for someone to take charge in the early stages of the game and allowed herself to get sucked into the role; she met more resistance and rebellion than Nick did and paid the price when the younger members in Helang, whose attitude frustrated her most, voted her off (before the tribe had got the full benefit of her armed forces skills and experience).

Simon Dunkley

Home: Tamworth
Age: 35
Occupation: Financial Services Area Manager
Marital status: Divorced, two children
Luxury item: Razor

PSYCHOLOGIST'S PROFILE: Very gregarious and confident in groups; usually open and tolerant with others but with an underlying rebelliousness and individualism; physically impulsive and adventurous; intellectually curious and flexible; likely to be underestimated because of his affable, humorous social style.

PSYCHOLOGIST'S PERFORMANCE COMMENTARY: Competitive and committed in the challenges; friendly and relaxed around the camp; successfully straddled the age divide in the Helang tribe; well prepared – e.g. had learned and rehearsed the names of all contestants and their families in readiness for a social quiz challenge; voted off seventh, just missing a role as jury member; the first Helang casualty of the Ular majority in the merged tribe

Uzma Bashir

Home: Rickmansworth, Herts
Age: 31
Occupation: Nursery Manager/Owner
Marital status: Single
Luxury Item: Tweezers

PSYCHOLOGIST'S PROFILE: Restless, impulsive energy combined with an intuitive thinking style; not one to research and plan; more inclined to see how things turn out; easily frustrated and bored; her motivation to take part in *Survivor* was more curiosity and fun than money or challenge; capable of dominating small groups but less gregarious than most in her tribe.
PSYCHOLOGIST'S PERFORMANCE COMMENTARY: The skills and confidence that have contributed to Uzma's business success in the UK were less evident on Pulau Tiga – partly because she was overshadowed by four very strong extroverts in Helang; and partly because she found the physical environment and tribe challenges harder than she had anticipated; although she was well liked, she was voted off early because she was not contributing enough or demonstrating her value to the tribe.

(note: Ages given were correct on 4 March 2001)

Introduction

As Sarah Odell took her seat at the Cultural Museum in Kota Kinabalu, she wondered what she was letting herself in for. She had been selected to be one of sixteen contestants in a game show she knew precious little about. She had heard about *Survivor*'s success in the United States. Indeed, she knew the show's producer, Mark Burnett, from the Eco-Challenges – endurance races across continents – she had taken part in, which he also produced. The races had been tough and gruelling and Sarah had been very successful and had earned a reputation as one of the best adventure racers in the world. Her experience and athleticism made her stand out from the 20,000 or so applicants who responded to press advertisements. But what was to follow in *Survivor* would be nothing like the races she had run before. There, she was part of a tribe, all of them pulling together. Here, she would be part of a tribe as well, but one whose members would tear each other apart. The physical challenges of the island held no fear for Sarah, who at thirty-three was in excellent condition. What did worry her a great deal, however, was the psychological aspect. As an introvert, comfortable with her own company, spending up to forty days and nights with a bunch of gregarious strangers was her idea of a living hell. It had taken her two weeks to fill in the application form, wracked with uncertainty over whether she would able to handle the social side of life on the island, and whether she wanted to parade herself, warts and all, on national television. She decided it was worth it.

But second thoughts were creeping upon her as she sat in the museum, waiting to be briefed on life on the island, its dangers and pitfalls, by two local guides and to receive an official welcome from the Crown Prince of Sabah, the region in which the island of Pulau Tiga lay. The next day, Sunday 4 March, she and the other contestants were to set sail. None of the sixteen had met. That afternoon was to be the first time they had seen each other and Sarah was eager to see who would be her challengers for the £1 million pound prize. It was a chance to get a first impression and identify the people with whom she would like to be grouped. A choice, unfortunately, which had already been taken by the programme's makers, with the help of a psychologist. Who their tribe mates were was not to be revealed to the competitors until seconds before they arrived on the island.

The next person through the door was Andy Fairfield, a forty-year-old pilot from Brackley. He made eye contact with Sarah but went and sat in a seat across the other side of the room. His demeanour suggested a military background, perhaps Special Forces. By his desire to sit as far away from people as possible, Sarah thought she recognised a fellow introvert. Andy was followed by Jennifer "JJ" Adams, wearing a baseball cap bearing the words "*USS Kennedy*", an American aircraft carrier. Andy noticed and, as a former RAF man himself, knew immediately that JJ had a forces background. Sarah thought her confident and strong. She was right.

Pete Farrar strode in. Sarah was immediately struck by his good looks, and correctly deduced he was a model. As a model herself, who had worked in Paris, New York and Milan, she knew one when she saw one. She thought he possessed a graceful energy and appeared quite self-effacing, with little hint of cockiness about him. Unlike the next contestant to walk into the room, Richard Owen, whom she instantly disliked. His eyes looked mean behind his round glasses and she couldn't help feeling that he resembled what she imagined the commanding pig in *Animal Farm* to look like. His presence set alarm bells ringing in her head. Often in relationships the same bells had sounded upon meeting someone for the first time, but Sarah had ignored them, to her cost. She vowed she would not let that happen on the island. Instead, she would follow her instincts.

Eve Holding bounded in wearing a huge smile, looking fit and self-assured. The contestants were forbidden to speak to each other but that didn't stop Eve speaking to the guides – a lot. Sarah didn't like her. Nor did she warm to Jackie Carey, who appeared unsuited to the physical rigours ahead, but had a look about her that indicated she was wise and savvy. Sarah believed she would be the sort of person who would be quick with a swift, cutting riposte should you say the wrong thing to her. Throughout the briefing she kept tossing her hair, nervously. An assassin in the guise of librarian. Richard, Eve and Jackie were the only three to have made an unfavourable impression with Sarah. She prayed she would not be stuck with them in her tribe.

Adrian Bauckham sauntered casually into the room, looking

slightly uncertain. He was wearing a singlet and his figure gave Sarah the impression he went to the gym for aesthetic reasons only. The room was filling up and as she looked around she noticed that not everyone had done as she and Andy had done, and sat apart from everyone else. Zoe, Jayne and JJ, in fact, had sat together. No one spoke to each other, but several asked questions of the guides or spoke out loud, not so much to gather information, but to impress their fellow contestants. Richard, a psychiatrist, though that was something he kept quiet on the island, baffled everyone by bringing up the subject of the first series of the Swedish version of the show. Apparently, he said to everyone in the room, the first person voted off committed suicide afterwards. No one knew if it was true (in fact, one of the competitors voted off did take their own life) but they couldn't understand why Richard would offer up such information, unless he wanted to unnerve them, which didn't seem likely. How little they knew him …

Sarah was not the only one to be forming first impressions. Charlotte Hobrough, a detective constable used to observing people and their behaviour as part of her job, was also mentally compiling profiles of each of her rivals. She claims to have observed every single person in the room – and not all of them favourably. As someone who considers herself a "smiley person", she made sure that she looked in people's eyes and noted their reaction. If they smiled at her then they were the sort of people whose friendship she would seek. Uzma Bashir fitted the bill. Her face could hardly contain her grin. Charlotte's immediate thought was "I like you" and she knew they could get on. Sitting next to her was Richard. Instantly she thought to herself "Erm, I'm not too sure about you." If first impressions were to play any part in voting people off the island then Richard was the prime candidate for a dinner in Kota Kinabalu in four days' time. Despite having a predisposition to people who smile, Charlotte was wary of Nick Carter, who seemed to be overdoing it somewhat, as if he was attempting to forge alliances with his eyes. Already he was trying too hard.

As an extreme extrovert, Charlotte tended to spot others who would challenge her for airspace. She recognised JJ as someone as loud as herself, talking a lot, cracking jokes. She claims that then she thought JJ would be "one to watch". But, again, she was smiling so Charlotte warmed to her. The thought crossed her mind that JJ "might not be someone who was easy to control". In contrast, Sarah stood out for her lack of confidence. Charlotte thought her ill at ease, as she constantly looked at the floor rather than into people's eyes throughout the briefing. Sarah was shy, not a problem that the twenty-four-year-old detective had ever suffered herself. All the contestants stealthily made a note of each other, trying to work out who did what for a living, who was harbouring some secret they could use to their advantage and, most importantly, who was the likely winner. While officially *Survivor* started the following day when the contestants boarded the boat to Pulau Tiga, the game had already started.

The whole *Survivor* story began, rather improbably, in 1988, a good twelve years before the programme finally reached British television screens. That was when Charlie Parsons, who would later set up Planet 24 and come up with *The Word* and *The Big Breakfast*, marooned four people on an island for the Channel 4 programme *Network 7* to see how they would get on. The soap opera star Simon O'Brien, who played Damon Grant in *Brookside*, the tennis player Annabel Croft, a former convict called Pete Gillett and a London stockbroker were sent for two weeks to a remote, inhospitable island off Sri Lanka and were filmed day and night. It was a few years later, whilst at Planet 24, that Parsons developed the idea from a series of short documentary films into a sophisticated game show, only to see it rejected. A year later, however, Sweden bought the show, renaming it *Expedition Robinson*. It was an instant hit and has now been running there for five series. Its success generated a lot of interest from other countries, some of whom made their own versions. One American network, ABC, even paid money to further develop it. Despite this, a British version failed to materialise – this was a time when the phrase "Reality TV" was some way from becoming the hottest buzzword in the industry. Very few people were willing to take the risk on such an obviously expensive programme. It was several years later, in the summer of 2000, after producer Mark Burnett had bought the format, that the game really caught the world's attention. It was shown on another American network, CBS, and was the TV sensation of the summer, a national talking point attracting sixty million viewers for its final episode. A British version had to be made.

The first that even the most eagle eyed members of the public became aware of the programme was when a trickle of adverts appeared in newspapers and on TV in December 2000. Bearing the *Survivor* logo, the ad asked, "One uninhabited island. Sixteen contestants. £1 million prize. Could you be the ultimate Survivor?" Interested parties were directed to websites from where application forms could be printed. The site received 20,000 hits in two weeks. Together with the completed form, applicants were also asked to submit a photograph. Meanwhile, arrangements were underway to mount the massive operation required to film such a show on a remote, tropical island. Nigel Lythgoe, of *Popstars* fame, had been appointed as series producer and director of the programme and immediately threw himself into the process of selecting sixteen suitable contestants to take part in the challenge. He and the rest of the selection panel waded through thousands of application forms and selected around 500 for auditions at several centres across the country, including Cardiff, Birmingham and London. From these auditions sixty-six people were put on the shortlist, representing a broad demographic range.

At this point, psychologist Stephen Flett entered the process. His job was to ascertain which of the applicants were pyschologically suited to being left to their own devices on a tropical island, without adequate food, in searing heat and oppressive humidity, with limited shelter, no contact with home, surrounded by strangers, not to mention poisonous snakes, rats and hundreds of insects. Each contestant would have to be robust enough to cope with such unique challenges and not consider quitting at any point. To discover this he interviewed each hopeful, questioning them about their family background and their upbringing, to find whether there was anything from their past that could affect their behaviour and stability on the island. To weed out those mentally ill-equipped for the stern psychological and physical challenges the island would provide, Flett subjected the applicants to the same psychometric test that NASA use to select their astronauts. The test had the benefit of being brief, while making it difficult for contestants to manipulate the answers, preventing them from attempting to appear a different character to the one they actually were. All sixty-six were given extensive medical checks to ensure they were fit enough to cope with the unique stresses and strains of island life, as well as security checks on their background to make certain that people were who they said they were and that no former axe murderers would make their way to the isolated island. As a result of these tests and checks, Flett arrived at a shortlist of thirty-five people from which the final sixteen would be chosen.

Then Lythgoe and Flett, joined by Planet 24 Managing Director Mary Durkan and Claudia Rosencrantz, the Controller of Entertainment at ITV, formed a selection panel to decide upon the final sixteen. The four interviewed each candidate, then shut themselves away and haggled until a decision was reached. Each had their favourites but the priority was to obtain a reasonable demographic spread and a variety of ages, backgrounds and personalities so that when the competitors were divided into two tribes, these would be as evenly matched as possible. If one tribe was to prove noticeably stronger or weaker than the other then the game would suffer badly as a consequence. Finally, a decision was reached and the last sixteen, plus four reserves, were summoned to London for a final briefing. At this stage, the contestants were also given further medical checks by Remote Trauma, a body that specialises in treating illnesses and injuries arising from extreme conditions, such as stings or bites from exotic plants and creatures. Nothing could be left to chance.

On 26 February the first batch of four contestants arrived in Kota Kinabalu, in the beautiful Sabah region on the north coast of Malaysian Borneo. None of that first group knew of each other and were strategically sat well apart on the aeroplane to avoid any contact. Unbeknown to them, members of the production team mingled among the other passengers to prevent any chance encounters, even though each competitor was warned against speaking to another. This routine applied to each of the next three flights. Security was paramount. Every contestant had been given a pseudonym, which would be the name they'd use to check into hotels, give to strangers who asked and use at all times while off the island. This would prevent them being tracked by journalists or any other investigators. Contestants were met individually at the airport by drivers bearing a card displaying their new identities, who whisked them to their hotels under strict instructions not to speak to their passengers under any circumstances.

The sixteen were spread across four different hotels and were confined to their rooms, forbidden to speak to anyone other than room service, Stephen Flett and Planet 24's Kevin Reid, who would act as their "babysitter" while they were on the mainland. Though the game was still a week from its official beginning, the challenge had already started. The contestants had little choice but to read books, watch TV and brood on the struggles that lay ahead. Human contact was kept to an absolute minimum and for some this proved a real ordeal. The more garrulous characters like Uzma and Charlotte found it nigh on unbearable. Sitting in their rooms with only the TV company, both felt a massive urge to pick up the phone and call their families, particularly Charlotte, who had never been so far away from hers without any company. But they managed to resist, seeking solace in room service and TV movies.

The more laid back didn't mind one iota. Adrian, for example, admits he was in heaven, being able to spend all day in bed, ordering five- star food to his door and with the TV on constantly. This was a man who on his application form described his perfect day as one that started with a lie in and who, after a night on the tiles, would ring his mother from bed on his mobile phone to ask her to bring him breakfast. Sarah also had no problems, and became nocturnal, sleeping all day and watching TV all night. At one stage she was astonished to see herself being screened racing on a sports channel and fervently prayed that no one else saw it. If they knew how athletically capable she was, and how impressive her credentials were, then she would be seen as a huge threat and would become a prime candidate for ejection. Mick, at fifty-five the oldest of the contestants, built an obstacle course in his room, using chairs and the bed in order to keep in shape. Andy and Richard had the opposite idea, stuffing themselves with as much food as possible to pile on weight they could then afford to lose on the island when the going got tough. Richard had been doing this for some time in Britain, adding two stone through a diet of junk food and doughnuts, perhaps explaining the "piggy" appearance that Sarah detected.

That night of 3 April was to be their last in a comfortable bed, with running hot water and decent food. It was not much of a night either, as the time they were due to be woken was 5.30 am. That night they were given walking boots, sandals, a waterproof top and a rucksack. All they were allowed to put in their rucksacks were two sets of long-sleeved tops and long trousers and two sets of bikinis/swimsuits or bra and knickers for the women, while the men had the choice between two pairs of boxer shorts or two pairs of swimming trunks. The rest of the luggage the contestants had brought with them from Britain was taken from them and stored safely until they left the island, whenever that might be. The only other piece of luggage each could take was their luxury item; an object they believed would give them most succour during the forty days and forty nights they might spend in the wilderness. For some it was a functional object, like a toothbrush to provide a refreshing tonic. Others, meanwhile, were more esoteric. Whatever they chose, it was to be their only luxury – though some succeeded in smuggling other, strictly forbidden items on to the island by a variety of means. This despite being searched thoroughly twice; once in an underground car park where they gathered in the wee small hours and then again prior to boarding the boat. A number of "illegal" items were found, loosely hidden on certain contestants, but not everything. In fact, one or two contestants allowed their least desired objects to be discovered easily so their more carefully concealed items would make it through. People can be very innovative when it comes to ensuring an element of comfort, as events were to bear out.

At 7.30 am, weary and wary, the contestants made their way to the boat, still forbidden to talk to each other, unaware which tribe they would be placed in and uncertain of where they were being taken. Their destination was around forty miles from the coast of KK; the island of Pulau Tiga (meaning "Island of Three"). Lying just above the equator in the South China Sea, famous for its pirates and brigands, until 1897 it never existed on any map. Then an earthquake on the Phillippine island of Mindanao triggered a volcanic eruption north of Borneo. The cascade of mud and rock formed a new island just twenty metres wide. Over the next four decades, subsequent eruptions of the volcano and two additional mud volcanoes expanded and coalesced and formed the island as it is now, about 2.8 miles long and 1 mile wide. Since 1941 the island's volcanoes have remained dormant, though at various outlets on the island, small methane pockets form mini mud volcanoes, from whose core a primeval ooze still pours forth with a satisfying "gloop". Legend has it that if you smear your skin with the mud then you become one with the island. Its minerals give it enriching properties. Bottle it to sell in the trendier parts of west London, and you could make yourself millions. It was an idea that entered the heads of more than one competitor.

Ringed by a coral reef that is home to 130 species of fish, the island is predominantly dense rainforest, which presents an ominous, dark canopy to those who approach by boat. In among that thick, creeping jungle live countless types of fauna and wildlife. Bordering the steaming jungle on certain parts of the island are thin sandy strips; the beaches which would be the contestants' home for the entire time on the island. Although the challenge would be filmed in the driest time of the year, rain sweeps in quickly almost every day, drilling down in huge drops as lightning forks across the sky. In a matter of minutes the jungle turns to swamp and all but the hardiest shelter is rendered useless. When the rain stays away a merciless sun pounds down, and the humidity levels rise so much, to around 85 per cent, that even performing the slightest task can sap the strength in seconds. The average temperature is 95 degrees centigrade. It takes days, weeks even, to acclimatise to the conditions presented by the island. This was not a luxury afforded the contestants. They would have to learn how to cope instantly.

Dangers for the unwary lurk behind every tree, under every rock and even in the emerald blue sea, from a distance so inviting, but with perils looming beneath its lustrous surface. Poisonous sea snakes, twice as venomous as a King Cobra, are perhaps the most visible threat, slithering on to beaches to mate and lay eggs. They are capable of killing a human with their venom in five minutes. Rats scurry everywhere, particularly at night where they are attracted by human food and waste. For those serious about surviving, these rats, revolting as they may be to delicate western sensibilities, would soon prove immensely desirable – as food. Chargrilled rat can be a treat when all you have to exist on is a meagre bowl or two of rice a day, and the fishing nets you have are proving useless. Mosquitoes buzz everywhere waiting to feast, while sand fleas and flies swarm around, biting and proving a constant source of irritation. Choose to cool off from the oppressive heat in the sea and you had better watch your step. Stingrays scuttling about on the ocean floor provide a sting so virulent that the only way the pain can be deadened is with morphine. Even sitting down on a rotten tree trunk has its perils, as more than one contestant can testify. Tiny mites are eager to swap wood for human flesh any day, and happily burrow their way into the human backside in numbers. The only way to get rid of them is to pour kerosene over the affected area, which doesn't do a lot for your dignity. And make sure you don't sit close to the fire afterwards. With all these inherent dangers surrounding the contestants, a team of medics experienced in the field of trauma medicine stood close by, ready to intervene should the hostile environment rise against any one foolish enough to become blasé about its testing nature. Welcome to paradise.

Among the less harmful island inhabitants are proboscis and macaque monkeys, flying foxes, bats, sharks, monitor lizards, sea turtles and a vast array of birds, including hornbills, megapodes and sea eagles. The island is home to fifty different species of tree and countless species of plants; while some are edible, others that look almost identical are deadly. Nothing could be more alien to each contestant, leaving behind the rain- battered shores of England in February. This setting, wild, untamed and yet breathtakingly beautiful was to be their home for this barbed popularity contest. A game where you swiftly find out who your friends aren't in an unforgiving and hostile environment. It's not the fittest, fastest, or even the most intelligent that survive. This is no crude experiment in Social Darwinism. It is, first and foremost, a game and what matters is how well you play it. How you forge alliances, and how well you break them. How you comport yourself is vital. Appear too strong or too weak, and it is likely your fellow survivors will eject you from the island without qualm. Linger anonymously in the pack for too long, however, and it becomes too late to make your move. Before long you're expendable and you're going home penniless, with nothing to show for your time on the island apart from a decent tan, mosquito scars and a taste for rat. Scant consolation when a million pounds is at stake.

Despite the rigorous selection process, no one, even the contestants themselves, knew how each would cope with the deprivations and Machiavellian machinations they would encounter. Some who appeared dynamic, forceful and successful in "real life" could collapse under the pressure of trying to survive in such an inhospitable climate, and the psychological ploys of their team mates, while making sure they don't get voted off the island. Others, however, with less forceful personalities could find unknown strengths and begin relishing the challenge, discovering qualities they had no idea they possessed. What was certain, though, is that all but one must go. Even firm alliances forged in times of hardship have to be broken. And throughout all this time ever-present cameras recorded every moment of harmony and discord, every joke and every insult, every cross and double cross.

The television crew, which numbered almost 130, had been on the island for up to four weeks before the game began, preparing for the *Survivor* crew's arrival. Equipment had been flown and then shipped to the island, edit suites had been built, together with the stunning Tribal Council building and accompanying torches, designed by art director

Chris George and his staff and erected with the invaluable help of local labour. The art team had also designed and built many of the props for the challenges, such as the huge figure of Surmanyat Appi, who formed the centrepiece of the first Immunity Challenge. The games themselves originated from a variety of sources. Some were adapted from the Swedish and American versions of the show, while some were devised by Nigel Lythgoe and programme executive Ed Forsdick. While conditions were much better for the crew, they were hardly five-star standard. Few of the cabins in the crew compound possessed air conditioning, there was no hot water and many had to share cabins, up to three to a room. Hot food and cold beer from the "Survivor" bar provided ample consolation, however. The Tribal Council stood yards away from the perimeter of the crew compound. To make sure the contestants had no idea they were yards away from a cup of coffee, chicken and chips or a cheeky glass of Chardonnay – and to add to the atmosphere at Tribal Council – all power on the compound was shut down for the duration of filming. Everything on the island seemed to stop for Tribal Council.

The rules of the game are quite simple: the sixteen are divided into two tribes of eight, each given a name – *Ular,* meaning snake, and *Helang,* meaning eagle. They are then housed on different beaches. Initially, the game progresses over a three-day cycle. On the first day, the tribes compete in challenges and the winner receives a reward. It could be a cold bottle of beer each, a phone call home or a mouth-watering meal to provide a relief from the daily diet of rice and rodents. On the second day the prize for winning the challenge is immunity. The losing tribe, however, faces an arduous hour-long walk in pitch darkness through thick jungle to join host Mark Austin at Tribal Council on day three. At this forum, the tribe must vote off one of its members, creating an unbearably tense and emotional atmosphere. The person cast aside by their tribe is then whisked away by boat to the mainland, in seconds becoming a distant memory while the tribe make the weary walk back to the beach, wondering who's next. On Pulau Tiga, friendship is a movable feast.

When only ten people are left in the game the two tribes come together and form *Sekutu,* Malay for "merged" or "joined". Now to all intents and purposes it is every man for himself, although old tribal loyalties die hard and members of the weaker tribe at merger can find themselves horribly exposed. The dynamics changes, as former enemies become teammates and the opportunity for forging new alliances arises. After the first person is voted off the island following the merger, the game shifts slightly. From that point those ejected will not embark on a journey back to Britain. Instead, they remain to form a jury that will vote for the winner when just two contestants remain. Each new outcast swells the jury's number until they form a panel of seven, who judge which of the last two contestants becomes a millionaire. The three-day cycle of challenges continues initially, except rather than winning immunity and rewards for their tribe, the contestants win for themselves. The importance of the tribe ethic recedes, the importance of the individual increases. The cycle comes to a close when only five contestants remain. At that stage, the challenges become daily and the only prize is immunity. Every night for four days, Mark Austin invites the remaining contestants to join him at Tribal Council until the last two are left standing and the jury gets to consider its verdict. Even for the two "finalists", past incidents can return to haunt, as jurors, voted off the island, have the delectable chance to avenge their rejection. Hell hath no fury like a Survivor scorned.

Week 1

Welcome to the jungle

THERE MAY BE worse places to suffer a hangover, but on board a ship on the choppy waters of the South China Sea must rank pretty high on the list. Jackie Carey felt awful. She had not slept the night before, foregoing rest in favour of a night in front of the TV drinking beer. A member of the production team visited her at 11.30pm to give her a rucksack and other equipment and informed her that she would be woken at 4.30am the following morning to be taken to the boat. Reckoning there was no point going to bed – for the past five days she had been sleeping all day and staying up all night – she ordered beer from room service and decided to stick to her routine and stave off boredom with a few drinks. It was a dreadful mistake. Five hours was a long time, and meant a lot of alcohol. By the time 4.30pm rolled around, she was drunk and when no knock came, she drifted into a drunken stupor.

So when she was finally woken an hour later she felt even worse; her mouth was dry and tasted terrible, her head ached and her stomach – she had not eaten a thing since dinner the previous evening – was churning. To make it worse she was still drunk when she left her room and was taken to an underground car park in Kota Kinabalu where the contestants were searched. A few hours later, as she sobered up, she was struggling to stop herself being sick as the boat, named the *Mata Hari*, bobbed up and down on the water. Was it still the hangover or had it been replaced by seasickness? She looked around the boat only to see fifteen bright-eyed and healthy faces. They all looked liked they went to the gym and worked out. A helicopter flew low past the boat, a camera recording every move on board. She could not believe how stupid she had been. Here she was taking a huge step into the unknown, being marooned on a desert island when the only thing she had ever done before that was remotely similar was a cycle ride from Land's End to John O'Groats. Surrounded by fifteen strangers who all seemed superfit, she had no idea when she would next eat and the cameras seemed to be everywhere she turned. It seemed certain that she was going to make a fool out of herself on national television in front of millions of viewers. She felt hopelessly, completely and totally out of her depth.

But there was no one she could confide in, should her embarrassment subside enough for her to do so. The contestants were still forbidden to speak to each other until the time came for them to be cast adrift on their rafts with the other members of their tribes, whose identity still remained a mystery. Sarah was wishing and hoping that she would be teamed with Andy, who, on her own admittance, she followed "like a lamb", drinking water when he did, scavenging equipment from the boat's deck when he did and waterproofing her rucksack when she saw him doing it. She sat alongside him watching his every movement. Her favourable impression of Pete from the previous day took a battering when he began to vomit off the front of the boat. As she sat downwind from him, something warm and wet splashed on her face. What it was she could not bear to think. Still, she did not move from her seat. That would mean moving away from Andy.

Further down the deck from Sarah sat Richard Owen, who was hardly helping to alter the opinion of several of the others that he was a bit on the strange side by singing to himself throughout the boat journey. At one stage he began to hum the Welsh national anthem, pricking up the ears of Cardiff girl Charlotte Hobrough, who was amusing everyone by pulling items she had managed to smuggle on board from all about her person, mainly from inside her bra, only for them to be confiscated. Charlotte was responsible for probably the most bizarre luxury item. While some had chosen toothbrushes, or something potentially functional like a razor, Charlotte had brought along a game of Twister. She asked at first if she could take a sleeping bag but was predictably told she could not and most of the alternatives she came up with were forbidden. When she mentioned a game of Twister as an option, the production team thought she was mad and agreed to the request. As it was, the sheet on which the game takes place turned out be an excellent ground sheet, keeping away sand fleas and became regarded on the island as one of the most useful luxury items, while objects like razors and nail clippers proved redundant because there were few things on the island that the contestants were allowed to cut down. It would not be the last time that Charlotte would confound expectations.

But everyone was ready – Jackie, and Eve, who had somehow managed to fall asleep, excepted – and waiting to be split into their respective tribes. Finally, after almost five hours at sea the tribes were announced. Initially, Richard, Eve, Sarah, Pete, Mick, Nick, Zoe and Jackie were told they were Helang and instructed to stand by their raft, while Andy, Charlotte, Jayne, JJ, Adrian, James, Uzma and Simon were to form Ular. Still the ban on speaking stood, as the tribes lined up either side of the ship. Then Nigel Lythgoe informed them they had two minutes to retrieve what they could from the deck before jumping in the water and rafting to the island. To complicate things further, Lythgoe then told them their tribes had been switched, Helang would be Ular and vice versa. This meant each tribe had to swap sides quickly, while making sure they retrieved all the equipment they could muster. For some it was too confusing. Jayne, for instance, jumped off the wrong side of the boat and had to swim around to the correct side as quickly as she could because her past as a rower – she counts Sir Steve Redgrave among her friends – would prove immensely useful for Helang as they paddled three miles against the current towards Pulau Tiga.

Salvaging what was on board was vital, though the contestants had no idea what lay in the crates scattered around. It was a case of grab what you can and hope for the best. The bamboo fish traps would be incredibly useful, if not essential. Not as attractive were the small wooden contraptions used for catching less tasty fare: rats. Among the other items the tribes had to grab were rope, machetes, wooden buckets and tribal banners. Also on board to be recovered were one pelican case and one survival kit per tribe. Some of the items were essential in ensuring that the contestants remained healthy enough to complete the game, while others were less so, but could help avoid a lot of trouble, like packets of condoms and tampons. The pelican case contained bottles of multivitamins, a first aid kit, the aforementioned condoms and tampons, water purifying tablets and a fire extinguisher. The survival kit held rice rations, enough to provide a meal a day for forty days, should it be portioned correctly. Each tribe was given a tin of fruit and a tin of corned beef each, together with kettles, cooking pots, a wok, three litres of kerosene, a diver's knife and line, hooks and weights for fishing. Among the other important items in this kit were a compass, mosquito nets, water containers, a map showing a route to a fresh water source, coconut bowls, a lamp and a small spade to enable each tribe to dig a latrine.

Because the island is protected by the government of Sabah, the survivors were forbidden to cut down any of the trees and bushes to make their shelters. Prior to the tribes reaching the island on their rafts, their respective beaches were strewn with bamboo poles and a local indigenous mate-rial known as *atap,* to be used for roofing, to build their shel-ter. A thirty-minute hike through the jungle from each of the tribe's base camps lay a fresh water source, which would be replenished every day. The problem for the contestants was to decipher their map and find it.

Other than what they had in the crates, the contestants had to forage for their own food. Hunting rats and fish was allowed, though any of the other wildlife on the island, such as monkeys and birds, was strictly off limits. If they could find it, sugar cane and tapioca grows on the island, providing a much-needed tasty snack. There is also one edible nut on the island. The local guides, on the eve of their departure from KK, briefed the contestants on the plants and fruits to avoid for the simple and stark reason that some species of plant, and fish, can induce paralysis, and, in some cases, death. Should any of the contestants fail to heed the warnings, fall ill or injure themselves in any other way, a medic experienced at working in such environments stood on alert throughout the game's duration. Unlimited supplies of sunscreen and mosquito repellent were provided for the contestants and all of them had been bound by contract to bring enough anti-malaria tablets to last for forty days and forty nights.

But the island's dangers were distant ones as the contestants plunged off the side off the boat into the inviting blue of the South China Sea. People ran to and fro screaming instructions. Within seconds a leader, for Ular, emerged. Nick held up his hand and announced immediately to his tribe mates that he was an experienced naval diver and, given his experience in situations such as these, he took control, immediately issuing orders. In one utterance he had completely blown his whole strategy for the game. That he was equipped to lead is not in doubt. A former diver in a part of the forces he cannot reveal for security reasons ("but I speak fluent Russian and have worked at Bletchley Park, draw your own conclusions") Nick is also a Falklands veteran and a lieutenant in the Territorial Army. As a hobby, he takes business executives on team-building survival exercises while still finding time to be a regional sales manager for a pharmaceutical firm in the Midlands, a career he started after ten years' service in the Navy. This wealth of experience was something he had wanted to keep well hidden, reasonably deducing that if it was to emerge then he would be considered a major threat and voted off the island.

Knowing this before the game's commencement Nick outlined his game strategy and said he would try and hide his leadership qualities. Instead, he aimed to be the "grey man", blending unknown into the background so as not to make himself a target for ejection. Rather prophetically, when asked on his application form what would be his biggest worry should he be chosen, he wrote, "That I have strong leadership qualities and this may overwhelm the other members of the tribe." Before leaving his home in Nottingham he had spent time reading *How to Win Friends and Influence People* in a doomed attempt to improve his social skills. In the end, he was not so much grey as fluorescent orange.

His second mistake was to lose the tribe's machete amid the chaos on the boat. He put it down, figuring that running around with a machete in your hand was not the way to make a pleasing impression on your new tribe mates. As self-appointed leader, he began picking up all he could and offloaded it into the sea where others could load it on to the raft. As the seconds ticked away he eventually was forced to abandon ship. Landing in the water, he realised he had left the machete behind but it was too late. He winced, knowing that if the others ever found out it could give them an excuse to vote him off. As a result, he determined not to own up to his error and hoped that no one would notice. But he did not brood on it for too long as he noticed that some of the tribe's kit was floating away in the distance and swam powerfully after it to retrieve it. Getting back to the raft he instructed everyone on their roles and the most efficient way to get the raft to shore.

Ular immediately got underway, establishing a steady rhythm to their rowing. Helang were far less organised – no one like Nick came forward to offer their services as leader – and they became confused over which bags belonged to them and at one point nearly overturned their precariously balanced raft. JJ, who had swiftly emerged as one of the more vocal members of the tribe, admonished the others for almost letting their oars sink. As they struggled to get everyone aboard the raft, and stopped their equipment from floating away, Ular sailed serenely off in the distance. A precedent was being set.

All the way to the island, as Helang floundered, Ular displayed the efficiency and organisation that would lead the production crew to label them, "The Germans". Helang, in contrast, were showing the type of behaviour that wold lead them to become known as the "Club 18–30" tribe, an apposite title given Adrian's liking for such holidays. Ular methodically inched their raft towards the island, with Pete rowing strongly at the front and Nick guiding their every move. Most were happy for someone to take control in such a confused situation, although Nick was given a warning that Ular would not be as easy to control and instruct as one of his novice groups of business executives when Richard turned to him and said, in everyone's earshot, "Can I be a Navy diver next week?" Already a chasm of distrust was opening up between the two. The island's first power struggle was beginning to develop.

On reaching the shore Ular were off like greyhounds. Nick had decided on the raft that he would try and retreat into the background. And just like most of us do when we want to become anonymous, he decided to start barking orders right, left and centre. He was unable to help himself after swiftly coming to the conclusion that no one possessed his experience and skills. He had already examined the sun's position and seen there was, at most, three hours of light remaining and if the tribe were to have built a shelter and found water by that time then they would have to start work immediately. Once again, he began assigning roles and instructing people what to do and, once again, most of the tribe were happy for someone to take the lead given they were tired, hungry and very hot. Most, that is, except for

Jackie, who was too dehydrated, dizzy and nauseous to be of any use due to her indulgence the previous night. She tried to join in, but was merely pretending to get involved. She confesses to being lazy when it comes to manual work. At home, if there is anything heavy to lift, she gets her boyfriend Martin to do it. Here she struggled to heave one bamboo plank across the beach, while Eve strode past her with four on her shoulder. It was clear she was physically the weakest of the tribe, even at this early stage.

She was not alone, however, in having doubts. Zoe Lyons, a twenty-nine-year-old bartender from London, was another who was overawed by the strength and fitness of some of those around her as they rafted to the island. As she saw everyone else pushing themselves to the limit she questioned how wise she had been to enter. Perhaps, she thought to herself, I should have tried harder to find some work as an actress in March. "I felt a bit overwhelmed actually, there were a lot of strong characters in my tribe and it was a bit much," she says. "Flashes of regret ran through my mind. It was hard work on the raft and I suddenly realised it was going to be a lot more physically demanding then I had previously thought. I considered myself to be average to reasonably fit, but I don't go to the gym. I can't stand them, they smell. And I don't run because it's bad for your knees and I don't go swimming because I'd rather not bathe with strangers. I like to play team games in the park, but I don't really do sport at all to be honest. I had thought, in terms of fitness, I was alright, but I was with these people who had run across New Zealand and things, which is a bit odd when public transport is quite adequate and advanced there. It seems a bit silly. I realised it was going to be quite physically demanding."

But she decided the best option was to put her head down and work hard. The shelter was coming along nicely, thanks to Nick who had not just taken charge, he had become a dictator. But under his guidance an A-frame shelter was erected that would, he informed the tribe, allow the cool air in from the sea for ventilation while repelling the humid air from the jungle. Pete and Mick had been the main builders of the tribe and Nick thought them good willing workers. Pete in particular was obviously very strong. Nick had set Jackie and Zoe, the two weakest in terms of physical strength, the task of making fire. He was trying to ascertain people's abilities, wondering if any had done as he had intended to do and were keeping their talents quiet. To find out more, he was asking people to tie knots to suspend the shelter, thinking anyone capable could complete such a "simple" task. It turned out no one was any good at tying knots, to Nick's surprise. Yet again this was another strategy that backfired massively. Many of the tribe members could not understand why he was ordering them to perform tasks and not doing them himself. Some, like Richard, came to the conclusion that it was because he did not know how to do it and Nick's talk was all an act. Either way, it lost him a huge amount of respect.

The list of Nick's mistakes on that first day seems endless. He wanted to prove himself indispensable, but while he was useful in exercises such as rafting and erecting the shelter, what would his role be when the latter was built? He had installed himself as leader and was there to be shot at. Before the sun had even set on the first evening discontent about his arrogance and dominance began to rumble around the camp, which Nick did little to dispel. He told Eve, condescendingly, on the first evening, "Eve, you're good, you'll go far." She couldn't believe it. Here she was still trying to cope with digging a toilet, finding the water and building a shelter to sleep in before dark and Nick was telling her that she could win a million. Her first instinct was to tell him to shut up but she held her peace – for then. An achievement for someone as upfront as Eve. "Nick wasn't seen as a threat by anyone," Eve says. "That was not why he became unpopular, although it was clear he was manipulating Pete and Mick. No, essentially he was voted off because he was a pillock."

According to Jackie, within an hour or two of being on the island Nick was talking about himself being in the final two to win the million. It had never occurred to her that she would be in the last two. Certainly, not that early in the game. Arrogance turned out to be a major factor in people being voted from the island. Jackie was not the only one to think that Nick thought he knew everything. Another mistake of his was to fill everyone in on the details of his extensive CV. But this just reinforced the idea in some that he was lying. Richard believed him to be a "Walter Mitty" character. "What is he," he said after the programme ended. 'A Navy diver, a lieutenant in the TA, a bloke who takes executives on team building exercises or a drug sales rep ? He told different people that he was one of those things." The answer is that he was all of them, but this game was about how you were perceived and, in that respect, Nick was doing appallingly.

After the shelter was built and water source found, Ular sat around talking to each other (apart from Jackie, who felt so ill that she went into the newly-constructed home to lie down). Outside there was rejoicing when Mick produced some sausages that he had smuggled on to the island and everyone tucked in heartily. At that stage, Mick did not reveal to them the method he had employed to get the contraband bangers through the search at KK. On the previous evening he had worked out it was to be last his square meal before he returned to the mainland so he thought smuggling a few sausages on to the island would give his tribe something to eat and keep them going, not to mention boosting morale. The rest of the story is best put in his own words.

"I asked room service to cook six well-done sausages, but I could only manage to get four up my backside. They weren't that big. I wrapped them in clingfilm and put some soap on them to lubricate them. It was considerably uncomfortable. I got them out on the boat, in the toilet and then stuck them in my bag. Though I lost one, I don't know what happened to it at all. In hindsight it was the wrong thing to smuggle. I should've smuggled spice, something to make the rice taste a bit different, maybe some curry powder or something like that. Or even spice up the rats, because once the sausages were eaten that was it."

Not having eaten all day, the sausages proved immensely popular. After Mick informed his tribe of his method of transporting them, however, everyone now claims never to have eaten one.

The tribe sat around telling each other about themselves as the sunset and darkness wrapped around them. There was little to do after dark, particularly before either tribe had discovered the means to make fire. Often everyone would be in bed directly after sunset. That first night, however, people stayed up chatting for some time. Bored, Richard decided to go and sleep. Due to the way the shelter was constructed, people slept in the order they went to bed. So Richard crawled his way along the floor alongside Jackie. She was in a pretty sorry state. Ill, tired and upset, she was on the verge of tears. "I've made a really big mistake," she told him. "I can't believe it's so early on and I feel so rough, so quickly." Richard consoled her with comforting and supportive words, telling her sleep was a good healer and that she'd be fine in the morning. They laughed about Nick. It was at this point that one of the most pivotal moments in the whole game occurred. Unbeknown to anyone else, and it remained that way long in to the game, Richard and Jackie hatched an alliance.

"We never said 'Right, we've got an alliance here,'" Jackie claims. "It was just that we naturally got on well and then because we felt comfortable with each other, we didn't necessarily need to spend a lot of time with each other on the island. We could concentrate on other people. He was supposedly in the male camp finding out what they were doing, and I was supposedly finding out what the females were doing. I mean, he didn't particularly get on well with the boys so it didn't work like that, and I didn't really get on with the girls either. But that's how it should've happened. But because I was weak that first night, he heard that they were going to vote me off."

It was always part of Richard's strategy to make an alliance early on with a female. He had done massive amounts of research and knew everything it was possible to know about *Survivor*, hence his cryptic comment regarding the Swedish show during the briefing at KK. After forging that alliance it was his aim to stay as true as possible to it and use it to suss out what was going on within the tribe. Even when making alliances within alliances, the plan was never to tell anyone about that original alliance. Richard, though he might not admit it, displayed a willingness to stand up for the underdog the whole time he was on the island, even when whichever underdog it was did not want his support. Jackie was feeling weak and vulnerable and her confidence had taken a hammering. But she was also streetwise and smart.

Richard knew that. In all, the perfect woman to fit his strategy. For her part, Jackie recognised Richard as shrewd, obviously intelligent and incredibly fit. He was a keen adventure racer, who had run in some staggeringly testing races, including one that involved racing across New Zealand, coast to coast. He likes to challenge himself. He lists as one of his best experiences the time running a marathon when he "hit the wall", enjoying the pain his body felt when it could go no further due to exhaustion. Of course, he did not give in.

So, as the rest of the tribe sat up swapping stories, and Nick told everyone how great he was, Jackie and Richard formed a team that would prove cast-iron strong. They deduced that if they could stay together through thick and thin, yet never let this on to anyone else, then their chances of advancing to the later stages were excellent. As they lay there, less than four hours after landing on that beautiful, remote island, they decided the first person who had to go, when the opportunity arose, was Nick.

Heard the one about the beauty queen, the drill sergeant and the old Etonian?

"If Ular were Bach and Mozart, then we were the Beach Boys," JJ said after leaving the island. What she meant was that while Ular were interested in survival, Helang were interested in fun. The tribe was divided nicely along age lines from the very beginning. On the one hand there was Charlotte, Adrian and Uzma. All of them were thirty or under, and loud, brash and intent on having a good time. At the top of the age range were Andy, Jayne, JJ and James. In the middle lay Simon, who might have been thirty-five but owns up to being twenty-one at heart. It was too early for these factions to be detrimental to the tribe's strength, that would come later, but their existence was obvious.

The first night on the island had been a rough one for Helang. Morale on the first morning on the island, day two, was low, nobody having slept due to hunger and the army of rats that trooped out of the jungle at nightfall and ran amok in their shelter. Helang opted to build a lean-to on Andy's initiative. His reward? Criticism from JJ, who believed they should have built an A-Frame. JJ was unable to bite her tongue, a trait that would cost her dear. While Nick emerged as putative leader of Ular, no one had yet come to the fore in Helang, despite the presence of a number of strong personalities. Andy, an airline pilot who used to fly RAF Chinook helicopters, had done survival training in the past and was more than equipped for the task. However, like a number of others, he was reluctant to push himself forward reckoning that he could be seen as a threat. His strategy was to play it carefully and try to position himself in the middle of the pack. Yet another grey man, though he was slightly more successful than Nick. Given his background, and obvious strength and intelligence, Andy was regarded as one of the favourites for the £1 million prize.

The other obvious leader was JJ. Third generation RAF, she had lived and breathed the armed forces until she left in 1996. She claims that her intention was to play down her military background, which had taken her all over Europe, to places like Berlin as well as to the Falklands, where she worked in a military prison. Playing down her past would not be easy, something underlined by Nick who was on the same flight as her from Britain and immediately knew she had been in the forces by the way that she stood at Kuala Lumpur airport waiting for a connecting flight, as if she had just been put at ease. She had also been a drill instructor, and after leaving the RAF she became a bodyguard to a high-profile person whose identity she refuses to reveal. Not the type of woman, then, to suffer fools gladly. Forthright and forceful, she knew she had to bite her tongue or risk alienating the rest of the tribe. That said, it was a curious decision by her, if she wanted to remain anonymous, to turn up for the boat trip dressed in full fatigues, aviator shades and her *USS Kennedy* baseball cap. All she needed to do to give the game away completely was to march on to the *Mata Hari*. Within seconds of reaching Pulau Tiga, Andy turned to her and asked, "So, how long have you been out of the military?" Not being a good liar, JJ was forced to reveal her past. "I was in the RAF for thirteen years. I was the bitch of the squadron. I was a drill instructor for a while," she told them, reassuringly.

Helang's arrival on the beach had its tensions. JJ, obviously capable and confident of her capabilities in a situation like this, with definite opinions on what should be done, was holding herself back. Others were seeking more consensual ways of making decisions, avoiding forcing their opinions on others. Charlotte decided a meeting would be a good idea. "Make it a little one," said JJ, who was obviously less than enamoured with the idea. Each of the tribe introduced themselves again, and were asked to say something interesting about themselves. James, a forty-year-old property developer, told them he had five children. This was news that shocked the Ular tribe when they discovered it because for reasons best known to themselves they had decided James was gay. JJ declared that Pulau Tiga was her twenty-ninth address, testament to her peripatetic army lifestyle. Adrian was asked if he had any children to which he replied that he didn't, only for Charlotte to say "None that you know of!" Simon then asked how many girlfriends he'd had in the past year. Sparing his blushes, Uzma said he didn't kiss and tell. "Not yet, anyway," was Charlotte's response. Then the discussion turned to guessing ages. Jayne, for some reason, appeared uncomfortable ...

The reason stemmed from her decision to lie about her age. She is forty-seven, but felt that if people knew that it would disadvantage her. She feared ageism, especially from the younger element of Helang, so decided a white lie was the best option. But rather than shaving a year or two off her age, she decided to say she was the same age as Simon, thirty-five. It fooled no one, but no one seemed to mind too much. What Jayne had to watch more than people discovering her age was her propensity to scold others and come across as rude. Speaking your mind is all well and good with those that know you well, but doing so to strangers whose affection and respect you still have to gain could be fatal in terms of survival. Already she had twice angered Charlotte on the raft. First, when Charlotte had been sitting on some boxes on top of the raft, Jayne told her caustically to get down immediately. Secondly, when she disapproved of the Welsh policewoman's rowing stroke. "Look Miss Blue Toenails, row properly," was her scathing comment. Charlotte claims, only half in jest, that she moved to the back of the raft away from Jayne at that point to prevent herself hitting her over the head with the oar.

Charlotte did not like being told what to do by anybody. As a determined, high-achieving woman, she has never subjugated the rebellious side of her character. As a teenager she was a beauty queen, winning the title of Miss South Wales, and a finalist in Miss Wales. Thinking of choosing modelling as a career, she was sent to London to try out for the same agency that employs Naomi Campbell. Despite being only eight and a half stone at the time, lighter than she was when she went to the island, she was told she would have to lose a stone in weight. After telling her mother about it all on the phone, she decided to take the first train back to Wales, but only after stopping off at the bakers to buy a box of cream cakes. Jayne's attempts to discipline her had been noted by Charlotte, and she had a willing ally in James who was also unfortunate enough to earn Jayne's ire. As they were building the shelter, Jayne said to him "You are a funny little man." James could not believe it. For a while he believed her, thinking he was completely out of place but then he stopped himself becoming paranoid. Within hours of the tribe's being on shore, a "Vote Off Jayne" alliance was beginning to form.

But the mood on the morning of day two was not one of tension, it was one of misery. No one had slept, no one had eaten and they could not fish because they had built the shelter on the raft. JJ was not feeling very well at all, and during one interview was sick. Another who was struggling was Adrian, a twenty-two-year-old barrister's clerk. For someone who values sleep more than anything else, the conditions were less than ideal. He says he forgot to wash out all of his hair wax before going on the island and it proved a magnet to the rats, meaning sleep was impossible. By the first night his thoughts were already turning to home. He vowed on that second day that if he failed to get a decent night's sleep then he would ask to be voted off. He did not want to stick around feeling hungry, surrounded by the ever-present rats which he hated, bugs everywhere, all the while being asked to perform tasks, like fetching water, by people who he did not even like. This was not what he had in mind. While he worked out at the gym he had not done anything remotely similar to this. The only holiday he had been on before was a Club 18–30 trip, where survival meant finding the kebab shop after thirteen bottles of beer.

But on that second day Helang's misery was alleviated by the first Reward Challenge; Plant Survival. Despite feeling awful, JJ decided she would not show it when they reached the venue for the challenge because she did not want to indicate any weakness at all to Ular. But the three-hour walk through the jungle to reach the site did not do her any good and she was extremely sick on the way. The temperature was way into the nineties, the humidity levels unbearable. In the jungle the sweat clings to you at all times, the cicadas blare like traffic at rush hour in Piccadilly Circus and dizziness and dehydration are a constant threat. But JJ made it – though the achievement was ruined somewhat when presenter Mark Austin asked her, "JJ, is it true you've been sick?" Austin also drove a nail into the rather spacious coffin that Nick was in the process of building for himself when he revealed to Ular that Nick was responsible for leaving their machete aboard the *Mata Hari*. Nick had planted a cover story after it emerged that Ular had taken a member of Helang's kit by mistake – Andy's to be precise. Nick said Helang probably picked up both machetes by mistake and no one was in any position to doubt him. Now, he was revealed as a liar to go alongside his other sins.

The challenge involved identifying which of twelve plants presented to them were safe to eat, testing what they had learned during their survival briefing on the mainland. Four of them were poisonous and would kill if ingested. In what was a bit of a lottery, Ular won but Helang were not too discouraged because the prize was a teapot, together with some tea and teacups. When you haven't eaten, tea is not a priority and the challenge at least had presented them with a chance to work together and bond as a group. This new-found sense of unity was sorely tested, however, by the three-hour walk back to their beach where they discovered that the incoming tide had washed away half of their camp. Clothing and bedding was soaked, utensils had been washed away and it all added to the sense of despair that hovered over Helang. Desperately tired and hungry, they knew that the next day could only be better. But then it had to be, because the first Immunity Challenge was due to take place.

Idol hands

As the game progressed, the day of an Immunity Challenge would always add an extra frisson to the atmosphere on both beaches as minds turned to who would be going should their tribe be defeated. If anything, day three crackled with more intensity because it was the first time the contestants had experienced it. Every single one of the sixteen survivors had said their greatest fear was being the first person to be voted off the island. For some, it did not matter when their time was up, as long as it was not after a paltry four days. The humiliation would be too much to bear.

In both tribes discussions had taken place. In Ular, Nick had wasted no time at all in marshalling his troops, Mick and Pete, both of whom were happy under his charge. They were, however, the only two. Nick needed two others to complete a five and he had turned to Zoe, whom he thought strong, capable and hard working. He approached her and Zoe agreed to join, reasonably deducing it was wise to go along with the strongest group to ensure her survival and at that stage it looked as if Nick was in the process of assembling one. There was some doubt as to whom the fifth person should be. Nick had developed a dislike and mistrust for Richard, which was mutual. Richard had taken the decision before the game not to reveal that he was a psychiatrist. He believes there is a stigma attached to work in mental health. He said after the game ended: "Many people think we analyse everybody. That's an over-generalisation, but it's fairly true. People will say 'Are you analysing me? And that can get a bit much. But there's no denying that you pick things up, you notice mannerisms and things like that. You pay attention. But I've been like that since I was twelve. It's not psychiatry per se, it's more a case of being very interested in people."

Richard felt guilty about lying about his profession on national television, fearing it would look as if he was ashamed of what he does for a living when in fact he is immensely proud. But he felt that if he were honest he would be treated with tremendous suspicion. His guilt was assuaged later when he joined the jury and discovered, after announcing that he was a psychiatrist, that every single one said they would have voted him off had they known that earlier. Instead, Richard claimed to be a family GP, believing his medical training would make it an easy disguise to adopt.

It would have been had Nick not worked as a pharmaceutical sales manager in the Welsh region where Richard claimed to have his practice. Nick already had his suspicions about Richard and so decided to test him with a few questions. Nick made up a name of someone who worked in the area and asked Richard if he knew this fictitious character. Richard said he did. Nick mentioned a drug, one that had only recently been made available which, he claims, should have been known by every GP in the land. Richard had never heard of it. Richard laughs off what he calls Nick's "pathetic" attempts to uncover him, but uncover him Nick did. He just chose not to make too much of it with the rest of the group at that stage, and it was clear that Richard had some medical training even if he wasn't a GP. Despite this, he decided to ask Richard to join his alliance. At first Richard said he would think about it, but then he returned saying he was interested and asked who else was involved. In reality, all he was doing was finding which woman Nick thought he had so he could then speak to her and get her to vote Nick off. Unwisely Nick revealed it was Zoe. So, Richard and Jackie approached Zoe, who was more than happy to swap sides because Eve and Sarah had also indicated they were fed up with Nick's over-bearing style. The writing was on the wall for the Navy diver.

Across the island at Helang beach, Jayne was rapidly emerging as the prime candidate for eviction. Charlotte had Adrian in her pocket, and had made good friends with Uzma. Charlotte and Uzma were both strong women, vocal and keen to have a good time. Andy and James tried to position themselves somewhere in the middle and Simon was tending to migrate towards the tribe's Club 18–30 element. JJ, like Andy, was seeking to avoid alliances. She had already made up her mind who she would vote for and that it would be for the good of the tribe. She sensed not everybody would vote in the same manner, and that personal feelings would come into it. JJ was adamant that people should vote on the basis of what benefited the tribe rather than being led by their like or dislike for personalities. For her either Uzma or Adrian would have to go because neither had contributed nearly enough to the tribe's wellbeing.

But the pall of dissatisfaction that hung over Helang had started to dissipate. They had managed to make fire on that second night, which meant they were able to eat and that immediately buoyed spirits among the group. Even better news was that people had managed a few hours of sleep, even Adrian, who was teased by Charlotte for his snoring. As a consequence, he felt stronger and thoughts of quitting began to recede from his mind. The whole spirit surrounding the tribe had become positive. There was acknowledgement that they lacked a leader, at that point there was a democracy but that meant there was very little action being taken. There was more sunbathing taking place than fishing, or adapting the shelter, much to JJ's chagrin. But everyone's focus was on the Immunity Challenge. Before leaving for the sand spit, the tribe put on their T-shirts and gathered round for a group hug. There was no doubting the amount of spirit that existed within Helang. The day before had given them their first glimpse of Ular and their impressions weren't favourable ones. In their view, the opposition were humourless and appeared to look down at them. For that reason, they were determined to wipe the smug smiles off their faces.

On the sand spit, a strip of golden sand that rises from the sea off the coast of Pulau Tiga, stood the huge and impressive figure of the Malaysian fire spirit, Surmanyat Appi. Out at sea were two large rafts, each carrying a large cauldron filled with fire. The two tribes had to start at sea and carry their rafts towards the spirit, lighting a number of torches on their way in. All the torches must be lit, ending with the one that Surmanyat held in his hands. The rafts were incredibly heavy and difficult to maneouvre, particularly in the sea. For Helang, Simon was the chosen torchbearer, with Nick performing the task for Ular. For almost the whole of the race, Helang led – indeed they never looked in any trouble. Until the time came for Simon to light the last torch. For some reason it would not light, and the hiatus allowed Nick to catch up and light the torch first. Helang were devastated. Charlotte and Uzma immediately burst into tears. Victory had been so close and to see it taken away at such a late stage proved too much for them, as did the whooping and hollering of Ular. They were truly despondent. They were given a thin shaft of hope, however, when a "steward's enquiry" was announced. Both tribes had to sit and sweat – literally, the sand spit affords no shelter from the sun and humidity – while the production team studied tapes of the race to rule whether an infringement had occurred.

Eventually, after a delay of twenty-five minutes, a decision had been reached. Mark Austin, the immunity idol in his hand, probably the most precious piece of equipment on the island, delivered the news. "The rules said that all the torches must be lit and stay alight. Ular, you failed to light one of your torches," he announced and handed the idol to Helang, who erupted with joy. It turned out that one of the torches had guttered slightly when lit and then extinguished itself. Ular had broken the rules and the punishment was making the long trek through the jungle to Tribal Council the following evening when it would be discovered who the first person voted off the island would be. With this on their minds, Ular trudged forlornly back to their beach, while Helang sank to their knees and thanked Surmanyat Appi for blessing them with good fortune. The victory brought the tribe even closer together, papering over the many cracks opening beneath the all-singing, all-dancing surface they presented.

How to lose friends and influence people

For Ular, however, or most of them, it was a chance to get rid of the division that was spreading an ill atmosphere through their camp. Nick had become irritated by the lack of application many of his tribe mates displayed. He was particularly perturbed by the habit of some female members of wandering off collecting shells and making necklaces when there was work to be done around the camp. Pete and Mick never did that, they worked willingly, and followed orders, just like the novices he took away for team-building exercises. With them he had reached the conclusion that Jackie was the weakest member of the tribe and had to go. She had got much stronger, mentally and physically, since shaking off the despair of her first night on the island, but Nick had explained that the tribe had to be at its strongest for all the challenges if he, Mick and Peter were to reach the last three.

But Nick had made enemies. Both Eve and Sarah were fed up with his orders and his condescension and wanted him off, if only to make the whole experience more fun. If he went, said Eve, "tomorrow would be day one". The tribe could start again, regain some democracy and all old alliances would be forgotten. This was the prevalent view among the other members of the tribe. Richard disliked Nick personally, thought he lied about his background and simply "had to go". The lynchpin was Zoe. Earlier, she had told Nick that she would join his alliance but when she was informed that there was a counter-alliance forming to depose Nick then she was more than happy to enter into that. She too found him too much to bear and had had enough of being ordered around, though she held less antipathy towards him than either Richard or Jackie.

"When Nick approached me for an alliance, I thought 'Bless him, he's trying really hard, he's done his research, he's seen this is how it ought to be done,'" Zoe says now. "Unfortunately, you can't anticipate how other people will react. However, I thought if he manages to get five people I will go with him. If not, I'll go against him. I think Nick's heart was in the right place, and he did work really hard, but he did not read the situation at all well. Initially, I said I would vote with him but I had no strong attachment and there was no problem switching sides."

Nick was unaware of this shift in allegiance. On the day of Tribal Council he spoke to the camera and informed people that "there would be no surprises tonight.' He believed Zoe was certain to vote with him, together with Richard, despite his distrust of the latter, because Richard had said he would. In reality Richard had no intention whatsoever of voting against Jackie, his main ally. Nick should have followed his initial feelings of doubt and unease over Richard's past.

The walk to Tribal Council was an hour and a half long through thick jungle. Occasionally, the contestants would have to stop as a six-foot long snake slithered across the path, or they would have to walk more quickly to escape hammering rain from one of the many storms that exploded late in the day. A number of contestants testified to how quiet and solemn those walks were, everyone locked inside their own minds, thinking of the vote to come. Ular's walk to Tribal Council on day four was even more silent, it being the first one and with no one knowing what to expect. Some would grow to hate the whole ceremony, Richard in particular, who said he despised it because it was denying people their dream of staying on the island, an experience he was loving and wanted never to end. Others, like Zoe and Jackie, and Uzma from Helang, loved the theatre, the drama of Tribal Council. For them island living, with its periods of inactivity and boredom, the petty personality clashes, was a place where fun had been taken off the menu. The jangling nerves and high tension of Tribal Council was a welcome relief.

One person whose nerves began to jangle on that walk to council was Nick. A growing sense of unease began to settle on him when the tribe stopped at the mud volcano, about two-thirds of the way to Tribal Council. He, Mick and Pete went to have a look but that was all. The rest, however, dipped their hands and smeared some of the cool mud on their face. Zoe and Jackie only made marks on their face, while Sarah, Eve and Richard went the whole hog and completely covered their heads with it. All laughed and joked as they smeared the mud on, leaving Nick to realise that all five did not seem to be behaving like a group that were about to vote someone they liked, Jackie for instance, off. No they seemed relaxed and happy and certain that their decision was a correct one. He began to worry.

The walk continued until the group reached the Tribal Council building. It shone to them from the jungle, a stunning sight for eyes used to pitch darkness. Then they noticed the line of cameras, and new unfamiliar, well-fed, healthy faces lined up outside the Council building; the production crew, eager to see who was to be the first person voted off. Mark Austin welcomed them and asked them to bang the gong to announce their entrance, before lighting their torches, placing them on the stand and sitting on the council seats. "Fire," he explained, "symbolises your life on the island." So long as a person stayed in the game then their torch remained lit. If they should be voted off, then it was extinguished. Hesitantly, Ular took their seats. Eve and Sarah, only their eyes poking through the dried mud on their faces, looked terrified, almost spellbound by the scene. Richard's mask of mud gave him a look of inscrutability, an air of rigid detachment from the whole proceedings.

Austin asked Mick whom he thought the tribe would most miss. "Nick," he answered, stating that Nick's skills made him the tribe's most useful member, and eliciting a smile from the man he had praised. Then it came to time to vote, each person leaving their seat in turn to climb the stairs to the voting booth, writing the name of the person they wished to see go on a scrap of paper and giving a short soundbite to camera explaining their decision before placing their vote in a pot. The vote went according to plan; Richard ("Nick doesn't say please, he doesn't say thank you"), and the four women voting for Nick, while the three other men voted for Jackie. Austin read out the votes and as the fifth vote for Nick emerged, he hunched his rucksack on to his shoulders and muttered "Interesting." As he extinguished his torch, it dawned on him that Richard was the man who had swung support against him, or so he thought. As he passed everyone, he mouthed the word "Bastard" at Richard, but the psychiatrist was looking elsewhere. Slowly, he made the lonely walk down the path away from the Tribal Council to a small booth – "The Confessional" – in which the ejected contestants spoke of their dismissal. After a short interview, Nick was taken to a boat which sped away from the island. Like all the following contestants he was taken to the mainland, accompanied by Stephen Flett, the psychologist. On the mainland he was driven to a five-star hotel where he was fed and watered and debriefed by Flett. The show's bosses did not want the contestants leaving Borneo in the order they were voted off, so as to leave no trace for journalists to investigate and discover who was voted off when. Nick had two weeks confined to a hotel, albeit a very good one, to contemplate being the first person to be voted off *Survivor*.

He says now that he made a number of mistakes, the biggest of which was becoming involved with Richard. "My first reaction to being voted off was immense disappointment, particularly on the boat leaving the island. But I was very proud of what we had set up. I don't know how the other tribe did but I know Ular were living very comfortably. I'm proud of playing a part in that. It is sad that we lost immunity because the next stage would have been one of calming down and enjoying the island a bit, which I never got chance to do. Had we won the first Immunity Challenge I am very confident that I would have stayed the course.

"I understand their decision. I would have voted me off too. I was a threat to everyone and it was my intention to win. I had worked out when the others were going off as well, including, I must say, Pete and Mick. But I had to survive that first challenge. I do regret that I didn't get to know people a little better and know how to keep them happy. And I certainly would not have trusted Richard. No way." Eve and Richard, however, reject the notion that Nick was voted off because he was a threat. Both claim he was voted off so the tribe could function better and more democratically. The lesson was there for those who wanted to learn it; people did not like being told what to do.

"She's just so bossy..."

Had JJ been able to witness what had happened to Nick then she might well have adjusted her behaviour. Or perhaps not, being the type of person, she admits, who can only be herself. Herself, as it turns out, is loud, gregarious, opinionated and forceful. A strong woman with a strong personality who liked to be in control. Unfortunately for her she was not the only female member of Helang to fit that description. Charlotte is equally loud, equally gregarious, though far less regimented and hates being told what to do. What's more, she likes control. A power struggle between the two was inevitable from the start.

Unlike Ular, Helang had not been to Tribal Council and

were unable to heal divisions in that way. Voting off Nick had done wonders for Ular's team spirit. People felt more relaxed and able to work together, think for themselves and take decisions collectively. After returning to Tribal Council, Pete and Mick understandably felt vulnerable and certain either of them would be next. Ular developed a routine after Tribal Council – one which would continue following the merger. They would get back and go skinny-dipping, cleansing themselves after the murky business of Tribal Council. It was so dark no one could really see each other, though Pete ("OK, I'm a prude") wore his trunks. As they swam in the sea both Pete and Mick were informed that their votes against Jackie meant nothing and they should not feel in danger. They had been extremely shocked and surprised at Nick's leaving. They thought Jackie's departure was a given and could not believe people had voted Nick off. Mick cleared the air in a heart-to-heart with Jackie and felt better afterwards, even though from that point on he was very wary of alliances of any sort. For Pete, in particular, it had been a huge wake-up call.

"I hadn't seen the game from a social point of view," he says now. "But as soon as Nick left, the very next morning it was different. I was thinking, 'Hang on, there's nobody I have to ask what to do. I don't have to ask for permission, I can think for myself, I can do what I want.' Which was good and we felt like a team rather than a bunch of people being dictated to. It made us stronger. But I had decided I was too nervous of alliances after what happened with Nick. I didn't feel comfortable with them at all. I decided I was going to vote for the person I thought should be voted off. If people came and asked me who I'm voting for and tell me and it turns out we're voting for the same person then fine. Or if someone can persuade me not to vote for somebody and give me good reason, that's fine. But I'm not going to go into alliances just for the sake of it."

So while Ular bonded for the second time, Helang's divisions on day four, and tensions, were exacerbated. While the victory in the Immunity Challenge was a welcome boost, it had also given the idea to younger members of the tribe that what mattered most was gearing up for Immunity Challenges. All the other times, the view seemed to be, people could take it easy. This was not a view that sat easily with JJ. Andy might have made a more emollient leader, but he was happy to sit back and watch JJ take charge. Charlotte, Adrian and Uzma, on the other hand, simply wanted to have a good time and JJ's berating was always going to jar. Jayne had made efforts to patch up her rifts with Charlotte, James and Uzma and it seemed clear who the new villain was for the youth alliance, as Uzma made clear to camera.

"The person who is really annoying me at the moment is JJ. She's just far, far too controlling and too outspoken for my liking, and really hasn't found out anything about anybody's personal life. All she wants to talk about is herself and the RAF and that's quite frankly pretty boring after a few stories. I like to get personal with people but you really can't get a word in edgeways with JJ. All she wants to talk about is herself, and I haven't got time for that."

Charlotte was also retreating from her antipathy towards Jayne on day four. The pair had spoken, got to know each other and reconciled their differences – at least for the time being. In common with most of the other women, Charlotte did not enter the game with any carefully planned strategy, unlike many of the men who had studied other countries' versions of the shows in the minutest detail. Richard in particular knew what was in store for many of the contestants throughout the game. Charlotte, however, only had a general plan: to vote off those that didn't like her before they voted her off. Apart from that she went in with an open mind, learning from her time in the police force that to approach any given situation with pre-conceived ideas was dangerous. But her mind was swiftly made up when JJ became unable to hide her impatience with Adrian, Uzma and Charlotte's inactivity. As JJ said to camera on day five, "I'm the sort of person that likes to say 'Whallop!' and things get done." Judging from the amount of times her voice had to be bleeped for broadcast, she was saying rather more than just "whallop". The camp was untidy, no one was replacing utensils, equipment was going missing and no one in the youth alliance was willing to put in any work to secure food. All these incidents started to accumulate and JJ began to snap at the likes of Uzma and Charlotte, calling them "honey", her voice barely concealing her growing contempt.

Kota Cuisine

It did not help that Helang lost the Reward Challenge on day five, though who won and lost are not the main reasons why it will remain in the minds of all the contestants who took part. In the jungle a table had been set; seven places for Ular, eight for Helang. There was no soft music in the background, just the screeching of cicadas. At the head of the table sat Mark Austin, *mein host* for the afternoon. He asked them to sit. In front of them sat small wooden bowls and bamboo cups of water. No one, except those who had performed thorough research, knew what was about to transpire. The last Reward Challenge, identifying plants, had been quite tame and viewed as a bit of a letdown. Those among the fifteen present who were seeking a physical test were feeling disappointed. Sitting down was what they did on the beach most of the day. To do it in a challenge was odd.

Their complaints were silenced when Austin unveiled lunch: a box of squirming bootah bugs. Tribesmen in Borneo view the creamy-white bulbous bugs as a delicacy. To both these tribes, however, they just looked like huge fat maggots. As the box was opened and people saw what was inside the blaring cicadas were drowned out by the sound of fifteen Brits going "Urggh!" in unison. The fat bugs wriggled in their box. Uzma looked around at everyone in disbelief, as if it was some sort of joke and the real nature of the challenge would be revealed. In her interview before the game's commencement Uzma said, unaware of what was to follow, that her greatest fear about life on the island was that she would have to eat bugs. Here she was being forced to do it within five days of landing on Pulau Tiga. They were hungry, but this was not what everyone had in mind as an ideal lunch.

The rules were explained; One-by-one the contestants must eat the bugs, in the style of a penalty shoot-out. The tribe with the most members refusing to eat loses. Should it be a draw then each tribe nominates the person they feel to be the most squeamish on the opposite tribe. These two then have a head-to-head contest, with the first to swallow two bootah bugs the winner. Uzma thanked the heavens that she had been prescient enough to sit at the farthest end of the table from Austin. She prayed that a couple of members of the Ular tribe would not be able to stomach swallowing the insects and she would be spared her worst nightmare.

JJ went first for Helang and seemed to relish the challenge. Picking up the bug by the head, trying to avoiding being nipped, she bit off the body and swallowed it, washing it down with a cup of water. Her example was matched by

Eve, the first to go for Ular. She had few problems and an example was set. Nobody now wanted to be the first person to refuse the challenge. These were early days and such weakness would be viewed harshly, especially if it cost a tribe a food reward that would give them strength for the following day's Immunity Challenge. So, no matter how nauseating it was, everyone was determined to eat the bug. At least it provided protein.

No one enjoyed the challenge at all, although Andy for Helang made a good attempt at showing that he did. While most bit, swallowed and then gulped water before they could taste the bug – though some likened it to Stilton cheese, others said it tasted of nothing – Andy chewed the bug, even stopping at one point to prise a piece of maggot from between his teeth. Obviously he was making a point, showing those around him that whatever challenges the island presented, he was not going to be cowed by them. In fact, he would try and show he enjoyed the challenges. Already he had been surprised by how much equipment they had been provided with and realised they would not be allowed to starve while on the island. Part of him was disappointed – he wanted a true challenge.

As the game progressed it was obvious to Helang that Jackie was the person who had struggled most to swallow the bootah, and would least like to repeat the feat. She managed to consume the bug, however, and before long Uzma was faced with the choice of eating the bug, or costing her tribe the challenge. It is an experience, she says, that she will never forget, no matter how much she tries. Inspiration, however, came from an unlikely source – the opposition.

"Peter was gorgeous. He is such a sweetie. Even though he was on the other tribe he was egging me on and all my tribe were chanting my name. The only reason I did it was for my tribe, the only reason. I couldn't let them down. I blocked my mind ... oh, it was awful. I can't believe I did it. Talking about it makes me feel sick. It didn't taste of anything though. Then when they said the most squeamish person had to do it again, I nearly died. I just knew it was going to me. For a second, I thought I might get away with it when someone from the other tribe pointed at Charlotte, but then they pointed at me."

Uzma's opponent in the eat-off was to be Jackie. It was a close run thing but Uzma was unable to force herself to swallow the bugs quickly and Jackie narrowly beat her, opening her mouth wide to let Austin see that the bugs had gone. Uzma looked distraught – not surprising because she had eaten three maggots, and for nothing – but was given a consoling hug by JJ. For Ular, however, the joy was unrestrained when Austin produced the reward: glass bowls filled to the brim with succulent fresh strawberries and topped with whipped cream. Despite being ravenously hungry, not one person wolfed them down greedily. They knew they might not eat something as tasty and healthy again for weeks, never mind days and they wanted to enjoy every single spoonful. Helang looked on despairingly, trying to stop themselves drooling. Their stomachs were hurting from lack of decent food and they had to suffer the torture of hearing the ecstatic groans of pleasure as Ular slowly devoured their prize. Uzma's suffering was too much for Jackie. In their discomfort, the two had developed camaraderie, a respect born of shared displeasure. Out of her bowl she picked the biggest, juiciest strawberry and handed it to her beleaguered opponent, who received it gratefully. To thank her Uzma gave her a kiss, any antagonism between the two tribes briefly forgotten.

Tempers flare

The next day Helang's losing streak was confirmed when a determined Ular tribe pipped them in the dramatic stretcher race named "Parachute Survivor". One member of the tribe was sent off into the jungle and suspended from a tree by a parachute, as if they had just bailed out from a plane. The rest of the tribe had to scavenge on the beach for materials with which to construct a stretcher, all in fifteen minutes. Four stretcher bearers then had to race to reach their colleague, guided by masks in the jungle. After placing the freed parachutist on a stretcher, the tribes then had to return to the temporary medical station on the beach. First one back would win immunity. Jayne and Eve were the ones banished into the jungle while Helang selected Andy, Simon, Adrian and James as their four. Ular plumped for Richard, Sarah, Pete and Mick.

Both sides struggled to release their "rescuee" but Ular managed it first. In freeing Jayne, Simon had scaled the tree and when he came back down James picked up the left front arm of the stretcher, where Simon was meant to be. Helang had reckoned correctly that the front of the stretcher would carry the most weight so their strongest members needed to be in those positions. For all his enthusiasm, James was the weakest of the four and he paid dearly for that split-second decision. Given the thick jungle it was impossible for the tribes to race side by side, so whoever led controlled the race. Ular offered Helang a glimmer of hope when they tripped over a fallen tree and Eve was ejected from the stretcher. As Helang bundled past, Eve's competitive nature took over and she rugby tackled Simon who was passing and did not let go. Simon, his hand on the stretcher, could only use his feet to free himself from Eve's grasp. In the chaos that followed, Richard claimed that Simon kicked Eve in the head even though she now claims that she did not feel anything and she does not blame Simon for anything he did because she was, in effect, cheating.

"I ended up on the floor. I thought our stretcher had broken and, therefore, I thought our race was over. I must have become aware that we could do something about the stretcher and I could get back on it but I wanted to delay Helang, so I basically stuck my body in the way as they came running along to block them. Sarah was in the way as well but she got run over and I got pushed out of the way. Then, as Simon ran passed me, he was at the back of their stretcher, I thought 'I'll trip you up'. So I stuck my leg out and he sort of stumbled and he was still moving so I wrapped my legs around his and I pulled him down. Only because I was determined that they weren't going to get away. It is alleged, though I know nothing about this, that he let go of the stretcher and then swung at my head with his foot. He didn't make contact – I don't even know that he kicked me or attempted to. It was only Richard's word. Richard got very angry on my behalf and it caused a huge argument, which I was never part of it. All I thought was, 'Here's a team that's going to beat us,' and the only thing I could think of to do was to stop them by pulling one of their people down. I was just trying to slow them down a bit. Which I did. I thought it was gamesmanship. The argument was between Richard and Simon – I never had an issue with him."

Simon claims he was acting like a rugby player, wriggling away from a tackle to get away and that any contact was purely accidental. "I'm a really aggressive character in challenges and I like to play hard and fair. It was tight in the jungle, not much path. They fell over and we went past them and as we did, one of them grabbed my leg and pulled me over. Then she got me in a rugby tackle and as I was trying to get back up – and I thought it was a man, I had no idea it was a woman – she was still holding on and I tried to move my leg and shake her off. They saw that as me trying to kick her. I was clear in my mind that I was just trying to shake her off."

Richard, however, did not see it that way at all. He was always keen to take up crusades on behalf of others on the island, particularly when he felt they were unfairly persecuted. As Simon got up and got away, Richard issued a volley of four-letter abuse in Simon's direction. Ular then set off in pursuit as the tribes neared the beach. As they turned on to what was in effect the final straight, James became exhausted, the weight of bearing the heavy stretcher too much. His legs crumpled. Next thing he knew, JJ was standing over him screaming "Get up! Get up!" Feeling like a cadet on parade, he somehow found the energy to get back up and get moving once more. A few yards on however his legs gave way yet again. This time he was brought to his feet by Jayne's exhortation to "Think of your five children." Yet again he stumbled to his feet, but by then Ular had overtaken them and in a mad dash for the line got their stretcher on to the station. Ular had won. James collapsed. He had never been so tired in all his life. The drama of that race stays with him even now.

"Usually after strong physical exertion, after twenty minutes you are on the way to recovery. It took me two hours to recover enough to breathe normally. I had gone beyond my limit of exhaustion. I don't think I could ever repeat it. From that point I first went down, I can't remember seeing anything. All I can remember is hearing JJ screaming at me, then I got up but it's like I was blind. Then it was Jayne shouting about my kids and I knew that I absolutely must get up. I gave it my all. I was carrying it with Andy. We were going at his pace and I was dragged along all the way by this huge strong bloke."

As a result of the phenomenal effort James had made during that challenge, not one member of Helang even considered voting him off. There were no recriminations, to James's surprise because he felt initially he had let the tribe down and would be punished accordingly. The only recriminations after the race took place between Richard and Simon, who had sought out the former to tell him never to speak to him again like he did in the jungle. Eyeball to eyeball the pair traded insults until they were separated by their tribe mates. The adrenaline coursing through their veins after the challenge had heightened their emotions and both admit to having gone too far. There was certainly no love lost between them and the consequences of that incident would be, in time, far-reaching and seal Simon's fate.

"I know exactly who voted for me..."

All these defeats served to draw out the underlying hostility in the Helang camp between Charlotte and JJ. JJ is scathing about Charlotte, particularly now, making insinuations about her behaviour with Adrian. She does not want to go into what the pair were actually getting up to, though during broadcast Charlotte admitted in a press release that she and Adrian did have a fling, which she regretted, and that she wished to patch things up with her husband Mark. Undoubtedly, the two got on very well. Adrian made her laugh, a rarity on an island where tension was the predominant mood. While Adrian was flattered by Charlotte's attention, especially during a time when he was struggling to adapt to island life, JJ says now that she thinks Charlotte is amoral, "a spoilt brat". Despite that, she claims she was not going to vote her off first.

She had taken the decision that Uzma was the weakest physically so she was the one the tribe could most afford to lose.

"If, however, it was down to characters, to put up with a nice life, I would have got rid of Charlotte," JJ says now. "On the island, she was lazy, she didn't listen, she was selfish and her behaviour was bad. It is a game and we all know that people are going to lie, cheat and manipulate. But when you have to live together, it is not fair to others if you don't play the game and help your team, it is not fair to others who are just as hungry and just as weak [as you are yourself], who are suffering just as much. If we had been in the final ten, after the merger, I would have understood that behaviour. But we were a team.

"She's a policewoman and I would have expected a lot more of her behaviour. I was disgusted. I would have expected that behaviour from a second-hand car salesman. You can be very singular and self-centred but there is a level you don't cross. That is behaviour that is immoral and disgusting. If she doesn't have any personal shame for what she did I think that is sad. I won't elaborate because it is not down to me, but there is a limit. This is a game, but even in life, people in extreme circumstances wouldn't debase themselves to do what she did. I think she saw this as her chance to gain maximum personal exposure. You can succeed in doing that by strength of character and presence. I was not happy with her selfishness and other behaviour, but that you can almost regulate. However, her personal behaviour went way too far for me."

On her behalf, Charlotte explains why she was so vehement that JJ had to go. "JJ was very capable. But over the three days before we voted her off she had become way too much. She was unbelievably bossy, telling me what to do left, right and centre. I don't mind her taking charge, but when it comes to telling me what to do, well, I thought she was trying to take control of me. She had such strong leadership skills, and she is such a confident, strong person that she is quite capable of bossing me around and the people who I had got supporting me. And she always talked about herself, no one else could get a word in edgeways. We knew everything about her, even though we had only known her for six days. I know more about her than Uzma. I remember Uzma came up to me one day and said, 'JJ has been whingeing about you, saying you're lazy, and you don't do anything around the camp.' Immediately I thought, 'She's got to go'. I saw her as a threat to me."

Perhaps the best person to ask about Charlotte's behaviour is Uzma, who was her best female friend on the island. She does not criticise Charlotte for her behaviour with Adrian – except when it was taking place next to her as she tried to sleep. "There was a lot of touching and groping going on next to me and the thing is when you are sleeping on boards then you can hardly lay down for fifteen minutes before you have to turn over because it's so uncomfortable and I couldn't because those two were carrying on. She told me what was happening. I asked what was going on and she said she was feeling a bit lonely and I said, 'That's alright, as long as you just be careful' and tried to give her all the advice stuff and she didn't take it. Everybody knew because they kept going off for water." Uzma does not condemn Charlotte's behaviour with Adrian.

Uzma does believe, however, that Charlotte is attention-seeking, but also feels JJ should stop complaining so angrily about her behaviour. "If JJ does what she says and has a go at Charlotte, then she will just look an angry, bitter and jealous woman," she says. Uzma suffered in Charlotte's shadow herself. James recounts how she complained to him about the amount of attention Charlotte was getting. As an outgoing, attractive and successful woman in her own right, Uzma was used to getting attention lavished upon her. On the island, however, she struggled to be herself with Charlotte around and eventually told James that it was affecting her self-esteem. JJ claims she wasn't jealous, but the prevalent opinion among the majority of the Helang tribe is that she was. Either way, the situation as Tribal Council neared became increasingly poisonous and the decision on whom to vote off increasingly murky.

JJ had unspoken allies in Andy – who wanted the strongest team to progress, which meant voting off Uzma, the weakest – and Jayne, who held no affection for Charlotte but felt Uzma was not enjoying the experience. The people who held the casting vote were Simon and James. James wanted to keep a low profile after having collapsed in the parachute race, not feeling he was in a position to dictate who went off. Instead he spoke to people individually, except Simon because time ran out, and discovered that there was a block of three voting for Uzma and a block of three voting for JJ. Despite not having spoken to Simon he deduced that he would be voting with the youth alliance because he seemed such good friends with them. James determined to make his decision on the walk to Tribal Council, after seeing how strong Uzma was. Satisfied that she was bearing up solidly he decided to vote with what he thought was the majority, rather than risk a split vote and the turmoil that could cause.

But what James did not know then was that underneath Simon's happy-go-lucky exterior lay, what James describes, as "a bit of a philosopher". His instinct was to team up with the younger, more fun members of Helang but he knew the tribe had to remain strong. While JJ was bossy and domineering, she was also strong, fit and capable. The positives outweighed the negatives. Uzma on the other hand, while a lovely girl, seemed to lack fight in his opinion. "As far as I was concerned Uzma had to go, she was weak," he says now. "I don't even know why she was there – she was complaining and whingeing from the start. The main thing about me is that I want to win and I wanted the tribe as strong as possible." Therefore, he had taken the decision to vote Uzma off in the best interests of Helang, even though he knew Charlotte and Adrian were voting for JJ. But he had underestimated Charlotte's dislike of JJ.

James misread Simon's intentions, a confusion that led to a highly dramatic and controversial couple of hours at Tribal Council. Had James found time to quiz Simon on his choice of vote on the journey through the jungle then it is likely he would have sided with the majority, and it would have been Uzma leaving the island, JJ would have stayed, and the youth alliance might well have been fatally wounded. But James stuck with JJ and the result was that the votes were split four-four. Mark Austin asked everyone bar JJ and Uzma to leave their seats and discuss whom they would vote for. At this point communications broke down drastically. James realised that Simon voted logically and decided that he would switch his vote to Uzma. On the other hand, Simon decided that the split in vote would mean the atmosphere in the tribe would be terrible if JJ was to return to the beach. The tribe would be split right down the middle. Unfortunately, neither told the other and so yet again the vote was split. The whole thing was becoming farcical. Austin asked all six to consult once more.

Tensions were running very high; JJ was furious. She thought it unfair that her tribe had not come to a unanimous decision whether to eject her or Uzma, leaving them sitting there "like lemons". Uzma, who was relaxed about the whole process, tried to calm her down, pointing out that in just a few hours one of them would be luxuriating in a five-star hotel with hot running water, fine food and clean sheets. Meanwhile, across the other side of the set the rest of Helang were deep in discussion. Andy and Jayne were arguing for JJ's retention, against Charlotte's pleading. In her view, to allow JJ back in would mean the tribe would have to cope with a terrible atmosphere. More selfishly Charlotte knew that JJ's return would almost certainly mean she would be voted off the island next. Her very survival on the island depended on whether her opinion would sway others. At her own admittance, she "begged" with the others to vote for JJ. Then she fainted.

Andy caught her as she fell and a medic was called instantly. Uzma ran over, worried about what had happened to her friend. As she was being treated, Charlotte came round. The medic passed her fit to carry on, detecting no signs of increase in heart rate or blood pressure or indeed, anything wrong with her at all. But that is not to say Charlotte fainted on purpose; the contestants had eaten little in six days, most were not taking on enough water and humidity and heat were severe. Given the tension at Tribal Council, it is conceivable that these factors combined to cause Charlotte to swoon. She is adamant this was the case.

"When there was a split vote I tried to influence James and Simon. I panicked immediately. I fainted, and it was a real faint. I had got myself so worked up, and we had walked all the way through the jungle. It was really humid and I had had hardly any water. I have fainted in the past. I remember breathing really, really fast and my eyes going and I just fell to the floor. The doctor came rushing over, but all I wanted to do was to get straight back up because I knew I needed to speak to them because Andy was going to try and change their minds. There was no way I would have fainted on purpose because I didn't want to be out of the conversations. I got back up and I was saying, 'No, Simon please. If JJ comes back it will be awful.' At the end of the day, I said to Simon, Uzma was still on our side, she was a friend and made life on the island bearable at that time. So, I just basically pleaded with Simon and James. I thought she [JJ] was having a detrimental effect on our team, because it was like having a teacher there. Three of us were being affected by her, and we were actively not doing stuff because she was telling us to do it all the time, and we were getting so sick of it. She had to go."

JJ, unsurprisingly, believes Charlotte put the faint on because she was losing the argument with Andy and that her "amateur dramatics" swayed Simon and James, who did not want to upset her further. "She definitely faked it. I have seen enough people faint on parade to know how people react when they actually faint. They do not land like that. The discussion between the six of them was not going the right way and she went for the sympathy vote," she says. But for the true story it is perhaps wise to consult other members of the tribe. Simon believed at the time that the faint was genuine and even if it wasn't, he says, then he began to see how badly JJ's return could affect the mood of the tribe, so his mind was swayed for good. Likewise, James says he does not know whether the faint was genuine but believes voting for JJ was still the right thing to do. Given her anger when she was finally voted off, he thinks she would have been unbearable. Andy says it is a question for Charlotte – at the time he was convinced the faint was real. Adrian, again unsurprisingly, claims it was real, but with less than 100 per cent conviction, citing the fact that Charlotte's brother has fainted before as conclusive proof that it was a genuine collapse.

Jayne believes Charlotte faked it. "It was all a set-up and no one else could see it," she says. "It was just ghastly. I was like 'Oh my God. I can't believe this.' She totally faked it. I said to Andy 'She's a drama queen.' It took him about another two weeks to suss it out, just what she had done. She is an attractive, pretty girl and I'm afraid they all fell for it, hook, line and sinker. But I had sussed her completely."

Also interesting is Uzma's verdict, considering how worried she was when the incident first took place and the time she has had to reflect upon it since: "I was quite flattered that Charlotte fainted. I knew what was going on. It was a put-on, I'm certain. At the time I didn't know that. I was really upset and in tears. It was scary. It was flattering that someone would go so far but I don't think that was for me. I think it might have been for the camera." If it was, it was unsuccessful, as it failed to make the final cut.

But whether it was genuine or not, the result was that JJ was voted off the island. On account of all that had passed at Tribal Council, she was absolutely furious, a reaction which made the decision to eject her more palatable. People could imagine what would have happened had she remained. As she left, she turned to the tribe and spat out, "I would like to say I know exactly who voted for me," before flouncing away in indignation. After she had left, everyone remained silent, shell-shocked almost from what had happened. The walk back to the beach was very quiet and pensive. This was a blow that Helang would take a while to recover from. Despite her personality being too much for some to take, JJ had been a leader. Helang were rudderless, and with Andy unwilling to step into the breach, that would cause them problems.

As they trudged back forlornly, JJ gave her final interview on the island, anger still coursing through her veins. In it she revealed that Andy had said to her that day that he thought she would get the million, and that two days ago Charlotte had said the same thing. She also claimed that Uzma had said to her, "You're the nicest person I know." JJ returned the compliment, describing Uzma as "lovely", not a description she applied to Charlotte. Since giving her confession, her opinion of Charlotte as "the fluffiest and most useless person I know" has not mellowed. If anything, it has become more emphatic.

"Charlotte realised my strength and the fact I had her sussed. She didn't like that one bit. I sussed her on the Saturday, at the briefing the day before we went to the island. I was something she couldn't control and she's a little madam who doesn't like that. I think she's a very spoilt young lady who has always had her own way. Whether it be from family, parents, or just life, she has always got and achieved everything that she has gone for. I think she saw me as someone who would definitely stop her from doing that."

Week 2

Two down ...

THE AFTERMATH OF JJ's departure was an uncertain time for Helang. Had they lost an organiser, a motivator, or a bad-tempered dictator? One person who subscribed to the latter view was Charlotte, but some of her tribe-mates were not so sure. It had been a bruising evening. The next morning, day eight, saw them lacklustre, lacking in energy and downhearted, particularly when they went off for that afternoon's Reward Challenge, T-shirts on a log, and lost. They had to watch Ular walk away with four tins of baked beans, together with a spear, a mask and a pair of flippers to help them catch fish. Hunger was playing a big part in the minds of the contestants now and Ular celebrated winning baked beans as if they had just claimed the FA cup. Boiled rice can become a very boring dish, even when it's your one and only dish of the day, and the chance to spice it up with some beans was most welcome. Watching Ular's delight only served to worsen the ceaseless gnawing Helang members felt in their stomachs. They desperately needed to break their losing streak by winning the next day's Immunity Challenge but without adequate food to give them strength they would struggle. Now Ular had been given an energy boost and the task had become even harder.

Helang were not aided by the gulf that was opening up between Andy, James and Jayne on one hand, and Uzma, Charlotte and Adrian on the other. For a start, the older members of the tribe, who had children, tended to rise earlier, while the younger members sought to snatch an extra hour or two of sleep. But that meant an extra hour of catching fish was lost, not that that bothered Adrian who, because he did not eat fish, refused to hunt it. When words were said to the young ones about getting busier around the camp they would have nothing of it. "We are not going to be bullied just because they're older. It doesn't mean they know any better," said Charlotte, perhaps expressing some residual contempt for Andy and Jayne's decision not to be swayed into voting against JJ.

Back at the camp, this atmosphere had Andy contemplating changing his strategy and taking charge of Helang. Simon said he felt Andy should step into the vacuum left by JJ's departure but for some reason that he could not fathom, the pilot was reluctant to do so. There was no questioning his credentials. He was at home in the conditions, having done combat survival training while in the RAF. Most of what he had learned was now fifteen years old, and relevant to a European theatre, also a lot of it had been forgotten. But importantly, he says, "I had done all that journey of self-discovery bit. When the deprivations strip away all the excess packaging of your personality you get to find out who you really are. I knew what was underneath and I was quite comfortable with it. That was the advantage of having done the survival stuff."

Survival was something he was always fascinated with. He had performed basic training, which involved spending six days and nights on the North Yorkshire Moors with just a single dinghy, knife and matches. He has also taken part in escape and evasion exercises, learning how to avoid capture in hostile terrain, and a three-week combat survival course, which meant spending six or seven days on Dartmoor. As a result of it all he became a Survival and Rescue Instructor for a special flight unit, briefing others on what to do should they have to land or crash on enemy ground. He had entered *Survivor* as one of the few, together with Richard and Nick, who expected life to be much tougher than it was. They expected to be given nothing – no rice, fishing nets, tools - and forced to fend completely for themselves. As soon as the game got underway, Andy realised that it was very much going to be assisted survival. He wanted the whole thing to get as tough as possible, however. At one stage he told one of the producers, "Nobody could make this experience too tough for me. There are sixteen people on the island and if you make it as tough as you can then fifteen people will drop out before I do."

Evidence of this arrived as soon as the first day when Andy, to his disappointment, got separated from his rucksack on the boat and it was mistakenly taken by a member of Ular. But apart from irritation at his own stupidity, it did not worry him unduly. He had the clothes he was wearing – T-shirt, shorts and flip-flops – and that would be enough for him. When he was told that, for safety reasons, he needed shoes and long trousers to walk through the jungle in, he borrowed some of James's clothing, which just about fitted. It cemented their friendship at an early stage. Andy was fully expecting never to see his rucksack again and did not care, but was pleasantly surprised when it was handed to him on day two by the Ular tribe member who had taken it. Again his thoughts were that this would not be as tough as he had expected.

Strong, quick-witted and capable, he was one of the favourites to claim the prize before the contestants arrived on the island. His experience also marked him out as a natural leader, particularly in a group desperately requiring leadership. His strategy, however, was to keep as low a profile as possible to avoid being voted off as a threat too early in the game. "My idea was that I did not want to be seen as a leader and I did not want people to know I had any experience of survival at all. I did not want to conceal it – I'm not a very good liar – but I very much wanted to downplay it. There are other things I wanted to make less off. I downplayed how much I was missing home because if you don't then there are some nasty people who don't need a reason to vote you off, but there are some nice people who do. And the fact you are missing your children is one of them," he says.

Andy, a father of three, was there for the money, and states that unequivocally. At first the idea of the game appealed to his sense of adventure and fun but as the game proper drew nearer his reason for competing changed."In the final analysis it was only what I could bring home to my family that allowed my conscience to let me take two months off work, and take two months away from my family," he says. "I was offered a one in sixteen chance of winning a million pounds and I could not have looked my children in the eye and say 'I turned it down.' I was there for the cash, and that was it."

Yet after JJ's ejection his tribe was floundering and badly needed leadership to unite the two factions or the money would be but a distant dream. At this stage, Andy said he was only willing to "tweak" his strategy to ensure his tribe went into the merger at least level with their rivals otherwise they would be picked off one by one. "I might have to play my cards a bit more openly," he told the camera crew before going on to slate the attitude of the tribe's younger members. "Why would you come here for a holiday? If I was to go on holiday, I wouldn't come here. I would take my family. I wouldn't come away with seven other strangers, even if it is free. I'm here to play a game. I'm here to play it hard and as well as I can. I'm not interested in a tan, or interested in lying on a beach. I'm here to win."

Across the island, the mood was strikingly different. Since Nick's departure, the atmosphere within the camp had been good, everyone appeared to be getting on and they were performing well in the challenges. They had managed to establish tribal unity, a sense of belonging to the tribe, which was serving them well when it came to competing with Helang, whom they had grown to dislike, at least according to Richard. "There was a very passionate tribal thing going on for Ular," he says. "We did despise Helang, we really did and anyone who tells you any different is lying. It was a tribal thing, like supporting a football team. We were snakes, not the nicest thing to be known as. But though they were eagles, their emblem was like some neo-nazi motif. It fitted them well."

Winning day eight's Reward Challenge had been a positive experience for Ular for another reason – witnessing Helang's mood. As Mick told the camera: "They looked demoralised. We understand they have lost their leader, although they might not have wanted her as leader. But when they lost that challenge today they looked totally shot away. I mean, when they walked down the sand spit their heads were literally hanging down." Morale within the Ular camp could not have been better going into the next day's

Immunity Challenge.

But the loss of the Reward Challenge appeared to produce a new, determined aspect to Helang's outlook. They ended the eighth day with Simon vowing "we will kill ourselves tomorrow to win," and by the next morning Andy was exhorting them to "dip into their reservoirs" of strength and aggression to win the challenge, although Uzma said she feared hers was merely a puddle. But there were signs that Andy's pride had been pricked by recent losses and he was coming more to the fore. "I'm going to die out there this afternoon," he told everyone.

Stirring words. The words might have been big. However, the deeds were small. Helang were dreadful in the Immunity Challenge. The task was to dive to the seabed and bring a treasure chest back to shore. Unfortunately the chest does not float and for much of the way the tribes had to drag it. Helang failed to budge it an inch, diving at different times and acting completely out of sync. In stark contrast, Ular were ruthless, efficient and expertly organised and seconds into the challenge it was over as a contest. Humiliated, Helang had to drag themselves back to their beach knowing someone would be going home the next evening and their losing streak was swiftly turning into a rout that threatened the tribe's very existence in the game.

Simon, in particular, was appalled at how badly they had performed. "We said we wanted to come out of there drowning, but we came out with our arses in our hands instead," he said bitterly. He was beginning to question the amount of desire some of his other tribe-mates had for the fight. For Andy, this was a positive response from Simon, whom he had wondered about before. He had initially seemed too keen to get on with everyone and maintain his own position in the middle of the tribe and therefore had ignored the fact that the factions within were slowly destroying everyone's chances. Simon, Andy felt, had more ambition than he had previously let on and this was exactly what Helang required. They needed to get rid of the person who was most holding them back and for that there was only one obvious candidate – Uzma.

Charlotte and Adrian did not want Uzma to go, for the obvious reason that that would weaken their position within the tribe. They wanted rid of Jayne, whom Charlotte disliked and Adrian *despised,* a feeling that was mutual. Andy and James were certain to vote for Uzma, as was Jayne, leaving the casting vote in Simon's hands. Charlotte and Adrian hoped to influence Simon and get him on side but there was no way he was going to be swayed once again. The first time they had gone to Tribal Council it had been his intention to remove Uzma and he was certain this second time that she had to go. Though he liked her, he believed she had no resilience or appetite for the fights and challenges ahead and that she would be a handicap to their chances. To be honest, even Uzma was certain that it was time for her to leave.

Uzma was never really on the island to win, and she knew she had little chance of doing so. By the age of thirty, she had already earned more than enough money running a string of successful nurseries and winning a number of Government contracts in the process. Her business success meant she had decided to take 2001 away from work and do something different with her life. Supremely self-confident – she often travels alone to places across the world – she was not fazed when she was chosen to go on *Survivor.* Not the sort of woman to spend hours in front of the television watching reruns of the American show, Uzma approached it with the intention of "having a laugh", which she did. Once, however, it stopped being a laugh, she then desperately wanted to go. She was also, as she says now, unwilling to get involved in the double-dealing and backstabbing required to go a long way in the game, wary of how this sort of behaviour would have gone down with her family.

"We are from a modern family but then we don't disrespect our Muslim culture. I took my sarong along and tried to wear it as often as I could. My culture and my religion is important to me. If anything comes from my time on the island at all, I hope that I have a been a role model to Asian women and for them to think watching the programme, 'If she can do it, we can do it.' All I wanted to do was be myself, and not compromise myself, be a bitch or be nasty. Maybe I wasn't the best of contestants. To win, you had to be a bit devious and I wasn't. Hence I got chucked out. But *Survivor* was fantastic. I've learnt about myself and I've learnt about my strengths and weaknesses." Interestingly, Uzma has told every member of Helang that they are coming to stay at her house in Hertfordshire for a weekend, and will not take no for an answer from any of them. She refuses to confirm whether JJ and Charlotte will be sharing a room.

The day of the Immunity Challenge Uzma told everyone to vote for her, though Charlotte and Adrian did not, deciding instead to put some votes in against Jayne. Should any contestant be in a tie at Tribal Council with another, then the person who has had the least overall votes against them remains on the island. Uzma, however, decided to vote against James for no real reason other than to ensure she was certain of going home. The others, all of whom said positive words about Uzma's warm and friendly personality while casting their votes, voted as expected and Helang had lost their second member, although Uzma's mood was wildly in contrast with JJ's. The smile on Uzma's face as she extinguished her torch testified to how happy she was to be going home. Then she bounded down the path to a waiting boat which whisked her back to Kota Kinabalu, where she enjoyed eight days of massages, facials, shopping and clubbing before returning to Britain. Off the island, out of Charlotte's shadow and away from the bickering, Uzma had returned to being her old self.

Ular start to crack

All had been going well for Ular, but in a sense Helang's losing streak began to have a negative effect on their rivals. Not going to Tribal Council for almost a week meant things were progressing steadily and, inevitably, some people got bored. The devil finds work ...

Three people were running the group, Richard, Eve and Sarah, or so the last two thought. In fact, Richard and Jackie were driving the group but their alliance was still a secret, no one having seen any signs of friendship between them. Eve had become great friends with Sarah, both being direct and physically active people. The pair had formed a "core three" with Richard. Sarah and Eve had little time for the less physically able among the group, though that is a charge they would deny, hiding behind the assertion that they were just saying what they thought. The group spent time one evening discussing which five of them would take part in the assault course if that challenge arose. Jackie suggested she should be part of it, prompting Sarah to respond with, "Jackie, you have no upper-body strength. You couldn't even get yourself up on a slippery log." Jackie was offended by this less than diplomatic retort. Sarah felt Jackie was harming the tribe by putting herself forward for a challenge. In her view, she was speaking the truth. Maybe so, but closeted with strangers in a hostile environment is no place for blunt-speaking. Jackie's dislike of Sarah was beginning to fester.

Her dissatisfaction was shared by Zoe. The tribe had agreed that should they have to go to Tribal Council again then they would vote a woman off, because to vote another man off would leave them at a physical disadvantage for the challenges. With Sarah and Eve in charge, Jackie and Zoe were the favourites for the chop. For the latter, who never shared the "Go Ular" mentality, it felt like being bullied by the strong people at school. The laws of the jungle had become diluted by the rules of the playground. Zoe felt like "dead meat" waiting to be cut off from around the edges. But she resented the fact that people were acting as if they were superior just because they were physically fitter and stronger. Their athlete's mentality contrasted sharply with Zoe's light-hearted, self-deprecating view of the world. But Zoe had one skill that neither Sarah and Eve possessed – she knew people and how to get on with them. She possesses a degree in psychology but dismisses its significance. "When people hear that you've got a psychology degree they go, 'Ooh, are you analysing me?' I'm like, 'No, I only know what happens when you put a rat in a maze and stick a blindfold on it.' " But she is good with people. If it came down to who could run quickest up a muddy slope then Zoe was going to struggle. But when it came to getting on with people, knowing what they were thinking and manipulating them, Zoe would survive. That was what the game was all about, otherwise, as she says, they would have given the programme the catchline, "*Survivor*: sixteen meatheads who go to the gym."

That evening saw the competitors experience their first torrential storm on the island. It had rained before, heavily, but it was nothing like the spectacular monsoon of that evening. The weather on Pulau Tiga has a dramatic beauty to it. First, the clouds gather in the distance. Then they burst; huge drops fall, slowly at first, then more and more heavily until it's like God has opened the sluices and the water is being fired at the earth by a million jet hoses. In seconds water is falling and cascading everywhere. The shelters built by the contestants were inadequate in the face of such a deluge. They would have to get used to sleeping in wet clothes, with wet bedding and the drilling sound of the rain on the beach, water and shelter roof. The storm that night lasted for twelve hours, ruining any chance of sleep for all.

The next morning dawned to reveal everyone sodden and bleary-eyed. Zoe was in a precarious position, which worsened following that day's Reward Challenge, Wobbly Maze, when Andy finally took charge of Helang and calmly guided them to victory. Their reward was three live chickens, sustenance that would give them extra energy and a renewed sense of determination for the following day's Immunity Challenge, which they simply had to win to have any chance of parity in tribal merger. The loss put extra strain on Ular. Cracks were beginning to show in their façade and Zoe got the feeling she was the one likeliest to go.

Eve and Sarah had formed their partnership with Richard on the way to vote off Nick, forming a three. Sarah had been the driving force persuading Eve to let Richard into their alliance. The pair were both adventure racers. Indeed, Richard admits to "hero-worshipping" the blonde model from London. He had heard of her and watched her race before going on the island, following the progress of her career closely, including the victory in the 2000 Raid-Gauloises race as part of a Finnish team. She had got into the sport when she realised she was lacking challenges in her life as a model. All you need to do is keep in shape and turn up to castings, people look through your portfolio and that's it, she says. "You are picked purely on your assets and you have to understand that if you don't fit the idea they have of the image that they want then they won't choose you. It's not a personal thing," she adds. "I needed more of a challenge and wanted to push myself a bit. I had seen these races on television when I was living in Paris and I thought it was an amazing opportunity. You can go to obscure parts of the world annd compete with a team. I'd missed out on travelling when I was younger, it was all luxury as a model and I just wanted to get lowdown and dirty. This summed up everything I wanted to do at the time."

Sarah initially tried to play down her past, thinking it would mark her down as a threat. Her cover was nearly blown on the way to one of the earlier challenges when one of the island guides recognised her from an Eco-Challenge race held in Sabah six months previously. Sarah denied it, and Richard stepped in to save her anonymity by telling the guide she merely looked like the woman he was thinking of. Later Richard plucked up the courage and shyly asked her if she was Sarah Odell, though he already knew the answer was yes. When she confirmed his suspicions she felt uncomfortable because it was clear just how much Richard idolised her but after a couple of conversations she warmed to him.

The pair began to strike up a rapport. The alarm bells that rang so clearly in Sarah's head when she first set eyes on Richard faded as the pair realised they had been to the same places and had mutual friends in the adventure racing sport. Compared to Sarah's achievements, Richard's were paltry, but he had raced coast-to-coast across New Zealand and knew of the hardship, struggle and dedication the sport required. He was delighted to have met someone he idolised, while Sarah was glad to have someone she had something in common with. They had something to talk about other than how hungry they were, or how little sleep they had had, something that was a million miles away from the constant scheming and backbiting that had slowly begun to envelop the island. So when Eve was not sure about forming an alliance with Richard, who she thought untrustworthy, she was persuaded by Sarah to agree to the idea. "He can be trusted," she said, though the sole basis of that assertion was that Richard was an adventure racer and therefore he would never stitch up one of his own. In her opinion, he knew the value of teamwork and working together. He wouldn't endanger that by doing something stupid.

Richard's inclusion meant the core suddenly became four because he brought in Jackie, again not entirely to Eve's liking. Eve and Jackie had disliked each other on sight and had enjoyed an uneasy relationship at best since arriving on the island. Jackie thought Eve abrupt and aggressive while Eve did not like the way she had to pussyfoot around Jackie, to avoid hurting her feelings. But there were still four of them and as long as they remained together they would get to the last four and then personal differences would not matter because it would be every man for himself. That was how Eve reconciled it to herself. But she still could not shift the nagging disquiet she felt about Jackie being in the alliance. She decided that she would speak to Sarah and Richard about it when the time came.

It came sooner than Ular and Eve hoped. On day twelve they went to the Mangrove swamp for the next Immunity Challenge to meet a revitalised Helang tribe whose hunger had been sated the previous day by a chicken meal. Twenty masks, ten for each tribe, had been positioned carefully around the swamp. In relay, the tribe members had to run and collect the masks – yellow for Helang, blue for Ular. The first to collect theirs won immunity. So rejuvenated were Helang that they trounced Ular, who put up a sorry performance. The days of inactivity, of not having to troop for an hour through the jungle to go to Tribal Council and go through the painful process of voting someone off, had made them lazy. Helang had to win and they did. It was if Ular wanted to vote someone off. As Helang rejoiced in their reversal of luck, Ular stood in stunned disbelief, watching them celebrate. Jackie and Zoe's wishes had come to fruition – things were going to get more interesting on Ular beach.

From Hero to Zero

Ular returned to re-establish their alliances. First up was a meeting between Sarah, Eve and Richard. Eve and Sarah had decided that Jackie was not to be trusted and they were tired of walking on eggshells in order not to offend her. They had decided that she should be replaced in the four by Zoe. Richard, however, was not happy about the decision. Obviously, this was because it threatened his (still secret) alliance with Jackie, but it also offended his sense of fair play. He asked what made them agree to Jackie rather than Zoe in the first place, to which Eve replied that she had started to believe Jackie had changed and gained confidence, but she had been wrong. "I don't think you can rely on her vote and how long is Jackie going to vote how we tell her to vote?" Eve asked him. "I think there's even honour amongst thieves," Richard replied, his eyes narrowing.

This volte face from Eve and Sarah was not what he had in mind at all. "I know it's daft but I don't have any loyalty to anybody here … I think you've got to be cold-hearted about it," Eve said, continuing the argument. But Richard was unconvinced that playing the game meant betraying someone so completely, as he saw it. "So, when do I become expendable?" he enquired pointedly.

Richard decided he did not like the way Eve and Sarah were running things and a different tack was necessary. Eve and Sarah had to be split up and because Sarah was more unpopular than Eve she was the one who they should try and squeeze out. There was no way he was going to break his alliance with Jackie. It would have meant rewriting his whole strategy, which until that point had served him well. This is how Richard said the plan was hatched to ditch Sarah

"Jackie and I were in shelter that night sleeping next to her. It was full. We couldn't talk so Jackie and me were writing on each other's hands, messages, like we did with Nick. I wrote on her hand, 'Can you get Zoe?' She wrote 'Yes, I think so.' We would have conversations like that for an hour and a half or something, and if we lost track we would just wipe off whatever was on our hands and start again. That night we hatched a plan to suss Zoe out, and then suss out Mick and then suss out Pete. Either of those two would have been fine. It became apparent that Mick disliked Sarah and it became a feeling of 'Right, we just don't like her, she's gotta go.' Which was a shame for me because, if it wasn't for her selfishness, she was good fun and we had a lot of things in common."

But Richard was not aware that at the same time as his flare-up was taking place, Zoe and Jackie were on a trip into the jungle to replenish their water supplies. After losing the Immunity Challenge, Zoe knew she had twenty-four hours to save herself. Reasoning she was not going to be able to influence the athletes, she decided the best way to turn things around was to form a counter-alliance with the weak and disaffected.

But Zoe needed to get Jackie on side. Little did she know that Jackie was as fed up with the "health fascists" as she was herself, and agreed with Zoe when she said they were acting as if the others were insignificant. It had been irritating Jackie since the Immunity Challenge that she was going to be voting for Zoe when the people she least liked on the island were Eve and Sarah. But she did not want Richard to go – she was keen to keep the alliance, sensing it was in her best interests. She suggested Sarah but Zoe disagreed. Richard should go, she said, because Mick would agree to vote him off. Jackie argued that Mick might agree to vote for Sarah and so would Richard, which surprised Zoe because she thought Richard's alliance with Eve and Sarah was deeply entrenched. But Jackie convinced her that she could sway Richard and, grateful for any lifeline, she agreed to seek out Pete and Mick's views on Sarah while Jackie took care of Richard. In the end, they communicated by using a smuggled pen, but the upshot was that Sarah was in real trouble.

Her cause was not helped by the fact that Pete and Mick had both become absolutely fed up with her condescending way of telling them how to perform simple tasks. Mick in particular, after twenty-five years' working with the police, did not want to feel as if he was looked down upon by a model twenty-two years his junior. He also felt Sarah was not pitching in around the camp and was only interested in her own welfare. Pete shared this view and he was the one suffering most from Sarah constantly telling him what to do. Much as he didn't like it, he admits that he let people walk over him a bit on the island. Not being the sort of person to provoke conflict he bit his tongue on several occasions, but when

Sarah began telling him how to swim properly he decided enough was enough. Pete was going to vote for her whether anyone else did or not.

Sarah had no idea her time was running out. After their row with Richard, she and Eve had decided to relent and stick with the Zoe plan, even though Sarah liked Zoe. The pair had shared an amusing moment a couple of days before when Sarah said to Zoe, "I wonder who the token gay person is?" To which Zoe, replied "It's me". That night Sarah and Eve checked with Jackie to see if she and Richard were still part of the alliance and happy with the plan. Jackie said that everything was fine. Zoe, despite knowing that Mick and Pete were voting Sarah with her, was still uncertain over whether her future was safe and that Jackie would be as good as her word. It did not help that Eve was not being very friendly to her. Eve is the sort of person who finds it hard to hide her feelings so when she knew she was voting someone off she found it difficult to pretend nothing was happening and all was OK. On the day of the Immunity Challenge she and Zoe had an extremely uncomfortable trip to the water hole. Zoe was quite resigned to going, talking of how she would bequeath her toothbrush to Peter and how she was going home. "It's been lovely to know you all," she said, rather dramatically. How much was genuine and how much was Zoe utilising her talents as an actress is a moot point, but Zoe claims that she really believed she was going home. It was only when Jackie reassured her, on the trip to Tribal Council, that she would be alright, that she knew she was safe.

On the walk to Tribal Council, Sarah walked with Richard and Jackie, chatting amiably all the way. Nothing seemed different, and she detected no awkwardness. She had brought a Tupperware box with her, into which she was going to put some mud. The plan was for her and Eve to cover themselves in it tomorrow, let it bake in the sun and then wash it off in the sea, rather than wear it for Tribal Council. She had always said that she would not wear any mud for the Tribal Council when she knew she was going to be voted off the island. Ironically, here she was, about to be voted off, and her face was clean. At the mud volcano she filled the box, as Eve and Richard and Jackie smeared mud on their face. The only one of the supposed "core four" not to join in was Sarah. Slowly and deliberately Richard smeared the cool mud across his face. As Sarah watched she became uneasy. Eve and Jackie put on the mud with a smile, laughing and joking all the while. But there was something sinister in the way Richard silently smoothed the mud over his skin. It completely masked the way he looked. He became expressionless, only his two watery blue eyes poking through. Soon Richard's ritual was over and the tribe was on its way again to Tribal Council. Eve came up to her and said that Zoe's torch had blown out several times on the walk. The tribe had become extremely superstitious about fire since the first Tribal Council and they took very seriously the part about fire representing their life on the island. Sarah began to feel sorry for Zoe and guilty about what they were about to do. She consoled herself that it was all part of the game.

As they took their seats, Sarah began to pick up a lot of hostility from Richard. It seemed as if he was avoiding meeting her eye. But still she felt safe and secure about her future. Being voted off never crossed her mind. She just thought Richard was behaving oddly and there was nothing new in that at all. One by one they went off to vote and still she was confident she was staying. At one point, she thought she heard Mick's voice from the voting booth say he was voting for Jackie. What he was actually saying was that Sarah was "stunningly attractive" and that any red-blooded male would delight in her company, but "not on this island". Sarah again dismissed the notion; no one could hear what was being said because of the noise from the Tribal Fire between the voter and the rest of the tribe. The only noises they could hear were what they imagined. A contestant would have to have a voice like a foghorn for the others to hear – and, anyway, Charlotte whispered her comments.

At one point, Sarah turned to Eve and they smiled at each other. Tomorrow they would spend time relaxing, getting rid of the previous evening's tension. A mud facial then a swim, the perfect way to prepare for the Reward Challenge. Then Mark Austin read out the names. First out was Sarah's. She didn't panic, it was never nice to be voted for but she expected that Pete, Mick and Zoe might vote against her. Next name out was Zoe, then Sarah, then another for Sarah – Pete's, who told the camera that "I've got one mother. I don't need another." That was probably the last of the three votes in her name, she thought. Zoe's name came out again, her second. Two more votes to go, both with Zoe's name on. But the next one said "Sarah". That was it, she was out. The next name out of the pot belonged to her as well and, before she knew it, Austin was speaking and she was extinguishing her flame. As she says now, she was utterly dumbfounded by what had happened.

"I was so shocked. I picked up my bag, and went through the motions. I wasn't broken, or felt like crying, it was just a really horrible feeling, like a bad dream. I was not supposed to be going home. I thought I contributed a lot to the team. I thought I was not a disagreeable person. I didn't want to say anything to anybody as I left. The whole island experience flashed in front of my eyes and my immediate thought was that Eve had betrayed me and that was just horrible, the thought made me feel really weak. Then it sank in that it was Richard and Jackie. I was like 'Why? I was your mate Richard.' I suppose that I must think that Richard was just playing the game but it is very, very difficult knowing that he stitched me up so completely. I really thought he liked me, not that I care now. I just hope I get to see him on the starting line of an adventure race in the near future then I will get revenge. I would beat him easily. The only thing he'd see of me was my backside, as I disappeared off in the distance."

She realised that she should have paid more attention to those around her and not taken it for granted that she would be on the island for any length of time. "My head was in the clouds," she admits. "And I suppose I became too absorbed in the island experience – it was amazing. I've been to so many different countries and experienced so many places but I have always been concentrating on the race. Here was a chance for me to absorb the island and its atmosphere. I love the elements so much. It was wonderful to be able to swim every day, being able to spill out of your little hut and fall into the ocean. I wanted to understand what it was like to have to fight for food. You can get by on very little and all the energy you spend thinking about food, pigging out and digesting, all that goes and you get a real clarity. I felt really alive, colours seemed very clear. I knew what it was like to be physically tired and weak and I knew I could push through that and come right. I loved playing in the sand, playing in the mud, picking up shells and making necklaces. It was an adult game of 'dens' as far as I was concerned.

"I very much removed myself from the group. I couldn't be bothered sitting around chatting all the time. Six weeks is a long time and I didn't feel the need to be in everyone's faces. I liked everyone, though not all of them were the sort of person I would choose to be with. Some I got on with better than others. But no one was making me feel that bad but I simply didn't want to be around them all the time. I didn't allow myself to get paranoid. If six people were going off to work the fishing nets I didn't go because we didn't need another person and I felt there was other things for us to do. After sunset I wanted to go straight to sleep. I just got up and went. I didn't want to have that horrible feeling about whether people were talking about me when I wasn't there, so you don't want to be the first to leave. Perhaps it would have been in my interests to be more like that. I thought I could be out of character and be manipulating and conniving. I really wanted to play the game but I couldn't."

As Sarah made her shell-shocked way back to the mainland, she was not the only person to be in a state of shock. Eve could not believe what had happened. She sat there shaking her head, her eyes ablaze with anger. Unlike Sarah, she knew immediately who had betrayed the alliance and got rid of her best friend on the island. The tribe trudged out of Tribal Council. Eve was far too angry to say anything then. Her silence did not last too long, however.

Hell hath no fury like Eve scorned

The trip back was an uncomfortable one, as everyone waited for Eve to explode. They did not have to wait for too long. "What the f*** happened there?" Eve shouted at Richard and Jackie when they got back to the camp. Richard's response was simple: Eve's alliance had not worked. She had played the game badly. Jackie's opinion was that Eve had not been as clever as she thought she was being.

"When we got back to the beach, Eve said 'Come on

Jackie, tell me what happened. I must have missed a trick.' I said, 'Yeah, Eve, you did miss a trick. You're not as clever as you think you are, are you? You were going to change your vote and vote me off.' And she said, 'Oh, you've been talking to Richard have you.' We all tried to maintain that there wasn't an alliance, that Sarah had gone because that was just the way the votes fell. But there was an alliance really because we knew we were going to vote Sarah off. Eve was furious, said she took it as a personal slight and it was a crazy decision because Sarah was strong. It was crazy as well. I should have gone because Sarah was a really good team member, in terms of the strength of the team. But she was a nightmare though and nobody liked her."

Jackie's words, and Eve's, became more and more heated and the row culminated with Eve saying to Jackie, "Basically, you don't trust me do you?" Jackie's response was a succinct "No". As Eve stormed off, Jackie turned to the camera and in her most malevolent voice she spat out, "And you're next." Eve went up to apologise to Zoe for voting for her. Her reason, she said contritely, was that Zoe was an actress and therefore she was unsure whether she was playing a role on the island or not and so she could not trust her. Zoe was, to a certain extent, flattered. She did point out to Eve, however, that if she was that good an actress then she wouldn't be stuck on a rock in the South China Sea with a bunch of strangers that she would normally cross the road to avoid. She would be on tour in England, sitting in a dressing room slurping a gin and tonic, saying "Aren't I marvellous?'. According to Richard, from that point on Eve over-compensated and "sucked up" to Zoe. The pair did end up liking each other more, though, when both were voted off later in the game in quick succession.

But Sarah's ejection had changed the whole dynamic of the tribe. Richard, Jackie and Zoe were now very much in charge, with Mick and Pete happy to go along with the majority, which left Eve isolated, with not an ally in sight. Should they go to Tribal Council before the merger then it was certain she would have been voted off, a fact confirmed by each existing member of the tribe. But Eve is, in Richard's words, a "tough cookie" and was not going to accept her fate meekly. She had been in the army for almost ten years, serving in Northern Ireland and Bosnia. Finally, she had left to regain some control over her life and to prevent long periods of absence from her partner, Sean. She did not miss the military life, but she missed the challenges and adventure that it occasionally threw her way, so *Survivor* was a chance to replicate that. By her own admission, she saw the game in very black and white terms, not thinking that people would have three or four alliances on the go, which explained her bitterness following Sarah's departure. It was a lot murkier than she had planned for.

The next morning in a candid and embittered interview on camera she said she would still give her all in the challenges but the way she viewed her tribal colleagues had changed unalterably, starting with Richard first. "Richard wanted an alliance – a core three of Sarah, myself and him. But now it is clear that he only wants an alliance as long as he is in command of it and we all must bow down to what he says. The instant we started to question what he said he turned tail and stitched us up. He was coming out with comments like, 'I must be seen to maintain the moral high ground – I am a professional doctor with 2,500 patients at home and I must be seen to be honest and fair." Actually with hindsight, I should have pointed out to him that he told us he was planning to emigrate to the United States where his girlfriend lives, so he doesn't care two jots about what's going on with his patients back in Wales ... I think Richard keeps trying to come across as the joker and actually he's very callous and he doesn't care two hoots. And trying to come across as a professional – rubbish! The man doesn't care about anybody but himself."

She was equally free of restraint when the subject turned to Jackie. "My opinion of Jackie has now been confirmed for what it was right at the beginning. I had her assessed as being the weaker member of the tribe and I gave her a lot of encouragement. I realised at one stage I was intimidating her and I was domineering, so for the next three or four days I backed off, gave her space, took the blame for things myself in order to support her. But she is very fickle, she'll float with whatever opinion somebody else comes up with. I don't think she is capable of having her own opinion. She's very temperamental, prone to tantrums, flying off the handle and she doesn't take criticism well at all. None of us likes to be told we're not good at something, but sometimes, if it's true and proven, then you have to sit down and go, 'Yeah, it's actually not my strong point.' You'd be respected more. But she flew off the handle at Sarah when she made the justified comment that she [Jackie] was not the fittest member of the tribe, which was proven in previous challenges."

Eve pronounced herself bemused by Jackie's initial response to her inquest into Sarah's removal. First she was told that she voted off Sarah to go along with the majority and that she'd never discussed it with anybody. Then she was informed that Jackie and Zoe had spoken about it. Then Richard was mentioned. Eve was unimpressed by every single explanation. Part of her was revelling in her martyr status because it meant that she did not have to pretend to like people.

"I don't owe you anything, Jackie," she said to the camera. "I don't like you, I'm not going to make an effort with you anymore. But I'm not going to give you and Richard the satisfaction of being a loner – I will still be a full part of the tribe. But my attitude is that I don't need those five and will stay here as long as I can .... In a very strange way I was almost envious of Sarah getting voted off last night. We were both lied to and Sarah was voted off, but Sarah's away from them now. And I've got to live with them. I can't stand the sight of them!... This is Ular breaking up. Whereas we would usually spend time like this doing something together, now we're at separate ends of the beach .... There's no one in the tribe that I'd even want to spend five minutes with once I leave this island."

The fact was that the tribe had to come together to take part in the Reward Challenge on day fourteen. Eve warned that without Sarah the tribe would struggle in challenges and predicted that they would lose that day's challenge, which involved diving underwater for letters which had then had to be formed into a word, because Jackie was "an absolutely useless diver". She was right to predict defeat, but how much of that was down to Jackie or was the result of Helang being well fed and invigorated is impossible to judge. What was certain was that Ular had to find some way to plaster over the growing fissures within their camp before the next day's Immunity Challenge or Eve would be gone. Not many at that moment in time would have minded that outcome, however.

Despite being re-energised by their recent string of successes, Helang's divisions still remained. Victory in the Reward Challenge on day fourteen brought more delights in the shape of chocolate (which was particularly well received by Charlotte, who had talked of eating little else on hungrier days), beer, and tins of alphabet spaghetti. But it had done little to heal the increasing rift between the tribe's elders and the youthful cohort. Andy had grown increasingly distrustful of Charlotte and sick of Adrian's almost comic laziness. Dismissing Adrian as not being the brightest character he had ever encountered, he saw Charlotte as the person who held the power.

As far back as day eleven, the morning after Uzma's departure, Andy had related this view to Jayne, who was more than sympathetic to his point of view. Jayne told him how Uzma had come to her on the day she left and said how she felt Charlotte had dropped her, because she was no longer of use. Andy noted that it was ironic that Charlotte had voted off JJ because she was bossy, then had swiftly become domineering herself, prompting Jayne to say it was "just like *Animal Farm*". The servants had turned into their masters as soon as they had wrestled control from them. "I think if we want to put an end to this factional stuff, then Charlotte has to be the next target," he told Jayne. "Cut off the head, the rest of the body withers and dies. I had been thinking Adrian up until now but I don't like what Charlotte is doing .... She is a destructive force and a luxury we can't afford."

Week 3

Helang s last stand

THE VIEW OF Charlotte being a "destructive force" persisted for a couple of days but victories in the challenges seemed to convince Andy that Charlotte's natural athletic ability and positive approach in the challenges was far too beneficial to lose. Winning the chickens and chocolate had shown the rewards of having a strong tribe and the challenges were becoming increasingly crucial as merger approached. On the day of the Assault Course Challenge, to boost their strength a chicken meal was planned. Andy had killed the first one but James insisted on killing the second. His zeal for murdering animals had earned him the nickname "The Terminator" from the rest of the group. Adrian called him the "Village Militia" for his bloodlust, although a vegetarian folk singer would appear bloodthirsty to Adrian, who could not bear to watch anything being killed or gutted. It got him teased mercilessly by Andy. It also earned the scorn of Jayne, who describes Adrian as a "wuss" and believes her seven-year-old boy Warwick possesses more courage. Adrian is dismissive of such talk, claiming that just because he did not like to see things killed does not mark him out as a coward. He had read that the human body could survive for twenty-seven days without food, so he wasn't going to volunteer to gut fish or kill rats until it was absolutely necessary. He still shakes his head, however, when he recounts James's strange relish for the kill.

James insisted on killing the chicken because he felt, after eating chicken bought from a supermarket on countless occasions, it was time he should experience the bit no meat eater considers when sitting down to a Sunday roast – the animal's slaughter. In such an environment, the idea of sparing an animal when the alternative was an empty stomach did not occur to the contestants, unless they were called Adrian. All of the contestants were suffering from a lack of food, existing as they were on a couple of small bowls of rice a day and whatever they could catch from the sea. What you caught had a direct influence on how well you survived. No food meant no strength and no victories in the challenges. No one was catching and eating rats for the fun of it – according to Zoe it doesn't taste like chicken, it tastes like you would expect rat to taste like – and no one was killing animals for sport. At least people had enough respect for their quarry to eat it when they caught it. Apart from the two rats Simon drowned in a bucket, something he is still not proud of, no animal suffered in any way. Though the chicken James killed might have had a more dignified death. Acting on Andy's instruction he twisted the chicken's neck and pulled. Unfortunately he pulled too hard and the chicken's head came off in his hand and the carcass ran around the beach spurting blood before eventually running into the sea, from where it was recovered. Exactly the same fate befell the chicken Simon slaughtered.

Day fifteen was a pivotal one in the game. Whichever tribe

won the Immunity Challenge, an arduous, exhausting assault course, would enter the third week of the game in a strong position. With only a few days to go before merger, and one more Immunity Challenge, the losers faced the very real possibility of being picked off one by one by their stronger rivals at tribal merger. Jayne had decided that if Helang were to lose then she might well ask to be the next person voted from the island, for several reasons, by far the most important being the fact that she missed her son desperately. If she was to carry on to the merger, and her tribe were numerically at a disadvantage then there was no chance she could win and the best she could hope for then was a place on the jury, which meant another month on the island. That was too much to bear. If she went now she would be at home with Warwick within a week. Not to mention thousands of miles away from Charlotte. She could not believe how vain both Charlotte and Adrian were. James had been allowed to bring a mirror so he could put his contact lenses in, but the only time she saw the mirror being used by anyone else was when Charlotte and Adrian borrowed it to look at themselves. "Every time I turn[ed] around Adrian was gazing at himself in it," she says. "It was actually quite disturbing."

Together with being the most crucial, the Assault Course was by far the most physical challenge yet. It consisted of five legs, each to be run by a different member of the tribe. The first involved a sprint along the beach, broken up by a log, under which both contestants had to dig. The next section was a race across a fallen tree. If a contestant came off they had to return to the start and cross the tree again. They then had to run up a muddy slope and tag the next contestant in their tribe, who was suspended high above the jungle canopy. This was the toughest part of the race, the contestants having to drag themselves along a rope, unhook halfway and haul themselves up another line to a colleague on a platform. The fourth leg was to race down a cargo net, down a muddy hill, through a muddy pool under two bamboo logs, touch a stone, then back once more to tag their final colleague. They had to swing across a rope ditch, then go over two log obstacles and under another before sprinting to the finish and picking up the immunity idol. It was severely punishing.

Jackie and Jayne were the contestants who missed out for either tribe. The remaining five walked the course and had the rules of each section explained to them. Helang had decided Simon would lead off, Adrian would run next, Andy would take the rope haul, Charlotte the next stage and James the final sprint. Looking at the cargo net on the way round Charlotte became unsure of whether she could cope with it adequately. James, willing as ever, said he did not mind running that section. Unfortunately, as the rules of the section were read out he had not been listening, his mind had been elsewhere and it did not occur to him to ask, he says. The rules for the final section, which he was to perform initially, were to go under and then over the log obstacles. Perhaps that order stuck in his mind and was responsible for the error. Whatever, his wandering mind would cost Helang the game.

Simon trounced Mick on the first section of the game and despite Adrian coming off the balancing tree, he still had a healthy lead to pass on to Andy for the rope haul across the jungle. But Andy was up against Pete, almost certainly the strongest and fittest competitor on either side. Lighter than Andy, he was able to haul himself across at high speed. He closed the deficit on the first part of the leg, before showing astonishing strength to shimmy up the rope at such speed as to make Andy, no slouch, look as if he was standing still.

When he tagged Eve, Pete had turned a fifteen-second deficit into a healthy lead and all seemed lost for Helang. Andy admits that on that section, "I took an absolute pasting."

Eve set off down the cargo net and down the muddy slope before James could be released. With no sense of personal safety James flung himself down the net, and barrelled down the slope headfirst. Any obstacles in his way he just flung his body over and as he reached the muddy pool, Eve was just exiting. James jumped in, almost landing on her. He then ducked under the first pole, but stepped over the second to touch the stone and repeated the error on the way back. Unaware he tagged Charlotte who easily caught up with Zoe and went on to win by a considerable distance. Helang, reunited on the beach, were overjoyed when she emerged from the jungle clutching an idol, as it meant that they were reaching the merger with at least tribal parity. The celebrations were raucous. Andy sank to his knees with relief that what he believed to be a poor performance on the ropes had not cost his tribe the challenge. Ular looked on, knowing they would be visiting Tribal Council for the second time in succession.

But word came through that another "steward's inquiry" was being held. James describes what happened next. " I was absolutely screaming with joy. But then Mark walked up to me and said 'James, the rules said on this assault course that you had to go under the two bamboos and you didn't, you went over one of them so that means you are disqualified. Give me back the idol...' and he gave it to Ular. We all fell silent. Amazingly we all accepted it rather well. And nobody blamed me, even though they said they all knew that rule. Everyone had heard the rules, I just didn't remember it. That's part of me I suppose, sometimes I do go off in a dream."

At first he felt certain that his mistake would cost him his place on the island, but while most were disappointed, every-one knew James's mistake was genuine. He put all he had into every challenge, often putting himself in danger of injury, so it was hard to find fault with him. "If I had been in Ular I would have been voted off for being weak or a liability, that was their mentality," James says. "But Helang's wasn't like that. I earned their respect and I loved that whole team mentality, the com-petitive aspect. It was the biggest thing I got out of the whole game. I've always dreaded competition and that sort of stuff, and I was terrible at games at school. But on the island it was what I really benefited from – being part of a team, trying your hardest and getting respect for that. I still feel that was the most positive thing for me, even though Helang did not win that part of it. In that respect, I learned a lot about myself."

A mother first ...

The fortnight Jayne Meyler had spent on Pulau Tiga had not been the biggest struggle of her life. That had come seven years before when, three months after the birth of her only son, her husband was diagnosed as suffering from a brain tumour. For a whole year she was responsible for raising Warwick and nursing her husband. It toughened her up and gave her a huge empathy for people with illness, which helps her in her career as a massage therapist and fitness instructor. When she came through that ordeal, she knew she could cope with anything.

As a result, extreme hunger, rat for breakfast, uncomfort-able sleeping conditions, all these were minor inconve-niences, which is why she became so fed up with Adrian's whining and whingeing. She believes he has a lot of growing up to do. Already having one little boy at home to cope with, she did not need another. But while she disliked the political side of the game, the scheming and plotting, she loved living on the island. The sea, the unspoilt jungle, the wildlife, even the smell, she adored them all. Following defeat in the Immunity Challenge the previous day, however, she had come to the conclusion that enough was enough. She had already lost ten pounds in two weeks and could not afford to lose much more before she was rendered physically weak. But, most importantly, as she told the camera, she was missing her son far too much to be trapped on the island, beautiful as it was, for very much longer. There are some things that are more important than one million pounds. Thinking she could cope, and urged on and encouraged by her husband, she had decided the opportunity to take part in *Survivor* was one she would regret missing. She taped video messages for Warwick so he could see his Mum's face on a regular basis and left presents that he was given at intervals during her absence. But it never occurred to her that the separation would affect her as profoundly as it did:

"I've always been very competitive all my life," she told the camera. "I've always wanted to be first – I hate losing, and that's just sort of been a natural instinct with me. I've always wanted to be ahead of everybody else. So from that angle, fighting the elements here has not been a problem. But what I'm finding creeping upon me is that I'm missing my son very badly. I'm going to start crying in a minute … I have learned that, although I have always been very competitive and there is huge fight in me, that motherhood has taken over and that is the first thing in my life. Although it's been such a huge adventure here, and I've loved it, I want to be with my son …. The first thing I will do when I get home is grab Warwick and cuddle him to death. As time has gone on I have felt the call of motherhood very strongly. I was OK for the first week but it's got worse and worse. It's not the sort of thing I can explain to all of my tribe-mates because none of them are mothers. A couple of them are fathers and from what I've gathered they are very good fathers, but the bonding is never the same, I don't think."

After weighing all these feelings in her mind, Jayne informed Simon, Andy and James that she wished to be voted off that evening at Tribal Council. She did not have to say anything to Charlotte or Adrian because she knew they would be voting for her anyway. There had been little love lost between Jayne and Charlotte from the time they were on the raft and Jayne scolded her about her rowing technique. Realising that she had put herself in a potentially dangerous situation, she had tried all she could to heal her rift with Charlotte and survived as a result. But two weeks of Charlotte's company – Adrian she could handle, he was merely a lazy little boy – had "distressed" her. While recognising Charlotte was a strong woman, she found her personality "suffocating". Being comparatively quiet and reserved – but then, most people are compared to Charlotte – she was unable to compete and did not want to have to fight for the right to talk. "I think she's very devious and clever," she said on the island. "She uses her attractiveness to keep in touch with the men and to bring them on side. She's playing the game a lot better than I am."

For her part, Charlotte claimed Jayne was constantly sniping at her, calling her an old woman on several occasions, and at one stage calling her a "dog", an accusation that Jayne denies. She also claims that Jayne's story about missing Warwick was conjured up to disguise the fact that she was to be voted off anyway, to make her leaving more palatable, a fact James verifies. "Jayne did not ask to leave," Charlotte says. "She realised she was going, and it was pride. People say 'I want to go' because it's better than being voted off, it looks better. But she knew she was going. She was the weakest one left at that stage, in terms of the physical challenges. It was the first time that she had ever said to me that she was missing her son. She was going anyway." Whether that was the case or not, who can tell? Jayne's upset did appear to be genuine. But relations between Jayne and Charlotte had broken down irretrievably. Andy's plan to vote the latter off came to naught and so it was that when the tribe marched through the jungle to Tribal Council the result was a foregone conclusion for the second time in succession for Helang and the person to be ejected was happy with the outcome.

One person who was distinctly unhappy at Tribal Council was James. His error on the assault course was still smarting with him and he lost his temper under questioning from Mark Austin. Having been asked whether he cheated or if it was a mistake, he became sharp and defensive in his responses, eventually telling Austin to "Stop asking such dumb questions". His tetchy attitude was not helped by his belief that a deliberate 'trick' had been played on his tribe when Charlotte was allowed to emerge from the jungle with the idol to the delight of everyone. He felt a theatrical trick had been played upon them; the sight of their joy turning to despair making better television.

In the voting booth, Andy paid a fulsome tribute to Jayne and pronounced Warwick to be a "very lucky little boy indeed". When the votes were announced Jayne gathered her belongings and made her way to the confessional. The person that she singled out for her final criticism was Adrian, whom she said would not be able to survive on the island on his own because he would either starve to death or be frightened to death. But then she was on her way on the boat to the mainland with Stephen Flett. Five days after that, she was on board a plane back to England for an emotional reunion with Warwick and her husband.

"I didn't bother to bring my shorts or shirt or cap or anything"

Three days lay ahead before the merger on day twenty; three days in which Helang had to recover their winning form or they would enter *Sekutu* – the Malaysian word for "merged" or "joined" – at a numerical disadvantage. If anything, as Adrian pointed out, Jayne was no great loss to the tribe in physical challenges so they should still be able to compete well with Ular – and they still had one more chicken to slaughter to provide valuable sustenance. But while they were determined to win to gain parity at tribal merger, Ular were equally focused on winning. A victory in the Immunity Challenge would give them the chance, after merger, to remove ex-Helang members from Sekutu one after another, leaving six of them with a chance of winning the million. A 6–1 chance of becoming a millionaire – slightly better odds than the National Lottery. It was a rare opportunity and one that no one wanted to pass up.

The next morning the show's producers decided that the two tribes had become too comfortable. Thinking that they had become too used to a daily routine, they woke the contestants up at 5.30 am and dragged them on a forty-minute hike through the jungle to the mud volcano. This had the effect of disorienting everyone, in particular the sleep-loving members of Helang. Simon admitted that pulling him out of bed at such an hour put him in a bad mood that he failed to shake off for the rest of the day. Adrian, meanwhile, did not seem to wake up for the rest of the day if his contribution to day seventeen's Reward Challenge was anything to go by. Mark Austin, waiting for the weary contestants at the volcano, explained the rules of the challenge. They had precisely five hours to return to their respective beaches and construct an SOS signal. Austin would fly over in a plane with a local expert, known as the dropmaster, and inspect the signals. (The dropmaster's normal job is to drop supplies out of planes, having spotted real distress signals.) The reward would be dropped to the tribe deemed to have created the best signal.

It called for the two remaining ex-military survivors to use their expertise. Eve, who became only the fourth woman ever to qualify as a bomb disposal expert while in the Army, quickly marshalled Ular. They were so tightly organised and ahead of schedule that there was time for some members of the tribe to take on other jobs, such as catching fish. Andy, who as a pilot knew what could and could not be seen on the ground from the air, had ideas for Helang. So did Charlotte, however. Her lack of military training did not stop her suggesting the idea of carving the words "Pulau's off Tiga" not realising the idea was to be seen and be saved, not have a pun admired from 2,000 feet. Andy was slowly tiring of Charlotte's verbal incontinence. "Charlotte will speak her mind and her opinion regardless of whether or not she has anything valuable to say," he complained. "It seems every challenge we have done has been a battle. Charlotte tries to take control." A muddled combination of Charlotte's "creative" thinking, Andy's reluctance to be assertive, Simon's ill mood and Adrian's inertia conspired to create an almighty mess for Helang and they ended up building a huge "X" on the sand that was pale in comparison with Ular's "Save Six Now". The latter were given the reward – though they would quibble with that description. The crate which they had to raft in from a quarter of a mile out at sea contained pillows, hammocks, a walkman with a CD of festive tunes and a battery-operated fan, and was described by a disgruntled Richard as a "heap of s***".

Helang were not to know how dire the reward was. They had failed and were slipping back into their old disorganised, fractious ways. Adrian put in a pathetic attempt – he thought the challenge "boring and pointless" – and spent most of the morning with his hands glued to his hips or in the sea, swimming while the others toiled. Little did he know that he was marking his own card. Andy had long grown intolerant of his idleness, but now James was railing at his lack of spirit and his selfishness. He was making the immunity idol look industrious. It did not go unnoticed by Simon either, with whom he got on extremely well. Together with Charlotte, the three were very close. Simon describes himself as "young at heart", a factor he attributes to playing football every week with men ten years, sometimes fifteen, younger than him. He likes to be one of the lads. But as a father of two, with a respectable position as a sales manager, there was more depth to him than Adrian realised.

But the Reward Challenge was not the important one; all rested on the immunity. Helang's view was that should they lose, they could bid farewell to the likelihood of winning the game. The night before they ate their last chicken, overruling Charlotte's idea of keeping it alive to act as tribe mascot. They were confident, certain even, that they would win immunity because they had managed in the past to pull off a triumphant performance when it was most needed. All they needed to do was make sure it was the vibrant, dynamic Helang that turned up, rather than the rabble they occasionally degenerated into.

The challenge was to be the Treasure Hunt Relay, which,

similar to the assault course, was raced in legs. First, one person had to swim to a buoy and dive down to collect a jar containing a map. After picking that up, they had to swim to a raft bridge, sprint across it and jump in a kayak where a colleague was waiting. The pair had to paddle back to shore and open a bottle to reveal two maps: one showed the position of a buried treasure chest on the beach, while the other showed the location of the chest's key in the jungle. One member must run to retrieve the key while the others dug for the treasure. The first tribe to raise their chest to a stand and open it with the key gets immunity. The key to the game, like the assault course, was to pick the right person for each task.

Helang's first problem arose in the familiar shape of Adrian. A keen competitor when he could be bothered, he was also judged the group's strongest swimmer. It was felt he would give the tribe the start they need against Pete, whose skills were viewed in awe after his heroics above the jungle on the assault course. There was, however, one major problem – Adrian refused to do it. James was astonished and still is. "Charlotte was a good swimmer, but Adrian was a strong swimmer and a strong bloke," he says. "I had seen him swimming underwater. Everyone said they thought Adrian should do the swimming part. He bottled it though. He said, 'Look, I swim in my local baths about the same distance as that and when I come out of the other end I am completely knackered. If I do it I won't be able to paddle back to the shore.' So, he said he wouldn't do it. Charlotte's face was drained, you could see the prospect of doing that leg terrified her but she is one good competitor and she did it for the tribe. Adrian couldn't care less. He could have done it any day of the week really yet he refused." What made it all the more galling for other Helang members, and added yet another complaint to a growing list of offences committed by Adrian, was that the next day he challenged Charlotte to a swimming race, which he won. "I knew I could beat you," he told her. "Why didn't you do that yesterday?" was her pointed response.

As it was, Charlotte swam excellently, beating Pete to the buoy. Her undoing was her inability to undo. The jar was secured to the buoy by a line and Charlotte was unable to untie the knot. Pete had no such problems and he opened up an unassailable lead as Charlotte panicked. Richard, whose job it was to locate the key, ran powerfully and had little trouble finding it. By contrast, Simon struggled to find the correct place of entry into the jungle, never mind the key. Reading maps never was his forte. By the time he found it and returned, Ular had located the chest, dug it out and secured a convincing victory. It was a classic case of Helang disorganisation and error. Quite fitting, considering it was the last challenge the tribe would undertake together.

Ular, understandably, were jubilant. They were compensated for their disappointment at the booty they had won the day before when the chest was revealed to be filled with beer and fruit. As they celebrated and toasted their increased chances of winning, Helang had adopted a philosophical outlook at their rapidly receding chances. "Who needs a million?" was the view. Charlotte said she had a premonition on the beach before the challenge that she would pick up the cash prize, which was swiftly debunked when they were trounced. James was not so quick to dismiss the idea completely. "You have it in you to win Charlotte, definitely", he told her. In his view, the only one of them that had a chance of infiltrating and eroding the seemingly impregnable Ular tribe was Charlotte. He recognised that she was a very strong competitor, who burned with fierce determination and had the ability to make friendships quickly. That looked unlikely with Ular, however, who thought her loud voice and range of coloured swimwear marked her out as vain and unbearable. "Bikini Babe" was the name they had given her, while Adrian had earned himself the name "Lycra Boy." With the exception of perhaps Zoe, who was the most vocal in complaining about Charlotte's volume before the merger, none of Ular were loud individuals. It seemed difficult to see how Charlotte would be accepted.

After the challenge Richard pondered on the prospect of four Helang members joining them. He had discovered through conversations with Helang members at the challenges that they did not have a toilet on their beach – Helang's method was to dig a hole, use it and then fill it in – and he said they would have to be potty-trained. Ular, efficient and methodical as ever, had built a latrine and were proud of it. Ular's somewhat condescending attitude to Helang's primitive toilet habits, inspired by Andy's adage of "Go animal early", still rankles with James now. In fact, much about Ular still rankles with James, but being told they had to be toilet-trained has him foaming at the mouth when he recollects. "They gave us all this rubbish when we merged about us doing potty training and learning to use a proper latrine. But we just dug a two-foot hole and when you crapped in it you covered it up. It was completely hidden and we never had any problems. What they did was dig this big hole and when the first person used it, it collapsed, then the hermit crabs got to it overnight and took all the crap out. And they're telling us that's healthy?"

Systems of sanitation were not preoccupying the minds of the five left in Helang after they lost the Immunity Challenge. A more pressing question was who to send home. Only

Simon and Charlotte seemed safe and they were in alliance with Adrian. On the surface, therefore, it looked as if it would be Andy or James that would not make the merger. Andy emerged as an early favourite to be jettisoned, but Simon decided that for him to have any chance in the merger he had to take Andy with him, because Ular might go for him first and therefore Simon would make the jury and at least have a say in who was the potential winner. So James was installed as the new favourite. His central role in losing two Immunity Challenges handed an excuse to the others to vote for him should they require one and they did. Adrian, who likes James, though he describes him as a "fruitcake", was particularly scathing about the error on the assault course. "My five-year-old sister could have understood the rules," he said to Charlotte, who agreed that James was the man to go. Three hours before Tribal Council on day nineteen it seemed certain that Simon would vote with Adrian and Charlotte. Adrian thought so, and decided not to go with him to fetch the water in order to shore up his vote.

Simon was in turmoil. If they had won immunity he would have certainly kept true to Adrian and Charlotte and stuck with them down the line. That was not an option here. He had three choices running around inside head: Andy, whom he quickly discounted; James, whom he liked and who had given his all for the tribe; Adrian, whom he also liked, had been in an alliance with, and who had given nothing to the tribe. He says it was "the toughest decision in my life". He admits that right until he walked up the steps at Tribal Council to vote he could have changed his mind. Andy was putting a lot of pressure on him to vote for Adrian, which Simon believes was "morally" the correct decision. But would it be better for his position in the game to vote for James and take Adrian through? He oscillated wildly between the two all afternoon, likening the decision to buying a car. To the camera he expressed all his doubts, even considering at one point voting for Charlotte.

"Charlotte has more physical abilities than the other women and a better personality than them as well. On merit, I think she deserves to be here. She has twisted people around to her way of thinking when she's aware that somebody doesn't like her. She will survive on her own .... Why should I vote her off?"

Everyone packed all their clothing and equipment in their rucksacks for the walk to Tribal Council that night – all, that is, apart from Adrian who was so confident of making it through that he left his cap, his shorts and a shirt. On the way through the jungle it began to dawn on him that this might have been a rash decision because he noticed Simon was unusually quiet and avoided his eye. James was resigning himself to going, though Simon had surprised him once by voting logically – for Uzma at that tumultuous first Tribal Council – and he was hoping that side of his personality would emerge again. As they arrived the tension was almost tangible. When Austin asked Simon if it was obvious who would be leaving that night, he replied "I don't think anything's obvious until you pick those names out of that basket and tell us what's written down on them."

The five went off to vote. As Simon picked up his pen he decided to vote for Adrian. With the benefit of hindsight, this is how he describes the reasoning behind his decision now:

"I was the one that talked Ade round to staying when he was having a terrible time at that start, so I took the power on myself to vote him off when his time had come. I supported him all the way through but you can only support him so much at the end of the day.

"James is such a character, such a personality. Out of all of us that were left, he was the least physical and had least physical ability. Yet, if somebody gives that much commitment, he really did give everything, and was superb around the campsite, then I could not bring myself to vote him off. Adrian was the exact opposite. Yes, if we had taken it to the letter of the law, because he lost the challenges for us twice, then we should have voted James off. But he was going for the win and I respect that. I could not justify voting him off and keeping Ade. James earned it."

Voting for Adrian, Andy said: "On day one your only topic of conversation was quitting. The only way you'd survive on this island alone is if a burger chain opened a restaurant here. At every opportunity of shirking your responsibilities at the challenges, you have taken it. I, along with the others, have carried you this far. I'm not prepared to carry you any further."

James named his reason as Adrian's "bad attitude" while Simon told him "You've got a lot to learn." Austin collected the votes and began reading them. The first two out were for James, prompting an anguished "It's me" from the forty-year-old. But his mood changed when two votes followed for Adrian. The smiles that had been in evidence when Jayne was voted off had been wiped from his face and Charlotte's. The final fifth vote saw Adrian's face fall further. It was for him and he was gone. "I've been shot," he said, a reference to Simon, his "assassin". He extinguished his torch, gave Charlotte a kiss on the cheek, shook the others' hands and sauntered away.

In the confessional booth, Adrian said he had not learnt anything about himself on the island, a testament to his self-belief and confidence. Every single other contestant said there was something, however small it may have been, that they had learned about their characters or physical abilities. Perhaps Adrian is not one for self-analysis. But he did reserve his criticism for Simon, claiming he was "betrayed". Over time, however, he has shifted the blame for it on to Andy, whom he felt applied undue pressure on Simon.

"I couldn't believe Simon had voted me off, I thought he wouldn't be able to," he says now. "I feel bad about Simon stabbing me in the back. I liked him. Andy bullied him into it, I think. He was always going to try and get rid of me, but I didn't care about him whatsoever. I'm just gutted I didn't stay on longer than he did. I was not interested in winning. I just wanted to be on the island longer than Andy. He's very sly. More than anyone else there, he was desperate for the cash. He tried to pretend he was respectable and responsible but the only thing he was there for was the money.

"If I had got to the merger I would have fancied my chances of winning the whole thing. I was saving myself for the last part of the game. Even though we went into the merger weaker I still think I would have done OK because the other group were a lot younger and friendlier, more like me. I bet not one of those other tribe members would like or respect Andy. That is something I know would not happen. Ular were more like Charlotte and I."

Adrian's antipathy to Andy seems unfounded. Sour grapes perhaps? Andy does not to try to hide the fact that the one and only reason he was on the island was to win the top prize. Adrian's prediction about Andy not winning Ular's respect also proved to be wide of the mark. To be fair, however, to Adrian's forecasting abilities, he did predict that Charlotte would do very well in the game, despite the odds being stacked against her when he left the island for the mainland, where he slept … and slept.

All together now

Charlotte bore Adrian's leaving in a stoic fashion considering she had lost her closest ally on the island. "He had to go sometime," she told the camera. This might have had something to do with the prospect of the imminent merger of the two tribes, which was occupying everyone's thoughts. The tribes had seen a lot of each other at the various challenges but had had little chance to communicate. The only time the opportunity arose for anything more than a cursory exchange occurred during the assault course as people waited to be tagged for their leg of the relay. But it was no chance to unearth anything other than a superficial knowledge of the personalities in each tribe. Ular knew Charlotte was loud, believed Simon was aggressive and Andy strong. For their part, Helang believed Eve to be tough, Richard a bit strange, Pete fit and able while knowing little about Zoe, Mick and Jackie.

On the eve of the merger James spoke to the camera about his fears for what lay ahead and the strategy that he and his fellow tribe members had devised for the merger. The plan was to disarm Ular's leaders, perceived to be Richard and Eve, and forge alliances while their defences dropped. "Our final plan is to go in there in all innocence and to give them the impression that they have beaten us fair and square. We know our time on the island is limited and they are going to knock us off one by one. But underneath we'll be looking for weaknesses. Hopefully, what will happen is that we'll develop a few friendships. Simon feels as if he could get close to Pete. Charlotte feels she gets on well with Zoe and one or two other people." Ironically, Zoe was probably the one member of Ular fearing Charlotte's arrival most, given her avowed dislike of loud people.

"I certainly see Richard as Ular's leader," James continued.

The beautiful island of Pulau Tiga in the South China Sea

Ular assemble for the first Tribal Council, which saw Nick
voted off

Uzma bites off more than she can chew during the Reward
Challenge on day five

OPPOSITE: Ular's ecstasy at winning the first
Immunity Challenge turned to agony when
they were disqualified for not lighting a torch

"Still, it beats a doner kebab." James prepares to eat rat for
the first time.

Exhaustion overcomes James and he collapses within sight of the
finish to hand Ular victory in the "Parachute Rescue" Challenge

"I know exactly who voted for me...." Furious JJ takes her leave after being voted off in dramatic circumstances

"You mean we won?" Helang gather in disbelief following a rare victory in the "Mangrove Scurry" Immunity Challenge

Caught on camera: James breaks the rules in the assault course by
going over the second pole rather than under

The "ayes" have it: The members of Sekutu vote unanimously
to live on Ular beach

HELANG

Charlotte Hobrough

Adrian Bauckham

Uzma Bashir

Simon Dunkley

Jennifer "JJ" Adams

James Stroud

Jayne Meyler

Andy Fairfield

"What? No black pudding Lord?" In between tears and prayers,
Pete gains sustenance from a much-needed breakfast

Tears flow as Charlotte watches a video message from her
husband and mother back in Wales

An astonished Richard unmasks his brother James
after the "Survivor Rescue" Immunity Challenge

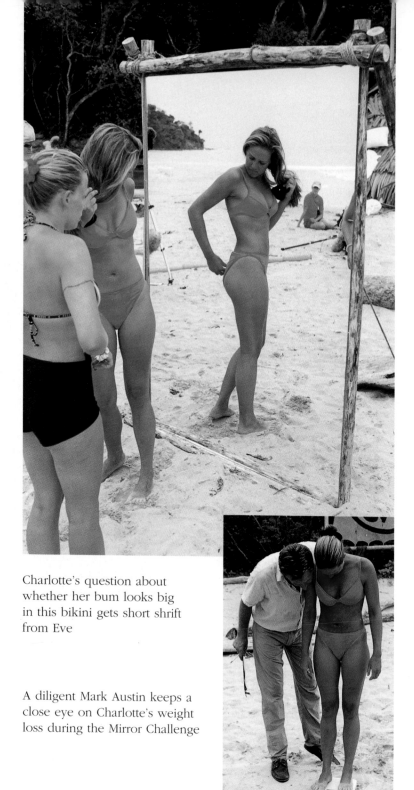

Charlotte's question about
whether her bum looks big
in this bikini gets short shrift
from Eve

A diligent Mark Austin keeps a
close eye on Charlotte's weight
loss during the Mirror Challenge

James, Andy and Pete show why T-shirt sales in the Kota Kinabalu region blossomed during the making of *Survivor*

Odd woman out: Jackie and Charlotte exchange tips on manicures while Eve ponders her impending exit

Richard and Jackie carve a farewell message into Eve's poncho. It didn't say "Good luck"

OPPOSITE: The devil finds work for idol hands... the "Hands On" Immunity Challenge, where tempers flared

Richard's dream of seeing the final sunrise goes as he loses the final Immunity Challenge, "Fallen Comrades"

Charlotte puts the finishing touches to her speech at the final Tribal Council while Jackie ponders her opening statements to the jury

"I mean, whenever we look around at a challenge he's always the one who seems to be explaining and taking the lead." He added that Helang had identified Jackie as the one most likely to be persuaded to reconfigure a new alliance with members of Helang because they had heard from a member of Ular that "she was only in it for the money", followed by Zoe. In James's view the best result would be for people to forget they were two tribes existing together and to begin to see themselves as one tribe. "It's certainly not impossible, it's certainly not enough to give up," he claimed. But Helang knew it would be very difficult to crack the tough outer shell that surrounded Ular. As they had already discovered, and as would be confirmed in the future, tribal loyalty ran extremely deep.

On the morning of the merger the tribes were woken early, before dawn. It was to be a long, strange and disorienting day. The two tribes were urged to raft to the opposing tribe's beach. After an inspection, the two would be brought together at an island council meeting where they would decide at whose beach Sekutu would set up home. The result offered no surprises. Helang were very impressed with Ular's home, and warmed to it immediately. Helang's litter-strewn home appalled Ular, in contrast. Eve described it as a "disaster area" and none could picture living there for any stretch of time. It confirmed the nagging thought that had been in all their minds that Helang were a slovenly, undisciplined bunch of "cheerleaders". Helang, in the meantime, had long mocked the humourless efficiency of Ular – though they did like the beach that state of mind provided.

While rafting to and from the beaches, Andy decided to play a trick on Ular. As a result of the distance between the beaches, and the strength of the current against them, both tribes had to be towed for some of the distance or else they would not have been able to make the journey before night-fall. Ular were very keen to discover which member Helang had discarded the night before. As the boats carrying the tribes passed out at sea, Andy ducked down to hide from view. Ular craned their necks, puzzlement spreading across most of their faces when they could not see Andy, who had been marked down as a major threat. A few of the faces brightened when it dawned on them that he might have been voted off, so saving them the trouble. Later as they approached Bird Island, where the Special Island Council took place, Andy hid once again, furthering the view that he had been eliminated. It was only when he strode up the beach as they all gathered together that Ular realised their best hopes had not been realised. They would have to get rid of him themselves.

Mark Austin explained the rules of the merger to the ten remaining survivors, one of whom would win a prize of £1 million and the title "Ultimate Survivor". The first few hours of Sekutu's existence were like the first few hours of the game, twenty days before, but even more important. From that point on, the shift was away from a tribe ethic and the emphasis was put on individual survival. To all intents and purposes, it was now every man and woman for themselves. Though in reality alliances were more vital now than ever before because a strong group could guarantee contestants safe passage through to the final two. To mark the merger, all the competitors burnt their tribal T-shirts and their tribal emblems. A vote was taken on which beach would be the new tribe's home and it was a unanimous verdict for Ular. In an atmosphere of unease and discomfort, the ten made their way back to their new home.

It was new because the former Ular shelter had been completely demolished by the production crew in their absence.

When Mark Austin mentioned this fact at the Special Island Council, his popularity sank dramatically. That was not all; some of their fishing nets and all the fishing baskets had been confiscated, meaning from that point on fish would have be caught "manually". Tapioca and sugar cane, a tasty snack, had been removed. The rice was in short supply as well and would soon have to be rationed. From here on in, life would get even tougher and the contestants would have to draw upon all their energy reserves to overcome the hunger and be able to put in strong performances in the challenges. They would also have to consider conserving energy by not over-doing it around the camp. As people became increasingly tired and hungry, patience and tolerance became even scarcer commodities. The veneer of politeness that had been evident throughout much of the game was stripped away as life on Pulau Tiga became a genuine struggle.

People's displeasure at the prospect of having to build a new home was pacified by the news that there would not be a Reward Challenge, and that a barbecue complete with steaks was provided to help the new tribe bond, though there was little chance of that. Eve had already told the camera that Ular's view was, "We've got visitors for a few days". The view was that in eleven or twelve days' time all the Helang members would be gone and it would be a straight fight for the million between the former members of Ular. It might not be that simple, however. James had already discovered a potential weakness in Ular's seemingly united front. On the ride back to Ular, he had fallen into discussion with Pete who indicated that when all the Helang members had been removed he felt he was certain to be the first Ular member to be ejected. James said little but banked the fact in his memory to tell Andy, Simon and Charlotte. Pete might be the one most easily petitioned to break ranks and join them if they could persuade him of the pointlessness of voting with a group of people who would then discard him at the first opportunity. It would be difficult because Pete's strong moral code meant his word was sacrosanct and he had given it to Ular.

In a decision that would have desperately disappointed Nick, had he heard about it, Ular (his former tribe) had seen Helang's shelter, which was also derided by JJ, and decided a lean-to would be much better than an A-frame. The shelter built and designed by Nick had turned out to be "absolutely crap", in the words of Jackie, particularly when the island had been buffeted by heavy rains in the previous week. So, Nick's sole legacy to his tribe was destroyed and a lean-to for ten was constructed. Or, rather, a shelter for nine. As he had done since the first night, James slept in a hammock under the stars. Come rain, wind, rat or snake, James had stayed in his hammock, watching the sunrise and sunset every day. He claims it was because he could not stand the claustrophobic conditions inside the shelter. Others joke it was because he did not wish his wife to see him sleeping in such close proximity to young, attractive women.

"I slept on the hammock because the shelter was really stuffy and I like sleeping outside. I didn't feel the need to be that cramped close together. To be honest, I think some people needed that closeness, in that situation. But I've been alone in jungles before and it doesn't spook me, though there were some quite spooky moments. I mean, I was lying in the hammock one night and I felt a person jump into the jungle behind me. It was the middle of the night. It must have been something else, but it sounded like a person. The night before there had been this blood-curdling scream. There was all this stuff about the island spirits flying around. People felt a tugging on their ankle at nights and then they got voted off. That night, Charlotte felt herself being pulled right through the shelter and sure enough her foot had gone outside the shelter. She started screaming in her dream or whatever it was and it set off a whole load of others in the same shelter. I was lying in my hammock when I head a series of screams and it shook me up. Because of that, people wanted to be close for comfort. Richard got into this big thing about watching the sunset and sunrise and the whole spiritual thing. But he was a bit of a fraud, because he only got into that about half way through while I had been watching it from day one without feeling the need to tell everyone about it."

Despite the juicy steaks and the forced jovial banter, the mistrust between the two tribes was palpable. Charlotte expressed her fears about Richard ('I don't trust him. I don't even like to look at his face. And he's a doctor. My God, I wouldn't go to him even if I had a heart attack!') Charlotte's voice, on the other hand, was already grating with some. Eve asked rhetorically, 'Does she never stop?' Had she directed that question at Andy, James or Simon they would have informed her that she rarely does. Eve rightly deduced that Charlotte liked to be the centre of attention and that was not a luxury that Ular were going to afford her. Particularly not Eve, whose no-nonsense style and lack of patience with vanity or anything "girly" would lead to her becoming incredibly annoyed with the Welsh detective.

Charlotte sensed her hostility and it affected her. The control and assurance she had felt while she was a member of Helang had been severely undermined by the merger and the cool response she had received from her new tribe-mates. No longer was she running the show. She told the camera through tears, 'It just feels really weird being here waiting to be voted off. We have to fit in with everything they do because there are six of them and four of us. I want to stay because obviously I've come this far but if I could go home I would. You get used to a certain group of people and I find myself clinging on to people who were in my old camp and just wanting to be around them ... I'm just feeling particularly homesick."

The next day, ironically, would be her birthday and the next morning the tribe sang *Happy Birthday* to her. It was without a doubt the strangest birthday she had spent yet – stuck on a desert island with nine other people, some of whom she had known for less than three weeks, and most of whom she had known for less than twenty-four hours and had no time for her. Back in Wales she knew her mother would be receiving phone calls from her extended family, asking where she was so they could wish her a happy birthday. The thought depressed her hugely. She wanted to be at home having a big meal surrounded by her family. Not on a beach eating rat'n' rice surrounded by hostile strangers. She was not sure how much she could take. Her birthday would get even stranger.

Andy logs on

From now on the Immunity Challenges were even more crucial, especially for former members of Helang who would have to win to guarantee their survival on the island. The ones facing the biggest threat on day twenty-one were Andy and Simon, whom Ular believed offered them the most potent physical threat. But in order of preference, they wished to get rid of Simon first for what many of them perceived as his violent, unforgivable act towards Eve during the stretcher race through the jungle, although Eve did not share those feelings of hostility herself. It was also clear that Simon was very strong and fit. He was a former apprentice professional footballer with Wolves and had kept himself in great shape ever since. Should he win immunity, however, then Andy would be going.

Andy was not ready to leave. The rules stated that the next person voted off left the island, while those ejected subsequently would form the final jury of seven and have a direct influence on which person would win the game. Andy, being a realist, knew he was high on the other's target list and that he could not hope to win every single immunity between this point and the final Tribal Council. But what he knew he could do if he managed to win immunity in that day's challenge was sit on the jury, still be involved in the game and have a say in who won.

The challenge was a simple one, the simplest so far, but it produced an epic episode of unforgettable drama that will long live in the memory of those privileged to witness it. All the ten contestants were asked to stand on a log, nine inches in diameter, out at sea. The last one remaining would be awarded immunity. Or as Mark Austin put it, "The last man standing on that log today wins immunity," underestimating the courage, willpower and stamina of some of those out on the log. "Tomorrow" would have been a more appropriate timescale, but he was not to know then just what would transpire over the coming twenty-four hours.

All ten swam out at 2.30 pm and hauled themselves on to the log. As seen from the beach, the six members of Ular stood on the left, Helang on the right. The temperature out at sea was well into the nineties, the heat reflecting off the ocean making it feel even hotter. As the ten mounted the log it instantly began to shake under the strain of all their weight and everyone atop it feared they would be unable to last more than a few minutes at best. Zoe was struggling even to get on her feet. After less than a minute she fell in and became the first victim. James, who did not fall in but opted to jump, followed her in within seconds. This was part of his strategy to make himself appear weak, not a threat, and encourage Ular to take their time in voting him off and thus allow him the chance to exploit any cracks that appeared in the Ular alliance. But he admits, given how much the pole was shaking, that he would not have lasted too long anyway. He and Zoe stood watching from the beach, cold beer in hand, predicting that no one would last more than an hour. Those on the log felt even that would have been rather optimistic.

"For the first few seconds on the log," says Andy, "I think everyone thought that they weren't going to last too long because Zoe got on it and she could not physically stand up. She was rocking backwards and forwards and the whole beam was shaking. I was stood next to Simon who was frozen. His arms were out in front of him to steady himself – he was petrified that he was going to fall in. I thought I would last five minutes tops because the thing was moving so much. Zoe fell in very quickly and that eased things a little but there was still a lot of movement. Maybe a minute or so later, James very shrewdly jumped in because he did not want to be perceived as a threat. That worked perfectly. It was not an option open to me, however, because I was always going to be seen as a threat."

To keep up their spirits, and to deflate their rivals, the six members of Ular began to sing and kept that up for some time. Simon, Andy and Charlotte did their best to ignore it at first, as they did when Ular began to wobble the log in synchronised fashion. Eventually, Charlotte, who started the game morose and uncertain, began to perk up in response, determined not to let them show their tactics were affecting her. She managed to cajole them into singing *Happy Birthday* once more. At one stage she leaned forwards and asked, "Let us know who you are going to vote off first so we know who has to stay on the log."

"We haven't decided yet," was Jackie's response, leaving everyone in no doubt as to which group was in charge of the game. This comment simply served to make Andy even more determined. The idea that Ular thought they could decide who stayed and who went on a whim angered him.

Charlotte succumbed to temptation after more than two hours on the log. The prospect of enjoying a cold beer on the beach to celebrate her birthday was a more enticing prospect than spending the rest of the day perched on a log. She knew that Simon or Andy would be voted off before her because of their strength and so she had at least three more days on the island. The beer was cold and provided a fillip to what had been probably the most miserable birthday she had spent in her life.

When Charlotte left, the thought in Andy's mind was that he would stay on the log "as long as it takes". Intentionally, he did not set himself a target like some of the others, such as Jackie who wanted still to be out there at dusk; Eve who wanted to last five hours and Pete who wanted to beat the ten-hour record set by the Americans in their second series of *Survivor*. "I never did that. I just knew from the first moment that I stepped on the log that I would be there until my legs gave way or I fell off because I fell asleep or something. That was my only target. It sounds straightforward but there were other things in the night that kept me going, because it was a bloody long night.

"One of the first things that inspired me took place when we got down to four – Simon and myself on one end, Pete and Rich on the other. I knew exactly why Simon and myself were there; we were the only two people who needed to win – nobody else needed to win or needed to be there. Pete was doing it for the ten hours and Richard, well, that came much, much later. Pete jumped in when he beat the record and then Richard stayed on the far end of the log on his own for the rest of the night. I thought that was fantastic because I had Simon there to talk to and keep me going. We weren't constantly talking. There were long periods when we didn't speak to each other, we just stood close to each other and were there for each other, supporting. I was encouraging Simon and he was encouraging me. I was aware that Richard had no one to support him and I thought, 'Great, jump in when you like mate.' Later he said he couldn't move along the log when it was dark because he might fall in. When it got a little bit lighter he sidled up to us and started talking to us. I said to him, 'Look, Simon and myself know why we are here. Why are you here?' He gave us some spiel that we didn't believe for a second, but finished off by saying it was for 'personal reasons'. I thought, 'Yeah, I know what those personal reasons are. You think you are better than me. Well, I'll show you that you are not.' "

Richard's "personal reasons" were not that he thought himself better than Andy. He says the reason he stood out there for so long when his future survival was assured was to break Simon, whom he had not forgiven for administering the alleged kicking to Eve – yet another example of Richard taking up the battles of others. "None of us needed to win that challenge, but we wanted to beat him. So Simon was first, he had to go for what he'd done. I wanted to stand there and watch him get off the plank, as a loser. It wasn't a case of 'If we don't get him this time, we'll get him the next time.' I wanted to beat him in that challenge and watch him go. But I actually warmed to him during that challenge. And when he got off the log he was crying, because that was him out of the game."

Simon was aware of what Richard was doing but initially that only served to spur him on. As night fell, and the tide came in so that the level of the sea rose above their ankles, Simon knew he was in for the long haul. "It was the toughest thing I have ever done," he says. "We went all through the night – storms, rains, thunder, everything. It was freezing cold – it was just desperate, absolutely desperate. It was mind over matter. At that stage I started hating Richard even more. He was shaking the log all the time to try and get me off. He was conniving, scheming all the time, thinking how he was going to win. Talking to us through the night. Every time that Andy leaned forward he would rock it to try and get him off. I had a decision to make. Every hour you think, 'I'll give it another hour' and you are just pushing yourself through. I was thinking of my kids, beating Richard, supporting Andy. I was thinking of seeing dawn. I wanted to make it through to dawn. I thought I could outlast Richard, his feet were in a bad way. I started thinking why Richard was still there, because he had no reason to be there. That played on my mind and Andy seemed immovable. Andy didn't want to talk to Richard, I think he hated Richard even more than me. But then I started thinking 'How can I win this?' "

Such thoughts had been banished from Andy's mind. He knew he was going to win. To keep himself focused on the task during the cold, wet and dark hours of the night, he developed an image in his mind. "I pictured that I was holding one of my children in my arms and the sea was acid. As soon as I developed that image, I knew that I could not possibly jump off. For some reason it became a very powerful picture in my mind and it made me very determined. One of the guides said in the survivor briefing before we even got to the island – I tend to latch on to the little things that people say and play them over in my mind – he said 'Your weakness is your strength'. I tied that in to what Nigel Lythgoe had said to me on the mainland about my children and how missing them could be a weakness. When I got this picture in my mind I knew, positively, without any doubt, that I would be the last person off that log. I needed to be there and I never even once thought of quitting.

"I was doing all I could to support Simon. There came a moment long after dawn when he became very emotional and he was just about to jump in. He was in a lot of physical pain. It sounds like standing on a log for twenty-three hours is just boring, and it is, but it is also very uncomfortable and painful. Your feet swell up, the balls of my feet were very painful and you cannot take the weight off them for one second. Simon's feet swelled up a lot and he could not stand it anymore. He got very emotional and he said to me, 'I always told my children that if they set their minds to something they could achieve it,' and you could see the tears in his eyes because he thought he had let his children down. I could sympathise with that because that was what was keeping me on the log, the thought of my children. Eventually Simon had to jump in and I was quite emotional at that stage."

Simon could not take it any longer. He had looked at Andy and seen there was no way that he would get off the log. Andy had already told the production crew that he was willing to stay out on the log for another night if necessary and hesitant plans were drawn up to delay Tribal Council, scheduled for that evening. Any chance of coming to an arrangement with Andy if Richard left were also unlikely, as Richard showed no sign of moving, despite the fact his feet had swelled and he was losing feeling in his toes. Simon was beginning to feel defeated.

"I kept looking at Richard thinking, 'He doesn't not need to be there.' He was coming out with statements like, 'It's my own battle now.' I thought 'This bloke is going to kill himself out here. He is that crazy. Andy wants to beat Richard and will do anything to beat him because he hates him and there's me, piggy-in-the-middle. So I then realised that Andy was stronger than me and Richard would never give up. So I thought I would get off. My body was giving me some signs. When I decided I was going to give up, my body relaxed and all my strength went and all my emotions kicked in. I came to the decision in my mind that Richard would beat Andy. I thought he would then reckon Andy was stronger than me and vote Andy off before me. I was wrong though. I had more time in me, and I should have tried to hold out a bit longer, but that was my decision."

When Simon jumped into the water, Andy and Richard began to applaud, joined by every single one of the production crew present who were astonished by such a feat of endurance. For twenty hours Simon had stood on the log, through all extremes of weather and emotion. Yet such a Herculean effort was not going to be enough to guarantee his future on the island. Back at the beach, the rest of the tribe were amazed that the three had not returned. They could see activity off in the distance but refused to believe that anyone could still be out on the log. James's prediction that no one would last an hour had been proved absurd.

Back out at sea, the battle had become a war of will between Richard and Andy. "We had been taking a rest every so often, leaning on our knees to try and take the weight off our feet for a bit," Andy says. " Simon had jumped in, Richard was stood next to me, and I was very emotional, my voice was cracking a bit. I said to Richard, 'I've got something to say to you.' And he assumed that he knew what I was going to stay. He said, 'You know that I really want to win this challenge and I know that you don't want to get voted off this island. I promise you that if you jump in that you won't be voted off tonight, it'll be Simon.'" Richard was telling Andy the truth, but Andy was not to know that – the motto "Trust no one" was being taken seriously by everyone.

"I looked at him and said, 'I wasn't going to say anything like that. I want you and me to stay on this log so long that it will petrify anyone who ever attempts this challenge again. I want you to encourage me and I will encourage you and we will stay on here as long as we possibly can. I am on here until my legs give way.' He looked at me and said, 'Oh shit.' I had said it very genuinely. I was not trying to psych him out but when he said that I knew had got him. We were there for three or four hours longer. It was after that conversation that Rich started saying he was having problems with his feet, that he couldn't feel his toes. He asked how mine were and I said, 'They're OK.' Even though I couldn't feel them either. Our feet went red and were filled with blood. He had told everyone he was a GP so he was saying 'This is serious,' and that encouraged me because I knew he was there to prove he was better than Simon and myself. I was determined he wasn't going to do that. Him saying 'Oh shit' gave me a boost. I thought I would be there until dusk at the earliest and my only concern then was that when dusk came I hadn't slept for thirty-six hours and could fall asleep or lose my concentration and slip in. Once it got dark again it would have been a lottery. He kept saying, 'I'm going to get off here soon,' and I think he was trying to psych me, play a game. Even when he was saying 'My feet are really hurting,' I thought he was playing a game. Eventually he shouted over to the sand strip and indicated he was coming off. I didn't believe him at first because I didn't feel too bad at that stage and I think I could have gone on much longer. I had said to him 'Richard, you go in and I'll be right behind you.' He said to me five minutes before we jumped in, 'Do you want to jump in together?' That was his last throw of the dice. I said to him 'Richard, I can't. I have got to win.'"

Right up until the stage that Richard hit the water, Andy did not believe that he would do as he said and give up. When he did, Andy took a long look at the empty log, trying to take in what he had achieved. At 2 pm, he slowly lowered himself to a sitting position, trying to bend legs that had remained rigid for twenty-three hours. It took him almost another minute to lower himself into the water and then he paddled his way to the shore where he was met by Mark Austin, who, after a few kind words, handed him the immunity amulet, which had replaced the idol at merger. He claims he felt no sense of elation, only relief that it was all over and he had secured another three days on the island at least. Asked what had kept him going, he said it was the thought of people back home. He also sent a message to his mother, given it was Mothering Sunday, thus ensuring his position as the "Housewives' Favourite". He was given some food and a cold beer, sustenance he accepted gratefully. All that they had been allowed on the log was water. If nature called, that also had to be answered while standing on the log. Slowly and painfully, he returned to the beach where he managed to grab a few hours' fitful sleep before he was called upon to make the trek through the jungle to Tribal Council.

Week 4

Loyal to what was Ular

SIMON KNEW WHEN Andy returned with the amulet around his neck that his days were numbered. For him it was very frustrating. He felt that after spending twenty hours on a log, he deserved more. Especially when he looked at some other members of Sekutu and believed they had reached that far, and would go farther than him, without expending half the effort he had done. In his opinion, the only reason the likes of Jackie and Zoe were still there was because their tribe had been strong. He was more deserving or so he felt. Now he acknowledges that that is the game's nature, and not necessarily the strongest survive.

Tribal Council on day twenty-two may have been a formality that night but it was also a chance for Richard, Andy and Simon to bask in the admiration their achievement had aroused. Mark Austin spoke for everyone when he told Sekutu, 'It's a shame we can't have triple immunity because Andy, Simon and Richard provided quite an extraordinary spectacle over the last twenty-four hours.' He asked Richard what made him eventually come off the log, and received the reply that he couldn't feel his feet – "a bad sign". Asked what he thought the rest of tribe would think of him as a consequence of what he did, Richard said: "I think they think I'm crazy. So, just the same as before." One person who did not seem too impressed by the feat of the men was Eve. Asked why she came off, she replied: "I did feel secure about not being voted off this evening so I wasn't striving for immunity myself. In the end it came down to the fact that I don't have testosterone so I didn't need to stay there." A thinly veiled sneer at Richard, which hinted perhaps that Ular's united front was superficial.

Mick said that the physical and mental courage displayed by Simon and Andy had contributed to a greater feeling of respect among former members of Ular for Helang. But any hope that the latter may have had of being accepted into the Ular fold were dashed by Richard, who said that he had turned down a suggestion to vote for Jackie that evening. "I stay loyal to what was Ular," he said ominously, adding the observation that his opinion would not change. Following that it was time to vote and predictably every former member of Ular voted for Simon. Some were kind – Jackie said he was "too strong", while Eve praised his competitiveness and congratulated him on how well he had performed. Others less so. "Life on the island has not been so long that your past crimes and misdemeanours have been forgotten," Richard told the camera. Simon continued the feud, his last words before being voted off the island being: "Richard, your scheming and cocksure attitude mean that you will not win the million pounds." Other members of Helang voted for several different people, the intention being to build up the vote histories of the others so should there ever be a tied vote, then there would be a chance that the Ular member would lose out on a countback. Clutching at straws maybe, but as James points out they had to do something. They could not simply accept their fate without a struggle.

One person who did struggle is Simon, who is proud of what he achieved during his twenty-two days on Pulau Tiga, and is only wistful that he failed to make the jury and have a say in the outcome. His other regret is that he did not use the floor as he left to denounce Richard in the strongest terms he could muster. "I had a bit of respect for Richard and I had only wished I had had the energy to say something to him when I left, a speech of some sort, to tell him what I really think of him.. I don't like him and he doesn't like me but we are both competitors and he beat me and, as a result of that, I have respect for him. But what I think of him as a person you couldn't print in your book."

He feels he did all he could to stay in the game considering the circumstances. Of course, he wished to go further and win the game but he feels he can hold his head up when he returns to the West Midlands and his friends. The whole experience, he says, was "sensational" right from the point when Nigel Lythgoe informed him that he had been selected. He was at work and became so excited that he went for a walk around the block to compose himself. As he got outside, he got out his mobile and rang his home phone number until the answering machine kicked in. For two whole minutes he just screamed down the phone to himself in celebration because he could tell no one else. This natural exuberance endeared him to all that met him on the island, with the odd exception. Had Helang gone into the merger in a strong position, he is one that could have made an impression in the challenges and potentially gone all the way.

Pete's dilemma

With Simon's removal from the island Charlotte had lost the last of her old Helang alliance. Consequently, she was finding the going far more difficult under the more austere regime laid down by the former Ular members than she did in her carefree, sunbathing days on Helang beach. James and Andy were both supportive of her but neither of them could offer her the attention she sought and got from Adrian and Simon. As married men with children, they could not be seen to be pandering to Charlotte's every whim. They liked and respected her – more and more as every day passed and her former flightiness was replaced with humility – but that was all.

More than any of the others, Charlotte was finding it very difficult to cope with life in Sekutu. She was getting a frosty reception from the female members of Ular, in particular from Eve who had little time for her. An argument arose over the amount of rice that was being cooked, with Charlotte being accused of cooking so much that Eve was throwing away the leftovers, which Charlotte feels they should have saved and eaten. Charlotte's way of salting the rice also attracted Eve's odium. People were getting extremely hungry living on rationed rice – Pete was becoming especially gaunt – and tempers were brittle. Someone as impatient as Eve was not going to fall for Charlotte's little girl lost act, or at least what she perceived as such. In fact, Charlotte was unhappy and often in tears.

"I just feel that I've completely had enough of the island and of the whole game. I haven't been happy since we merged. I've been severely homesick. I really miss my family and my husband and I feel there's no incentive for me to stay. There's no chance I've got to win the million pounds and I knew that when we were going in as a minority. But even so the atmosphere is horrible. We're on a beautiful island with the sun shining and everything I love and I'm so miserable. The people in Ular are picky and funny .... They're being very silly, Eve especially with all her little catty comments and the little bossy madam she is. She's an absolute nightmare. I don't know how they've put up with her ... I will do my damnedest to make sure that she doesn't win the million pounds. She's a bossy little crow – she's the littlest one here and she's ordering everyone around and they just take it."

To Eve and Zoe it was as if they were carrying three passengers in the shape of James, Andy and Charlotte, though these three's inactivity might stem from the realisation that they were being systematically picked off. "I'm just pissed off with them," Eve told Zoe. "I'm just looking forward to them going. I just want to get these next three out of the way," Zoe agreed. They thought Charlotte loud and irritating, James eccentric and odd, while Andy they wanted off because of his strength. The "them and us" division was growing.

Andy started to become annoyed at the attitude of Ular members towards the three of them and Charlotte in particular. Andy was noting Charlotte's behaviour with interest. At the start of the game he was no fan of hers, but as she became the victim of sniping comments from Ular he began to alter his opinion. "Right from the first moment that I saw her at the briefing," Andy says,"I came to the conclusion that if she could play the game then she would be very dangerous because of her looks. I always thought that an attractive woman who could play the game would win it. Initially she was not the type of person that I warm to. I find it hard to say why exactly. From an early stage she was distracted to the exclusion of lots of other people on the tribe. I really did not get any chance of getting to know her. I admired her athletic ability – she is a very strong girl. However, from the moment of our final Tribal Council she developed a vulnerable quality that made her far more appealing. My feelings changed a great deal. I mean, I didn't dislike her before, but I didn't warm to her. But once she discovered this more vulnerable quality that she did not have before, then I really warmed to her. I was quite protective of her, especially when I saw how people were disrespectful towards her.

"Charlotte is a bubbly, pushy kind of person and in the early stages of a game you tolerate that," Andy continues. "After merger, people did not have to tolerate it and they made that clear to her, very bluntly, which I felt was not necessary. Ular were smarmy. There was an issue over cooking rice, salting rice, because Eve did it one way and Charlotte another. She was in tears a few times in the early days and that made her more appealing to me. I think she did remarkably well to come through that."

A few members of Ular – Richard and Zoe among them – realised that being nasty to Charlotte could be counter-productive in the long run. It was likely that all three members of Helang would be voting on the jury, granting them a strong power base. It was worth taking the trouble to befriend and get on with them if people had any desires of winning a million pounds. The person that got closest to them would have three extremely valuable votes come the final shake-up. One person who was not going the right way about winning those votes was Eve, who was swiftly turning into Charlotte's biggest bugbear. She was heeding a warning offered to her by Jayne before she left to keep a watchful eye on Charlotte because she was extremely devious. The pair had already clashed over cooking the rice, forcing Charlotte to get her feelings off her chest to James, who was constantly encouraging and cajoling his former tribe-mate into remaining upbeat and positive about their – and her – prospects.

Away from the cattiness around the campfire, James, Andy and Charlotte appeared to have been offered a glimmer of hope from their main chance of smashing Ular's impenetrable alliance – Pete. A devout Christian, Pete was never one to sit in huddles cooking up elaborate schemes or fighting to salvage his place on the island. As a consequence, he had always felt a bit of an outsider among Ular despite getting on very well with Richard (he was only person on the island to call him "Rick"). Speaking to the same people and hearing the same stories for three weeks had become tiresome, so when the opportunity arose following the merger to meet new faces and have some new conversations, discovering other people's experiences on the island, Pete welcomed it. He instantly formed a very strong friendship with Andy and felt there was nothing wrong with doing so because he had no intention of breaking his word to his old tribe about sticking together and divesting themselves of the others one by one. He had already created suspicion among his old friends on the first night of merger, as he recounts.

"Anybody who tried to make friends with Helang was perceived as trying to win a vote. Helang were gone, they were just there for the ride, filling out the numbers. I honestly believe that people knew I was just being me when I was being friendly with them. The first night I dumped my rucksack in the shelter though I didn't have plans to sleep anywhere. We worked out that when we built the shelter each person had four planks each of space. I realised that and told Charlotte that she would have to move apart and make a space or move closer together so we don't take up too much room. She had a Twister mat and I asked if she minded me going next to her. I was happy to sleep on the mat. When I came back to sleep that night, Andy was sleeping where I was going to sleep so I ended up going the other side of Charlotte, and it ended up as Simon, myself, Charlotte and Andy in a row and suddenly I realised I was with Helang – sleeping with the enemy, while the rest were over the other side of the shelter. It was the only place available that night. I couldn't really say, I'm sorry but you lot are Helang, I want to go back and sleep over there. To be honest, I wasn't that bothered, it was quite nice to be next to Simon and Andy who I didn't know and chat to them. I don't think Ular thought I was ingratiating myself upon them. I think they thought Helang were trying to win me over to their side. Especially when it came to the first vote to vote Simon off. Just before we went to Tribal Council Simon came to me and tried to persuade me to vote on merit and not what people decide to do as a team. Rick collared me and told me not to change my vote. I think they were a bit worried I would change my vote. They were worried for the next one with Andy.

"I got on with him, and that was probably one of the reasons that started my downfall with Ular because I started getting on with Helang. Ular felt, 'We've got the majority, it's our campsite, this is our beach, this is how we do things.' People from Helang were asking what do we do here, can we do this? It was everybody's beach but they felt they had to ask permission. Even when it came to things like rice, they would ask 'How do you do the rice'. Charlotte had been doing the rice for Helang for loads of weeks but she still she had to ask. Eve was not welcoming. She was very unpleasant to Charlotte and that made me very uncomfortable, almost to the point where I stepped in and said something. I couldn't see the point. You don't need to be nasty, you can just get on. If you're trying to win then you're not doing yourself any favours, because when Simon went the people that you're being nasty to will form the jury and they won't vote for you. It's not in my nature to be horrible to anyone anyway, I hope. I just like to be friends with people."

That day's Reward Challenge was one Andy was desperate to win. He knew that immunity had to be achieved once more to offer any prospect of him remaining on the island and therefore he needed the reward (presumed to be food) to build up his strength for next day's encounter. He and Richard both woke with sore feet and ankles and were stiff from head to foot. But Richard was OK within the Ular unit. Andy possessed no such luxury and had no time to rest up, though he made a conscious decision not to join in much of the work around the camp in order to preserve his strength.

The Reward Challenge was, quite simply, a test of who could hold their breath longest underwater. The members were taken to a raft parked off the shore of Snake Island. The game involved groups of three diving in and swimming down to the bottom of the sea where there was a fixed bar to hold on to. The person who stayed down there the longest won the heat. After the three heats, those with the three longest times took part in a final with the winner getting the reward. Many of the competitors fancied Mick to win his first challenge. He is a keen diver and at home underwater. He was quietly confident of grabbing the prize but in the end he never even made the final, a disappointment for him. Instead it was James who surprised everyone by winning the final in a time of 1:52 minutes, more than 21 seconds ahead of his nearest rival, Andy, who finished ahead of Zoe, achieving her best performance in a challenge by some distance. James was delighted with his victory and utterly shocked.

"The three of us went in the first heat and I do this form of meditation and part of that is controlling your body function, making your heart rate calmer and regular," James explains. "It's very good when you are in a stressful situation, like going into a challenge, and when you need to calm yourself down you can repeat these mantras in your head. You can feel your heart beat calming. When I first went underwater I thought this was the perfect challenge to use it, because the last thing you need is adrenaline when you're trying to stay underwater. It's the exact opposite you need. I went underwater, closed my eyes and started doing this meditation bit. I held my breath as long as I could then I came up and thought I can't do this any longer. I was amazed when I came up to hear clapping. Then Mick was in the next one and I thought he would be down for ever but he came up like a beached whale after about thirty seconds. Suddenly I was in the final and Andy was next to me and I managed to stay down even longer. It was totally unexpected. It was the most fantastic award you could imagine."

Mark Austin told the tribe that the reward was treatment similar to what someone would expect from a five-star hotel. James was asked which other person he would like to take with him and before Austin had completed the question, he had blurted out Andy's name. His friend had been suffering ever since his epic last stand on the log and he wanted him to be given a reward that he deserved. Richard criticised James's decision afterwards, claiming he should have taken Charlotte with him because she was distressed. But James knew Andy was more in need of recuperation. It never crossed his mind for a second that it might invigorate Andy so much that he would win immunity the next day and that James would be the next member of Helang to be evicted from the island. And even if he had known that he probably would not have cared. It was a chance to enjoy a night of normality with a good friend.

If, that is, normality includes a four-poster bed, a hot tub and a dining table on a strip of sand situated in the middle of the sea. Not to mention a masseuse, aromatherapy oils, a three-course meal, a bottle of Chianti and cigars to follow. "It was so bizarre," he says. " Here you are in the strangest place in the world, being filmed by God knows how many people, then you are taken away for this bizarre experience, with a helicopter flying over you while you're in the hot tub. It was like *The Truman Show* with Chianti. Naturally, I took Andy because he stood on the log for twenty-four hours and he was my mate from Helang, if you like. Charlotte did not even enter my head, though I did feel a tiny bit guilty because Richard said I should have taken her."

The next morning, after experiencing the best night's sleep of the entire game, without mosquitoes buzzing everywhere, their clothes having been laundered and ironed, the pair were treated to a breakfast of pancakes, fresh fruit and coffee. Noting the sugar, Andy sprinkled it liberally on his pancakes and heaped about five or six spoonfuls in his coffee to provide an energy boost. Following his example, James poured the entire contents of the bowl into his mug, an amount Andy estimates as being the equivalent of twenty-five or so spoonfuls. Both men were on a high when they left, not all of it naturally induced. Andy was delighted by how things had turned out and was relishing the challenge ahead. If it was to be a physical challenge then no one was going to be in a better condition than James and himself. Their spirits were buoyed further upon their arrival back at camp to find the other tribe members sitting down to a breakfast of rice and rat, which Pete had killed by spearing it through the head.

While her two friends had been away, Charlotte had been condemned to spending a night with the very people – Pete excluded – who were making her life a misery. As it turned out, she found Ular more accommodating than usual, in particular Richard who had genuine sympathy for her. As the pair both know Cardiff extremely well, he began to ask her about places she knew in the town, pubs, clubs and other sights they had a shared experience of. Charlotte found it reassuring, a chance to talk about the home she was missing so severely. She was grateful to Richard for offering her warmth that no other member of Ular, Pete aside, had shown her. After that evening she felt better about herself and being on the island.

But it did not alter the fact that she, James and Andy were still no nearer to breaking Ular up than they had been at the merger. Andy was becoming increasingly accepting of his fate; he knew he could not win eight immunity challenges consecutively and that when he lost he was going. As a mark of pride he had taken to wearing a yellow band around his hat, a symbol of his former tribe. "It reminds me of what were really much happier times," he said. "I like it – it reminds me of something I was very fond of." His main focus was still winning that day's immunity challenge, which Ular were praying would not be a physical challenge so that all six of them could gun for Andy rather than it being just Pete and Richard. The latter also felt that a test of mental agility might not be the pilot's strong point. It is unlikely that Pete asked for it, but Ular's prayers were answered.

Andy logs off

A quiz was probably the last thing Andy wanted, but a quiz it was. The contestants were asked questions on what they had learned on the island so far, covering topics such as what plants or animals to avoid or eat, local geography and emergency medicine. The survivors stood on logs arranged in a pyramid formation. Moving backwards and forwards depending on their answer to the question. The person left nearest the tip of the pyramid won immunity, and in this case it was Pete.

Andy wanted no desperate measures to save his life on the island and said there were sacrifices he would not make to stay there, referring to the suggestions that he could abandon his former Helang tribe mates and form an alliance with members of Ular. In a short period of time he had grown even closer to Pete, to the point where Andy made him promise that after the game he would come and visit him down south for a few pints. He also told Pete that he should do all he could to reach the last two because he was someone who deserved to win the million. If he did so, he could be sure of Andy's vote and those of the rest of Helang. Pete was not happy to see Andy leave at all. In his opinion, anyone who could stand on a log for the length of time that he did in order to survive was deserving of far more than the fate awaiting Andy. The idea of shifting sides and throwing in his lot with the "other three" was tempting, even though Ular would have trumped it with their five and Pete would certainly be the next man voted off for his betrayal. Pete's trouble was his conscience and in Zoe's opinion, 'This is not really the place for a conscience … you make the rules up as you go along."

A vague sense of unease was spreading itself among the Ular group and eventually to ensure that Pete stayed "on side", Richard had a quiet word on the beach to make certain their plan stood. He and Pete had got on very well from that start, becoming firm friends and Pete still views Richard as the one person in Ular he could trust wholeheartedly. The pair devised a rough-and-ready games of Boules, using stones. At first everyone laughed at them, but soon they were all playing it. Pete describes it as a "northern thing" – Richard is originally from Merseyside, Pete is from Manchester – and both have an interest in football; Richard supports Liverpool, the place of his birth, Pete, from Stockport, supports Manchester City, which gave the former plenty of ammunition with which to tease the latter. So when Richard urged Pete to stick to the original plan, Pete was going to listen, no matter how difficult the decision was. The fact that it would be a vote in vain also deterred him.

"I felt all the way the maths were against me siding with Helang," Pete says. "Had it been five and five then maybe, but I suppose what was stopping Helang voting me off when they had got rid of everybody else? Why risk it? And the bottom line was that I'd given my word that I would stick with Ular and in times of doubt, when I was thinking about whether I should vote Andy off or not, I would think 'No, I gave my word. I will do it.' I won the Immunity Challenge when Andy was voted off. I didn't expect it to be a quiz at all. I expected it to be physical. I said to Andy that day, 'Whatever's happening, just stay with me. I'll be there at the end.' I was going to throw it at the end so that he would win immunity and be able stay on. That way I wouldn't have to break my promise and vote against him. But when it turned out to be quiz there was nothing I could do. He lost."

That evening of day twenty-five the remaining nine made their way to Tribal Council. Upon arrival they were informed that from that point on, every person voted off would join a jury that would decide the winner. Richard had been unhappy at first, wanting clarification on the rules. If the jury were able to watch video footage of what happened on the island after their leaving, he said it would affect the way he would behave from that point onwards. He was reassured that that would not be the case and the jury would only know what had occurred from observing Tribal Council and hearing the latest news from others after they were voted off the island.

Given there was no way he could alter the vote, Andy decided to take a defiant attitude at Tribal Council. When asked by Austin about his position, he answered: "If I could start my answer by saying that, in all my life, I have never personally felt less vulnerable than I feel this evening. I have never, or very rarely, in my life employed as much self-respect as I have this evening. However, I will be voted off the island in the next few minutes, the reason being that the majority of people here who will vote for me know that if they fail to do that, I will punish them severely in forthcoming Immunity Challenges, so I will take that as a compliment." In a pointed warning to the rest of Sekutu, and a reference to a promise he had made Pete make to him, he added, "I have already started forming views as to who I might like to see win the first prize, and who I might like to not see win the first prize."

Richard paid tribute to Andy when asked about his vote. "He was my nemesis for twenty-three hours, he's going to remain my nemesis for quite a long time to come. I've got a lot of respect for Andy after that night [the log stand] and it's difficult to vote him off. I've told Andy to his face that I'm going to vote him off this evening and it's out of respect rather than any drive or malice." Richard was disappointed about the manner of Andy's leaving, believing losing out in a mental challenge was not becoming for such a strong competitor, despite the fact it was what he had been hoping for on the morning of the challenge.

"Andy was my biggest threat. He went out to a 'girly' quiz, poor bloke," he says now. "Quizzes were always going to be my stumbling block. I felt let down for Andy when he went – that he didn't go out on a better challenge, doing something more dynamic and physical. I felt sorry for him, but he wanted to be on the jury, that was his goal. I think he felt he was a in a no-win situation. In terms of the game, though, I was very pleased he was out because he was a strong rival." Perhaps Richard's disgust at "girly" quizzes could stem from the fact that they were to be his downfall too?

All six former Ular members voted for Andy. All paid fulsome tributes to his competitiveness and his personal kindness. He had certainly earned their respect and acknowledged this as he left, thanking them for the compliment they had paid him and wishing them luck for the rest of the game. Slowly, he made his to way to the confessional booth. He was sad, but he had known he was leaving and so had had time to prepare himself. What regret he felt was for his failure to win the million, a goal he had come with the express purpose of achieving. He claimed to feel no regret for not taking control of his tribe at an earlier stage.

"The only way that I could play the game, and particularly in the early stages, was to keep my head down, to be a quiet person. That, in many respects, wasn't just a game, that is me, and it was the only strategy that was open to me. So I have no regrets about the playing the game in that way." As to the failure of Helang to enter the merger with at least tribal parity, he accepted his share of the responsibility. He tipped Richard to go on and win the game but added "he is not a person that I hopes wins the game." His epitaph was: "The people he loves, and his friends, can respect the way he played the game and respect the way he conducted himself. Theirs is the only verdict that is important."

Andy was taken to the mainland where he did what many others did and went straight to the hotel bar, where he stayed until 2.30 am. He then carried on the party in his room, polishing off a bottle of whisky, and finally staggered down for breakfast. After recovering from that he was ready to take his place on the jury. On the evening of the next Tribal Council he was taken back to the island and a camp was built on a neutral beach a ten-minute walk from the Tribal Council complex. Andy spent the night there before going back to the mainland where the next person to be voted off would join him. From that point on the jury spent their time in KK and Tribal Council afternoons and nights on the island. From day thirty-seven onwards, when four consecutive Tribal Councils took place, the jury spent every night at their camp on the island. It was a stark contrast to the harsh life on Sekutu beach. People slept in comfortable tents and were fed well three times a day. Despite being out of the game, Andy was determined to make his presence felt on the jury and began to hatch a plan ...

And now James ...

Pete's vacillation over Andy and seeming uncertainty about where his loyalties lay had earned him the scorn of a couple of his former tribe-mates. Zoe and Eve, who were getting on better and better as the days passed, were getting fed up with the way he seemed to hold Andy in awe for his achievements in the physical challenges. For Zoe, the game was about far more than being the biggest and strongest; it was about mental endurance. As someone who knew what it was like to be threatened with being voted off, and the efforts required to turn it around in your favour when all looked lost, she knew what was required to remain in the game. Nowhere was it written in stone that the "Ultimate Survivor" had to be the fittest, or the fastest runner, or the most agile. The game was to stay on the island for as long as possible, any way you could, and the people who remained at the end were the most deserving winners, full stop. They had survived when others had not. Strong did not mean being able to stand on a log for the best part of a day; strong meant picking your way through the psychological games being played by other people, forming the best alliances, knowing what everyone else was up to and acting accordingly. People who got into a position of having to win Immunity Challenges every time in order to stay in the contest had the wrong strategy. What was the best ploy after all, jumping off a log after forty seconds, having a cool beer and a decent night's sleep or staying on it night and day, exhausting yourself in the process? Zoe knew the answer.

"The thing that is narking me at the moment is that Pete is having all these dilemmas about who to vote off because of their log-standing abilities and it puts the rest of us down," she complained to Eve. "Pete's never once had to fight or think about his position on this island, he has never once had to approach anyone about insuring his position on this island. Pete hasn't got a bloody clue what is going on ... he's pissing me off. It's just this whole who's deserving to win sh** from people who don't have a clue .... Pete lives in a little 'Boy's Own' comic. But if this happens again next time with James or Charlotte, maybe the time has come, maybe we should cease this pain for him." Eve's reply was succinct. "I wouldn't be averse to it all." Pete's position as the first person to be voted off when James and Charlotte were gone was becoming surer every day.

Hunger was beginning to play a very real part for everyone left on the island. Rice had been rationed so it would last, with only one bowl of rice at midday and one in the evening allowed. Fish were becoming increasingly hard to come by as few people had the energy required to go out and fish, apart from Mick whose skill for catching lobster was providing indispensable. With Reward Challenges being granted on an individual basis, there had been no replication of the team stage when rewards were handed out among the tribes. The only thing that had been shared was Andy's cigar from his night of luxury on the sand spit, the butt of which he gave to Charlotte, a confirmed smoker, to satisfy her craving for nicotine.

With this in mind, the eight remaining survivors approached the Archery Auction Reward Challenge with a generosity of spirit. The challenge was divided into two stages: first each contestant fires a dart from a blowpipe at a target. Depending on which part of the target they hit, they are given amounts of cash ranging from £50 to £250. Secondly, they were allowed to spend their money in an auction of fast food and other small luxuries – burgers, pizzas, chocolate and a phone call home. On hearing this, Sekutu decided that the plan would be for people not to bid so high as to price others out of the market, or outbid people for items they desired, and then save the food for a feast afterwards which would be shared among everyone. Unfortunately, people were overestimating everyone's generosity and underestimating their hunger.

The problems started when Richard bid for a pizza and got it. He decided to take a bite before passing it around for others to have a slice. In James's view, however, he "wolfed it" and then only passed it on to selected members of Ular. In Richard's view James was being "anal" in expecting him to sit with it in his lap until the game had been finished and then dissect it into eight equal pieces, weighed and measured. Whatever the truth, James's reaction was to bid his £50 for a burger, and share it with Charlotte and Pete. Zoe could not resist outbidding everyone for chocolate. From that point on it was anarchy, with people eating their own food, ignoring the others. Pete was expecting Chicken Tikka Massala to be among the prizes, only to find that it wasn't and he had £100 in his pocket, useless in the middle of the South China Sea. Some fellow members of Ular did share some of their food with him, but he was shocked at how they had behaved.

Afterwards the inquests were long and in-depth. The idea of sharing the food had been Jackie's, which irked others who thought it was easy for her to suggest such a ploy when she had done little in any of the Immunity Challenges. Zoe's view was that it was an individual reward to do with as you wished. "With regard to human nature," she said, "It just shows how shallow we are ... what it highlighted to me more than anything is that if you take everything away from people and then give them little bits back, they'll rip each others throats out in public, they'll tear each other to pieces."

James was appalled by what he had seen. Fair play means a great deal to him and what he had just witnessed was far removed in his opinion. "They behaved like a bunch of animals, complete and utter animals. What happened when we got back to camp? They all sat around and shared it with Pete, we weren't even considered. Even I was surprised at their behaviour but they all behaved perfectly to character. Eve was fussing about how much of her tomato ketchup I was putting on my hamburger. She said she won it with her £20. What is that woman on? What is she f***ing on?" Despite his disgust, James saw how Pete had been marginalised by his former tribe-mates' behaviour. The intention once again was to persuade him into abandoning his loyalty to Ular on the basis that they would jettison him as soon as it was practical to do so and that breaking his word with people who behaved in such a way was no crime.

Pete, however, was not open to persuasion. His view was that he did not want to be seen to break his word and if he lost then that was the price he would pay for retaining his dignity. "I'd rather lose and keep my dignity because a million pounds can't buy that back afterwards can it?" was the way he put it to James. The Reward Challenge had proved to him what could happen when people lost their self-control and became selfish. "I was very upset by what happened," he told the camera, "because it was supposed to be a bit of fun and it's tainted the day really. For me the game was getting more exciting regardless of the fact that people are going to turn on each other." The million pounds in his view was begin to muddy the situation and get in the way of people's friendships. He was disappointed to see what people were prepared to do to try and win the million pounds but he put that down to the situation they were all in. "It's only a game, but there is still a lot of reality happening." he said. "Emotions are real; excitement's real; hunger's real, and people are prepared to do what they have to do to get food and the upper hand. It's real life magnified 100 times – there's very big highs and very big lows and it's steering a course through those. It's easier because I know there is a finite date at the end of it all so I think everyone should take hold of the fact that it is only a game and soon it will be over and they will have to go back to being themselves."

For this reason, Pete did not want to switch his affinities. Blocked in that direction, James decided his last chance –

other than winning immunity – was to approach Richard and try and cajole him into joining him and Charlotte and bringing Pete along to make a four. First of all, however, James went all out on day twenty-seven to try and win immunity in the Fast Fire Challenge. Eight small holes were dug in on the beach to act as fire pits. Each had a rope wick stretched horizontally above it, attached to a flag. The survivors were given two minutes to collect driftwood from the beach and place it in the pits. No wood was allowed to touch the ropes. When the two minutes were up the contestants then had to swim out to sea with their torches and light them from a burning cauldron on the raft. After they returned from the pits they had to stick their torches in the sand, light a piece of their kindling and use that to light the fire. When the fire burned through the rope wick a flag was raised. The first person to raise their flag won immunity.

James's fate was sealed when he failed to light his driftwood quickly enough, for reasons he cannot quite fathom. He recovered well and managed to get his fire burning but just as his flag was about to be raised, Richard beat him to it. It was the first individual immunity won by the psychiatrist and triggered a winning run for him. James knew then that his time on Pulau Tiga was going to end. He accepted it, he says, because he felt it was pre-ordained from the start. Island living had made him very fatalistic, things occurred for a reason. Getting on the show had happened so easily for him, or seemed to have, compared to everything else in his life, his business, his family, which he had to work extremely hard for. He was ready to leave.

But not so ready that he did not make a bold, if doomed, bid to stay. The morning of the Tribal Council, day twenty-eight, he had gone fishing with Jackie and she had told him that they had decided he was going before Charlotte. Intriguingly, she caught a large fish and handed it to James and said he could claim he caught it. This would make him look like an expert fisherman and curry favour with the rest of Sekutu. But Jackie, James feels, was seeking his vote on the jury. Richard was the person he wanted to try and cosy up to. That afternoon, he attempted to sway him by saying that he and Charlotte wanted to form a four with him and Pete. Richard's response was to inform him that it was his belief that Pete would never form an alliance. He continued to give James the impression that the game was being run by Jackie, Zoe and Eve – whom he dubbed the "Witches' Coven" – and they would conspire to get rid of both Pete and himself once Helang had been wiped out. James decided the time was right to make his move.

"The deal I would like to put to you is that if I spoke to Pete and said 'I've spoken to Richard and Richard will join us,' then I really think he would go with it," he said, before playing his final card. " I would like to threaten you with the fact that you know if you stick as you are then you will not win the million and we will make sure of that." Richard was not be blackmailed though, and told James that. He also pointed out that in the last four it could all fall apart, and the alliance's aim could switch from putting Pete and Richard in the final to Charlotte and James making the final. Tantalisingly, he told James that he might have been open to persuasion had James not introduced an element of blackmail. But he shook James's hand for his effort, unsuccessful as it was. Even then James did not stop trying. As Richard emerged from the sea James went up to him and said, "Richard, I have one last thing to say to you. If you vote me off tonight I think you are a coward because you are scared of me." What James was thinking of no one knows. He claims that he was hoping that Richard would be so stung by the criticism and subsequently wish to prove he was not a coward by allowing James to stay on the island and then beating him in all the challenges. Things had become truly desperate for James, unaware that he was trying to psych out a psychiatrist.

For a third time, Tribal Council that evening would not yield any surprises. James admitted to Austin that the last few days had possessed an air of inevitability. The only surprise was Charlotte's announcement that her feelings of homesickness were disappearing as the time when she believed she would be going drew closer. She wanted to enjoy her last few days on the island and not sit about and mope. Any lingering doubts that Pete might change his mind at the last minute were dispelled when he voted for James, telling the camera in the booth, "We said we would fight for Ular to the end and that's what I'm doing now." Mick said James was "exhibiting the first signs of madness" and Charlotte and James continued the policy of trying to build up the vote count of members of Ular, Pete excepted, in the hope that it would help either Charlotte or Pete in the event of a split vote. When the time came for James to leave he had trouble extinguishing his flame, evidence of his reluctance to leave the game.

Looking back now, James can only draw positives from his experiences on the island. "I think it's made me more confident with strangers. Before I went I was anxious that people wouldn't like me and it's quite clear that I was not the most unpopular person on the island. It's quite refreshing to know that outside the context of your family and friends. They were very different kinds of people and I've been able to get on with them all. It surprised me because I really enjoyed the team games when I never expected to, while the individual aspect I thought I would excel at but I never really got a chance to. Well, I did get a few chances but I missed them. I enjoyed it more than I expected, though as time passes you realise that it is just a game and you want your reality back." Before going on the show he was worried, the thought lodged in his mind that it might be in some way tacky. But he is glad he cast aside his doubts and took on the challenge.

One of the things that gave him most pleasure was watching Charlotte's progress. To James, she seemed to mature before his eyes and when he left he believed she was a fully rounded woman, as opposed to the rather spoilt, immature girl he had met exactly four weeks before. "She grew as a person and she was the only person who could have won the game however it turned out. Whichever tribe got to tribal merger strongest, she could have won it either way. You could not say that about any of the other sixteen. She is a very strong competitor and her personality helped her in the sense that she formed friendships very quickly. It could have worked the other way, but she managed to form friendships enough to help her. She grew enough to get around the bit with Andy and me. When finally Simon went, it was if she was on her own. You would not have said that on day one the Charlotte that you saw at the beginning of the programme would have dealt very well with that situation. She had a bad day, she got very depressed. But I encouraged her and said she could do it. I said that even if there was only her left, she could still do it and there were still alliances she could make. Richard was a target – he was a guy who would make an alliance when there was only one of us left. That is actually what happened. My last words on the island were, 'For me this has game has been Charlotte's journey. I hope that you continue that journey and win a million pounds.' "

Pete was another of his favourites. But while respecting his moral outlook, James believes he was terrible at playing the game because he refused to make alliances of any sort. Other people in the game impressed him less; Richard he says he still cannot work out, while Eve shocked him. "I could not believe how she played the game. She was bossy, forthright and could not make an alliance to save her life. Even right at the end, if someone had said to her that the only way she could win the whole thing was to make an alliance, then I don't think she would have done it. She could not do. I think she was incapable of seeing that side of the game. She did her best, on the performance side of things, but she was rotten to Charlotte, she really was. When she came on the jury I warmed to her a lot – she's a very nice woman. Looking back, I feel proud that I was the second to last person of my tribe to be voted off. That to me was far more significant than being the third one of Ular to be voted off. They just happened to get through by a thread."

Week 5

Disloyal to what was Ular

JACKIE HAD GOT bored. For nine days, since the tribes merged Tribal Council had been a foregone conclusion. For the three days leading to it, and on the walk there, there was none of the intrigue and secrecy and nervousness that she liked. Without it life was rather dull, an endless cycle of lying about on the beach feeling hungry, arguing about rice rations and fishing. She was looking forward to the time when Helang had gone and the bloodletting within Ular got underway in earnest. That would be much more interesting. She was in a good position if she sat tight; her alliance with Richard, forged on that first night, was still going strong, and no one really knew they were as close as they were. Rarely were they seen speaking to each other and Jackie often spent a lot of time going on about how weird he was to put the others off the scent. Jackie's best friend on the island was Mick. He was funny, often unintentionally so, and was kind. He played the game but never in a way that angered others. But he was not with her and Richard. Zoe was the other part of their threesome and they were confident of reaching the last three if they stayed solid. That would not make Jackie's boredom go away, however.

Pete wasn't bored, he was hungry. He was so hungry it hurt. Two days before leaving England for Borneo he had had a modelling assignment to fulfil. That ruled out any notion of putting on weight before going to the island, like Richard and Andy had done. His body, which he took care of for the sake of his career, already possessed little fat as it was. The first three weeks or so on the island had been fine and he felt strong. But following the merger, when the fishing baskets were taken away and the rice rationing was enforced, it had become a real struggle. His beard had disguised just how much weight he was losing, weight he could ill afford to lose. When he shaved it off everyone saw how gaunt and cadaverous he had become. Previously energetic and industrious around the camp, he took to lying in bed all day to preserve his energy, only rising for his meagre two bowls of rice a day. He buried himself in his bible, seeking solace in his faith, which had remained solid the whole time he was on Pulau Tiga.

A born-again Christian, he made it clear before leaving for the island that he would not do anything to compromise his faith. He had played, semi-professionally, in a Christian rock band for six years, an antidote to his day job as a crisis loans officer for the Department of Social Security, before he left to follow a career as a model and actor, worlds not known for their Christian ideals. But Pete was keen to retain his principles. "The island can be quite a test; it can be quite a fire to go through," he told the camera. "I've certainly developed as Christian – just in my own personal thoughts …. I suppose lately we have had quite a few religious discussions, simply because I've brought my bible with me. James asked the other day if he could have a look at it – he wanted to read 'The Sermon on the Mount', so I passed it to him and we started having religious debates. I've enjoyed that. I've not felt persecuted and a lot of people, including Rick, have said that they don't believe what I believe. In fact, most of them have said they don't believe in anything and that's a thing I'm used to."

Pete's inactivity did not go unnoticed by the others, nor did his moaning and complaining about being hungry. They were all hungry as well and nobody else was making the song and dance about it that Pete was. Nobody minded the fact he was a man of strong religious convictions, but some began to feel he was going on about God a bit too much. Zoe and Eve especially had already voiced their reservations about his mental strength. No one, they said, was going to die on the island. Pete should just got on with it and shut up. "My five year old stepson would probably handle the situation in a more mature manner than Pete does," Eve told the camera. "It's like, 'Get a grip, grow up and deal with it.' He is thirty years old going on thirteen, he just needs a sharp lesson in dealing with life. He still lives with his mother and father when all the rest of us have moved on from that." Patience was wearing thin.

Despite her reservations about Pete, Eve was confident that the "Ular Six" would hold strong. Charlotte was still grating with her, particularly her tendency to cook way too much rice. Realising stores were becoming very low, she had measured out all the rice that they had until the winner was finalised. A few people grumbled when they saw her do it but it had to be done, she said, to ensure they did not run out. Mike, Richard, Jackie and Zoe were fine, their attitude was to get on with it and cope with the rationing. No one said winning a million pounds was going to be easy. Eve had not yet given serious thought to what would happen when there were just the six of them left. She did not trust Richard and she did not trust Jackie and she knew they would be forming alliances and making them safe. That was not Eve's plan. When it come down it she would have to win every single Immunity Challenge, which was impossible. But, after what happened with Sarah, the last thing that she was going to do was try and forge an alliance with the two people she had least respect for, Charlotte excluded. Only Zoe and Mick did she have any time for.

Pete's trials did not bother Richard either, though he did not like to see his friend suffer. The rice situation was helping Richard because it was sapping Pete's strength and Mick was looking more and more tired with every day. That gave him a very good chance to win rewards and immunities. The girls managed the situation better than the lads, Richard thought. But he liked the way he was placed with the girls. He liked and trusted Zoe and Jackie. If Zoe turned on him all well and good, she would be playing the game, but if Jackie did then he would be very disappointed because he felt he had risked his neck in the early part of the game to save her.

Another person who was delighted with the way things were going was Mick. The retired police officer from Kent had placed himself perfectly, in his own view. He was well liked by everyone, which meant he was no target for the others. He was neither too weak nor too strong so he did not stand out in any way. His strategy had worked. Initially, his intention was to thieve and steal around the camp, spread suspicion and discontent, and pin the blame on others. Realising it was a high-risk strategy, he then decided to "fly low under the radar". Not wanting to be seen as a threat, he had, he claims, devised a strategy of projecting the image of a bumbling old man. "I had a few genuine accidents where I cut myself, I had quite a few more than I needed to. I would lose things a lot on purpose, the most infamous time being when I was running around asking people where my glasses were and they were on top of my head all the time," he says now. It certainly worked – even now people still think Mick was a bit forgetful and clumsy. "Mick's really nice, he's a bit of charmer. He claims he adopted this really different persona on the island. I don't know how much this accident-prone old man strategy was him and wasn't. I reckon he's probably a bit clumsy and forgetful in real life as well," Jackie says now. Intentional or not, it was working. Mick was never seen as much of a threat and is the only person on the island that everyone has a good word for now.

Zoe was another who was coping well in the circumstances. She was on a high since winning a satellite phone call home to her partner Sindy in the auction after it descended into a free-for-all. The phone call reconnected her with home. "It was really nice, it was a real morale booster. She was up and happy to hear from me and so positive and told me to keep going, it was wonderful because I was fading a bit. It made me realise there was a reason for me doing this. It was great to hear a friendly voice." Zoe is someone who places high value on a sense of humour and frequent laughs were something Pulau Tiga did not provide. "Tension Island" as she called it. Belly laughs were few and far between. She thought there would be plenty of opportunity to laugh and joke but she was wrong. "I thought that because we were in this very bizarre situation it would produce some hilarious moments, laugh or cry situations, but most of the time it was cry. There was lots of tension and I think it's because we were so different. None of us would have been friends had we not been there and you get used to your friends and what you all find amusing. You can say things to your friends, with strangers it's more difficult. But I wish there had been more humour, it would have made things more bearable on occasions." To keep herself sane, she wandered the beach singing "Agadoo" to herself over and over. In normal circumstances, she admits, that would be enough to drive her mad.

After James left, Charlotte became less keen on leaving and more determined to fight for her future on the island. Eve's snappiness was bothering her less and less. As a police officer, she is used to hostile behaviour and swiftly developed a thick skin to deal with all the insults and sneering that go with the job. Deflecting criticism is a skill Charlotte possesses in abundance, and was one that earned Jackie's admiration. While Charlotte laughed off Eve's comments, so winding Eve up even further, Jackie could not resist responding with a biting comment of her own when she was the one being criticised. Charlotte was getting over the worst of her homesickness and had become good friends with Pete following the obliteration of Helang. She even began to sense that her tearful stage had gained her sympathy in some quarters. Certainly they were being perceptibly less hostile towards her, Eve excepted.

"They perceived me as quite a weak person and also it brought out the human in them and they realised there were emotions involved in this," she says now. "Perhaps they didn't show them, but people still had feelings and some of them did become more approachable and friendly and tactile. It really broke down a lot of barriers for me. I was able to chat to people, like Richard. I was genuinely quite upset – it wasn't put on. I really wanted to go home at one stage. I knew they would leave me till last. Actually, they said when it was James and me, 'Is there anyone that wants to go first?'. I said to myself, because I knew before going that it would get hard, 'No matter what, you have got to put in 100 per cent, no matter what.' So I said that I wanted to stay. I knew I had been sad but I always knew I could get through it. I'm the sort of person who's either really, really happy or really, really low, it's all or nothing. I know I can snap out of it, it just takes a little while. James and Andy were fantastic and I probably drove them both insane, because I was so miserable. I did snap myself out of it and we did have a good old laugh about things. It's such a weird situation. The whole experience was like a huge emotional rollercoaster. You're either really happy or really sad, so many different feelings, and at the same time you're hungry. The million pounds is so far from your mind that it is unbelievable.

"I started talking to Rich about the time I was sad, and he was really good and we talked quite a lot. I thought 'Hang on, I'm getting a bit of an inroad there,' and Jackie and I had started talking. At that stage, I didn't know that Jackie and Richard had an alliance. I approached Eve at one stage. I asked her to come in an alliance with myself and James. We had a big discussion, we discussed everyone. We were saying 'You're someone who wants to win, who deserves to win, let's get down to so it's just us three of us at the end and do it on who wins immunity, rather than all this alliance thing.' We had a good chat but she declined, which I was expecting but it was still worth a try. I did it even though she snapped at me all the time. I just laughed it off and didn't react, which drives people mad. I'm certainly not going to lose my pride and have a catfight just because she's so snappy. She didn't seem to care what she said to anyone, or how she hurt their feelings."

Pete's prayers are answered

At the tribal council at which James was ejected people had been puzzled. Sat on the jury stand, in a bright yellow T-shirt was Andy, looking fit, tanned and well fed. On his T-shirt was the picture of an eagle and below that was a number, 14.29. Those on Tribal Council wondered if there was some sort of hidden message in the shirt, either that or it was an extremely odd design. No one could make head nor tail of it. On the way back to the camp it was suggested that perhaps it was some sort of biblical reference. Pete thought about it for a second but did not give it any more consideration until after the Reward Challenge the next day.

For days he had been praying for food and when he learned before the challenge that the reward would be a full English breakfast he became determined to win, build up his strength once more and dispel the understandable view among his tribe mates that he was becoming a dead weight. The challenge, named Bamboozled, involved racing across slippery bamboo beams over the sea. Only Eve managed to stay with Pete, who won the final leg by hauling himself along the last pole, a trick he picked up in the Boy Scouts. His prayers, he felt, had been answered and he eagerly awaited the feast that would be put before him on the beach the following morning.

Returning to the beach, he began to ponder once more the meaning of Andy's T-shirt. He could not remember what the numbers were, but when he was reminded of them he immediately dug out his bible in case his friend was trying to relay a covert message to him.

He tried to guess which book of the bible it would be in and whether it would be Old or New Testament. He could not unravel the significance of the eagle, or remember any reference to one anywhere at all in the bible. He decided to look through the New Testament and in the first book, Matthew, he looked up chapter 14, verse 29. It was the story of the feeding of the five thousand and Jesus walking on water. "Peter called to him: 'Lord if it is you, tell me to come to you over the water.' 'Come,' said Jesus. Peter stepped down from the boat, and walked over the water to Jesus." He remembered the challenge which involved him walking across bamboo poles *which had been suspended above the sea.* He was astounded. His prayers for food had been answered and the man who had brought God's message was Andy. Andy was sending signals from God. Pete couldn't believe it. How did Andy know the challenge would be on water?

The truth, as always, is rather more prosaic. Andy was trying to send a message to the remaining contestants, but it was not from God and it was not directed at Pete. After being voted off Andy had sat in the hotel cogitating over how he could still influence the game. What he wanted to impart, albeit obscurely, was a message to Ular, warning them that that they should treat the other members of Helang with respect, something he believed they were failing to do while he was still in the game. He wanted them to know that the way they behaved towards the ex-Helang members would affect their chances of winning, because each person had a vote. With seven members sitting on the jury, it meant each person's vote was worth 14.29% apiece. The T-shirt's colour, yellow, and the eagle insignia were references to Helang. In a rather convoluted way it was a warning. No one got it, however, apart from Pete whose interpretation was somewhat fanciful.

But if Pete's prayers for food had been answered, then he was soon to be given a nasty wake-up call. His moaning about food had irritated a number of people, Zoe, Jackie and Eve in particular. To them, Charlotte was weak and not a threat. Pete however was a very real threat. He was able to win immunity and despite being stricken by hunger he had managed to win a number of challenges. They were not simply physical challenges either. He won the island life quiz that Andy had been so desperate to win, disproving the opinion that was forming that he was a brainless male bimbo. It was always the idea among most former members of Ular that he would be voted off after Charlotte was ejected, but the thought had crossed people's minds that it might not be that simple if Pete were to win immunity, which he was capable of doing.

It did not help the next morning when he was served his full English breakfast. He was so thankful to God for the meal that he spent most of the time crying rather than eating. His tearfulness just served to increase the disdain of several Ular members towards him, who just saw a thirty-year-old man crying, perpetuating the view put forward by Zoe that he was just a "whingeing girl's blouse". There was also the fear that the meal of sausage, beef bacon, mushrooms, eggs, orange juice, coffee and croissants would reinvigorate him and give him renewed energy for the challenges ahead. So when Richard again won immunity in the Underwater Scavenge Challenge on day thirty-one it was decided amongst the other members of Ular that Charlotte would be spared the following day. They would vote her off the next time they went to Tribal Council and get rid of Pete now. Ular's superficial façade had cracked.

Vengeance is mine, sayeth Pete

Zoe, Jackie, Eve and Mick all agreed that Pete had to go. Faced with a fait accompli, Richard had no choice but to go along with the plan. First, because he would find himself voted off if he did not go along with the idea, and secondly because he knew the plan was to vote off Pete after Charlotte anyway. But, he claims, Pete was a good friend of his and he did not want to see him go in such a manner. He was looking forward to battling it out with Pete for immunity in the challenges to come because when it came to the physical games, he was his only competition, which Richard thrives on. Zoe's decision, he says, angered him a great deal. "Jackie brought me the bad news that Pete was going next. She said that if I wanted Charlotte to go, that was fine by them, nobody would be bothered. And I thought 'That's bollocks'. If I go against them then I'm just going to be the next Pete."

Pete had always said to them that if it was his time to be voted off then he wanted someone to tell him before he left so that he could have a chance to prepare; he wanted to watch his last sunset and sunrise on the island and soak up every last second of the whole experience. But it was decided that no one would tell him, for varying reasons. The main one was that the person who told him would stand a good chance of gaining Pete's vote on the jury. Others were too scared to tell him, while some just did not want to do it because no matter how irritated they had become by him, everyone thought he was a good, honest man. But Richard, as his friend, was not willing to allow Pete to find out he was leaving at Tribal Council and he decided to tell him.

The next morning, day thirty-two, Pete was up early collecting wood. As he returned to the camp he was met by Richard who silently ushered him into the jungle. Richard whispered, "You're going tonight." Pete burst into tears. Richard told him they were going to use the excuse that he was weak, when in fact the breakfast had made him much stronger. The decision still smarts, even now. "It was a complete shock. The fact that no one had spoken about who we were voting for had indicated to me that we were going to follow the plan through and vote for Charlotte. Richard said I couldn't tell anyone that I knew because they would know Rick had told me and they would vote him off next. The first thing I did was throw the wood I had in my hand to the floor and kicked a log and cut my foot open. A couple of hours later Rick came back to me and said he could switch it. I didn't believe him, I thought they'd broken their word already, why would they change back? I thought the only thing that could come out of it was it not working and Rick looking bad in front of them and getting voted off next.

"I was very hurt that the Ular people would vote me off. I didn't feel like they owed me. I felt I had really pushed myself harder than I had ever done to win Immunity Challenges to get people through and I knew that out of the people voting me off, two of them had done the square root of nothing in the challenges. Jackie had done nothing, and she was voting me off, and Zoe as well. Rick and myself had got us through the immunities. I had bust a gut for them and for them to turn round and say 'Thanks very much, off you go' was hard to take. One of the reasons I was weak was that I had done so much. I felt betrayed. But I didn't say anything to anyone because I didn't want to land Rick in it. I really wanted him to win." Richard vowed to Pete that he would get revenge; he would do his best to get the person responsible for Pete's leaving voted off next. Once it had been breached, the whole Ular edifice had started to crumble.

Charlotte had been watching the comings and goings of everyone in the camp very closely and knew something was afoot after Pete lost immunity. After the Immunity Challenge, as she swam in the sea, Jackie came up to her. The pair had discovered they had a lot in common and were slowly becoming good friends. Jackie, while knowing she should not, could not resist telling her that she would not be going the following evening. It would also help Jackie's chances should Charlotte be on the jury. Instead of telling her Pete was going, she lied and said it would be Eve because she did not want Charlotte to tell people that she knew Pete was going. They would know it had come from Jackie and that would put her in peril. Everything was beginning to get extremely murky.

The next morning Pete and Charlotte were in the sea. "I was in the sea and he told me, 'You won't be going tonight,' and I feigned ignorance, because I told Jackie I wouldn't tell anyone," she recalls. "I asked who was going, and he said, 'I am. Rick's told me.' I thought, 'Oh my God,' because I thought Eve was going. And I was thinking 'Oh no!' because Pete was my only friend left that I knew I could trust 100 per cent. I didn't think I had much chance of winning at that stage. I wanted Pete to win. So, I told him I didn't want him to go and I was really upset but I couldn't show it, otherwise I would have dropped Jackie in it. I didn't want anyone to say anything to Jackie because she might not have spoken to me again had she found out."

Charlotte saw immediately that this was a golden opportunity to stir up some trouble among the others. She immediately sought Richard out for a "quiet chat". "I approached Richard, and he didn't know that anyone had told me anything and he told me that Pete was going. So I feigned the whole "Oh really" routine for the third time. I said to Richard that I thought he would be the next to go because I knew I had to side with him at that time. I didn't think I could side with Jackie because I still thought she was with Mick and Zoe. So I knew I had to get Richard on side. I said, 'You're going to be next, they're voting off the strong people. I want you to win, blah, blah, blah.' I was a spare part and superb for him to vote with. He'd seen me as quite weak, as quite vulnerable and didn't see me as a threat at all. That suited me down to the ground. I was nobody's threat at that time. He lied to me, and I know he lied. He said, 'I've approached Mick to try and get him to keep Pete here but he won't.' He knew I liked Pete and he was trying to keep me sweet. But I knew that secretly he wanted to get rid of Pete because Pete was the major threat to him. Pete was really good at the challenges so this was a wonderful opportunity for Richard to vote for Pete, get rid of him, but keep him sweet for the jury. Pete had a lot of influence with Andy; Andy and James got on very well, so he thought he had a little in there, and I was the only other person he had to keep sweet and 'Bang,' he had four votes. I knew exactly what he was planning and I thought, 'Sorry mate, it ain't going to happen.' Even if I was voted off I was going to go up to the rest of the jury and tell them exactly what he had been up to. James and I knew what Richard was like – you couldn't trust him at all.

"I was busy making Richard feel he was vulnerable and I acted all concerned about him. I was being a bit evil, but it wasn't my crew, my friends, they were all stabbing each other in the back. I was just stirring it a little bit, being a little bit devious. Richard then comes up to me and says, 'Jackie's on our side'. I was like, 'Excuse me? What's going on here.' Then I realised there was something going on. I was thinking, 'Jackie's not with Mick and Zoe, I don't know who she's with but I'll work it out. The fact was he and Jackie had the alliance all the time."

Even better for Charlotte, was the fact she knew about Richard and Pete's forbidden conversation – a fact she knew that she could use against him any time she wanted. But for the first time since the tribes merged, Charlotte had been given a whiff of a chance. Pete's misfortune would allow her another three days on the island in which she could get stuck into Richard and try to sway him into forming an alliance with her and another. If she could get a split vote then the policy, devised by James, of building up other people's vote tallies would have worked. Charlotte and Pete were the only people on the island not to have any votes against them, a strong position for Charlotte to be in for the Tribal Council after next. Only if she managed to get two people on her side, though.

The rest of the day continued with people pretending to Pete that everything was going as planned, Pete pretending that he did not know he was going, Richard pretending that he had not told Pete he was going and Charlotte pretending that she did not know she was staying. Zoe confessed to the camera of her doubts about her alliance with Jackie and Richard. The latter she trusted, but Jackie she "couldn't trust as far as I could throw her". Richard told Zoe that Jackie, in her boredom, had begun to play a few games, suggesting that they liven things up a bit by swapping Zoe for Mick "just for a bit of a laugh". Jackie, said Zoe, was "fairly useless but fairly ruthless". In response to this news Zoe had confirmed with Jackie that they were still solid. "I tried to insinuate that, if we weren't, not to mess with me because I hold all the cards! I've got Eve and Mike where I need them. But it's really soured things. I've got a bad taste in my mouth and God knows after thirty days I had a bad taste anyway." But she felt secure with Richard – "together we are strong. I trust him, which is nice."

But what Zoe did not know was that her "chat" with Jackie did not have the desired effect. Jackie reported back to Richard about Zoe's "I hold all the cards" line. Richard was already upset, or appeared to be, about the manner of Pete's leaving and in a conversation the pair agreed Zoe was getting too confident and something would have to be done. She was trying to run the show, drive it along and as Sarah and Eve will testify, that is not behaviour that Jackie and Richard were prepared to tolerate.

Whatever shocks and surprises were in store for future Tribal Councils, the one that evening promised to be the most dramatic for a some time. As Zoe said, "Richard will cover his eyes with mud so nothing can be read about his emotions. Jackie and I will fall about laughing with hysteria and Eve will go (*Schoolma'm voice*) 'Well, you know. It has to be done! Back to camp everybody'. And Charlotte will go, 'Pardon? Pardon? What do you mean I won't get any chocolate tonight?' " Ironically, she and Jackie embarked on a water run together that day where Zoe urged her not to divulge any information about what was going on to Charlotte "Because I swear to God she will use it. Don't mention anything to her because she takes it all in." Zoe was right, but it was too late.

Pete spent the last day with his friend Richard. They talked and reminisced about all that had gone on over the past thirty-one days on the island. It brought home to Richard, he told the camera, how angry he was about the situation. He decided from that point that he would "turn up the heat to the maximum." He indicated that he was tempted to enter into an alliance with Charlotte ("she's a clever girl, she's not missing anything") and that he trusted her. He predicted that the three days following Pete's dismissal would be the hardest of the game so far, as everyone began to jockey for position for the final week. Richard was relishing the prospect. "I've gone from being really bored six days ago to thinking, 'Oh my God, what is going on? This is fantastic.' " From now on, he declared, he would be going for immunity every time because he feared he would become a prime candidate to be picked off.

At Tribal Council that night James had joined Andy on the jury and both were wearing T-shirts. This time they *were* wearing references that referred to the bible, but it was too late to save Pete. Jackie admitted to Mark Austin that splits were appearing within Ular, adding with a gleam in her eye that "it makes it very exciting". Zoe said it was "a volatile beach", Richard confessed that he was unable to hold back his competitive urges. The atmosphere was becoming febrile. Then it was time to vote. Pete voted for Charlotte, keeping his word even when he knew the others had broken theirs. Charlotte kept to the Helang strategy while the rest voted for Pete.

As he left, Pete stopped in front of the people who had just ended his stay on the island. Clearing his throat, anger flaring his nostrils, he said "I consider it an honour that you considered it worthwhile breaking your word that we held to vote me off. I consider it a personal insult that none of you could tell me face to face. So, keep your word in future." With a flourish he then threw his bible in the direction of Richard, to everyone's amazement. They believed Pete was truly upset and that Richard was the main focus of his anger. In fact, he explains, it had all been planned.

"The theory was that if Rick was to have any chance of survival it would be good if they didn't think I would vote for him when I was on the jury, because they would get rid of him then. They knew Helang quite liked him, because he was a good player. They wanted to get rid of the popular one. I wanted them to think that I felt betrayed by Rick. I made out I was angry with him. Rick was aware that I shouldn't do something that was too crass and obvious. It was lucky the way things happened, with Andy and James sat there with what we thought were bible quotes on their T-shirts. I packed all my stuff away that night. I pretended I didn't. Because I thought they were doing these bible quotes, I thought if Rick had the bible it would help him. But I thought there was no point having that if people didn't understand what it meant. I thought I could speak to people through the T-shirts, through the quotes. I decided to throw it at Rick in a huff. It worked quite well – it was funny looking at everyone's eyes when I did it – they were petrified. I had always been mild-mannered Pete. Up until then I hadn't said boo to a goose. It was the first bit of acting I had done on the island. I like playing the nasty guy, not being it."

His reluctance to be the nasty guy cost him the chance of a million pounds. Physically, he was the strongest person on the island, by some distance, until the ravages of island life began to sap his strength. Had he been prepared to get involved with the political scheming on the island then he would have gone much, much further. For instance, after finding he was being voted off he could easily have entered into an alliance with Richard who could have hastily configured a group of four to guarantee Pete stayed. But he did not want to do that and feels it would not have suited him anyway. His word was more important, even if it was a word no one else was prepared to stick to. He wanted to maintain his self-respect and feels he did so, taking comfort in the fact that he could vote for the person he felt deserved the money most when he joined the jury.

The plan to cover the scent of suspicion following Richard was successful. On the way back to camp, the others were attempting to come up with names of other people in history who had suffered the ignominy of a bible being thrown at them. All of them thought Pete's wrath was genuine – perhaps he does have a future as an actor, as he wishes. As they arrived back the heavens opened and an almighty storm unleashed itself upon the island. It threatened to wash the whole camp away and at one stage Sekutu were certain that they must be rescued before they were swept away. One person who was not worried was Richard, who was giving the others the impression that he had lost his grip. "I was shouting 'It's Pete, it's God.' I was running up and down the beach. It was superb, absolutely superb. I was laughing my socks off. It was one of the best nights I spent on the island, if not the best. It was spectacular – lightning lighting up the sky, snakes appeared everywhere, they were all around us. Everyone else was scared but I loved it. It was just a really exciting night both from the point of view of personal dynamics and the natural force of the island. I think it was probably, with hindsight, the best moment I had on the island."

"She lost the plot ..."

Richard and Jackie decided that the time had come for Zoe to go. The latter in particular was in her element as the plotting and treachery became more intense. "Basically Richard said to me, 'Don't you speak to Charlotte, I'll speak to her and set up a threesome,' " Jackie says. "I was saying to Charlotte, 'If we could get Rich it'd be fantastic because then we could get rid of Zoe.' So I put the seed in her mind and Rich spoke to her and it was all on. The three of us would vote against Zoe and she had more votes against her name than Charlotte." For Richard it was simple, "Zoe changed completely. She was, I think, malnourished. She lost the plot, she was using Eve liked she owned Eve, and she had Mick in her pocket."

For Charlotte, this internecine squabbling was the best information she could hear apart from news from home. She decided to stir things up a bit to encourage Jackie and Richard to turn even more vehemently against Zoe, knowing that Eve and Mick would be swift to follow. "I said to Jackie, ' I know who is going to win this, and so do Andy and James,' and Jackie went, 'Who? Who's going to win it?' And I wouldn't say. But that set her thinking that they would have to vote someone off their team because it seemed as if that someone had three votes on the jury already. I was dropping little things like that in to the conversation, even though I had no idea who was going to win. It was little things like that to make people paranoid. Zoe went because she had become very confident that she was going to win it. I said to Rich and Jackie, 'Zoe thinks she's going to win it. She told James on the sand spit.' She'd told me she was going to get down to the last three, and that a woman was going to win it. Which turned out to be true. They did themselves no favours with their over confidence."

On the sand spit, James had actually said to Zoe that he did not want Richard to win it and that she should do everything in her power to prevent that occurring. "It won't happen," had been Zoe's reply. She was confident that their alliance was still strong – at least until they got rid of Charlotte at the next Tribal Council. Zoe began to notice small indications that not everything might go to plan, however. "After Pete went, Jackie didn't speak to me for a few days and I found it really weird. I was like, 'Why isn't she speaking to me when I'm the person who she wants to vote with.' I couldn't understand what was going on, I lost it a bit. She seemed awfully confident. Then she and Charlotte became best buddies and it seemed obvious they had ganged up. I couldn't work out why they had done that to form a two, because that wasn't enough. They started mimicking each other. That's the way Jackie works, she's quite like a chameleon, she attaches herself to people who can help her."

Eve had also noticed the blossoming relationship between Charlotte and Jackie. She was not approving. "Charlotte was seen as completely insignificant and expendable. There was no sense that people saw her as a threat. What happened is that Pete left and the instant he had gone Jackie sidled up to Charlotte and actually isolated herself from the rest of the tribe. From that point, Charlotte and Jackie were inseparable for about seventy-two hours. That's what put everyone's back up against Jackie. What we didn't realise then was that Charlotte and Jackie were manipulating the situation. Jackie knew she had Richard in the palm of her hand and she knew she could get Charlotte in the palm of her hand because Charlotte wanted to stay as long as possible. Jackie started copying how she did her hair. She had a reversible swimsuit, which was blue on one side and black on the other. Up until Pete had left, she always wore the black on the outside. Charlotte's bikinis were all very bright colours, and all of a sudden Jackie turned her swimsuit inside out. They were minor little things, but you think 'Oh Jackie, that's pathetic.'

The increasingly poisonous situation on the island was forgotten for the Reward Challenge on day thirty-two which turned out to be an emotional experience for everyone involved. For all apart from Zoe, who had "bought" a conversation with her girlfriend, home had come to seem a very distant place indeed. The prize for the "Sixty-Second Assault" – a short assault course constructed in the jungle – was to be a fifteen-minute video from home. A film crew had gone to the homes of the contestants and taped a short snippet filled with news from home, words of encouragement. As the wives, husbands, mothers, boyfriends, brothers and sisters all knew their loved ones had reached a certain stage in the game they had been asked to sign confidentiality forms.

Unbeknown to the contestants, they were all at that point waiting at a hotel near Heathrow. Whoever won the challenge would have their loved one or ones flown out for a surprise reunion the following day. To whet the appetite of the contestants and to stir them for the challenge ahead, the contestants were shown a thirty-second segment of the tape. The winner would get to see the rest of his or her video.

First up was Mick. It was his wife, Jean. Before going on the island, Mick had told the camera about news he might or might not want imparted to him while playing the game. He said: "If my wife became terminally ill then I'd want to know; but the decision we came to was that if she died, my friends would get her put on ice until I got back – and that was a mutual decision." Any thoughts of Mrs Easton being put on ice were forgotten when she appeared on the screen, telling him how his treasured Ghost Carp fish had been eaten by a heron. Mick was overcome with emotion. He started crying and that set everyone else off. Afterwards he spoke about how much it had affected him, unexpectedly. "I've been married to Jean for something like thirty years but I think it takes something like this to make you realise how much you love and miss someone. It was difficult, difficult. I'm not sure how I'd have coped with looking at the whole of it.

"It was only a short glimpse but instantly everybody's emotions were enormously high, there was nothing hidden. Most of the people left here are mentally hard otherwise they wouldn't still be here but it was quite an eye-opener to see their reactions. I think just about everybody burst into tears so it was quite interesting."

Mick admitted that he made a faux pas with Zoe after the tape was played of her girlfriend Sindy. 'She doesn't look like how I imagined," he told her. "Oh, why is that Mike?" Zoe asked. "She's very attractive," was his response. His face fell, mortified, as it sunk in what he had said. "What did you expect, a right old badger?" Zoe shot back. Fortunately for Mick, she was not the kind to bear grudges or take herself too seriously.

Everyone else had the same response as Mick. Jackie's boyfriend Martin was on her tape; Richard's brother James delivered his message, summing up the whole of the last four weeks' news in thirty seconds so Richard did not have to watch the rest. Charlotte was probably the most emotional. Until recently, her homesickness had been acute. She had never been away from home on her own before and that had been tough. She burst into tears when she saw her husband Mark and her mother on the screen. Thirty seconds wasn't enough for her and she was determined to see the rest of the tape, even if it killed her. Richard had told her he was not interested in winning because he felt he could not handle watching the rest of the tape. With him out of the way she was confident she could win it. She got the best time, running over a slippery log. But Richard, as competitive as ever, could not resist. He took off his boots and ran in his socks to give him extra grip and he went on to beat Charlotte's time. Winning was a habit for him, a fact he underlined when he said he did not want the prize and gave it to Charlotte instead. Charlotte could not believe it – now she cannot believe Richard's competitiveness – but seeing the full video was extremely emotional for her, as she told the camera.

"That's the most incredible thing that's happened to me since we came to the island. I miss my family so much, my husband, my Mum, my Dad and my brothers and sisters and just to see their faces and hear their voices has taken my breath away. I just want to sit and try and take as much of it in as I possibly can, remember every word they said. I can't believe Richard was that generous .... It just makes things a bit more real on the island – it seems totally crazy being on this island so something like that brings you back to normality. If I were to make a video for them I'd say I was doing fine, I miss you all and love you loads and I can't wait to see you and I'm never ever going to do this again. I'm never going away from home again." At this point she began to sob. "You know how much you love people but it's amazing how difficult it is to be without them, especially for this period of time."

Given the prevailing mood of cynicism and distrust on the island, the others saw Richard's generosity as a blatant attempt to win Charlotte's favour. Richard denied it at the time but now admits he was motivated by the fact it would earn Charlotte's thanks and she would now owe him one, particularly when she reached the jury. For Charlotte it was the turning point in the whole game, regardless of what Richard's motives were. "Richard and I had been chatting and he realised just how much I was missing my family. Before the challenge they told us what the prize was. I thought, 'This is one thing I want to win,' more than food even. But he said he didn't want to win it, he didn't want to watch the video. I thought that was great because I thought I could beat the others. It was a balancing assault course and I got the furthest of anyone. Then Richard put his socks on and beat me, the logs had become slippy and socks gave him extra grip. I thought 'You git, you're too competitive for your own good.' Because even though he had said he didn't want to win the video he still wanted to win the challenge and then give me the video because he knew how much I wanted to see it. He gave me the video and I'm sure there are a number of reasons for that. At the time, it was just fantastic because it was Mark and my mum. My mum was saying, 'I know you can win it love, I know you can do it.' And Mark was urging me on. At that stage, I was a bit vulnerable and then I watched this and I snapped back into myself. I had become this pathetic little wimp, moping about. But the video gave me strength, I thought 'I can win this. There is always a chance.' "

Shared emotion over, it was back to the scheming. Mick expressed his reservations about Jackie's recent behaviour, how she was playing a "dangerous game". "She is becoming extraordinarily friendly with Charlotte who is, was, Helang and is actually our next target, so the way it is going Jackie is making herself the next target after that. Jackie may have a strategy for the game but if she has it's certainly nothing that I'm aware of. I can only think that the reason she did that and the reason she is behaving as she is, is insecurity." The reason was that boredom had led her to start playing games, swapping alliances to make things more interesting. As a result of her behaviour, the others were beginning to shun her, driving her closer towards Charlotte. On a water run with Richard after the challenge, the pair thickened the plot further, discussing how to get rid of Zoe.

The night before, on the way to Tribal Council to vote off Pete, Zoe had spoken with Eve and told Richard that Jackie was playing a "silly game". Richard's response was to think Zoe was playing a worse game because she was acting as if "she owned everybody". He then outlined what he thought the strategy should be to Jackie. "We've got two days. We need to play a really quiet game now. We need to let Zoe think she is in charge. With a bit of luck she won't win immunity tomorrow, so that means in two days' time … if it ends up with us and Charlotte in the last three she will win hands down. But I think it's far more dangerous keeping Eve and

Zoe on because they are just not nice people in this game ....
Zoe, OK she looks like a megalomaniac at the moment, but I
think she's playing a wise game. I think that she probably
thinks that the actress 'ha ha ha' image will win it for her if
she gets to the last two .... Mick, I think there is a bit of stunning cunning there. He's a clever guy. I don't think his stumbling around and losing things is an act because he's too
good at it. But I think he knows what is going on ... I think
that if I win Charlotte over and I announce that it's you I'm
with then I think she'll be happy with that."

It was becoming clear that what happened at the next
Tribal Council would dictate who would go through to the
final three. Elsewhere on the island, Zoe spoke to the cameras and outlined her reasons to distrust Jackie. "She's not
exactly flavour of the month at the moment for various reasons. I had an alliance with her and Richard, which I no
longer have because she sort of wanted to get rid of me and
have Mick instead. I found out that she told Charlotte that she
wasn't going yesterday so I think she's playing a very funny
game ... I think she thought she could have an alliance with
Rich and Mick but she underestimated my cunning and I have
poisoned her path in that direction and any other direction so
ha! Don't mess with me ... in her own words she 'just wanted to have a bit of fun and stir things up'. Well, go stir up
somebody else because I've got a different sense of humour
than you ... I think she has ruined things for herself."

For the next forty-eight hours Jackie kept an extremely
low profile, often being seen on her own or with Charlotte.
This was done on purpose, avoiding conflict with the other
three. Richard was making Zoe believe that he was still with
her, while at the same time buttering Charlotte up. Jackie,
however, was feeling paranoid, even though, as she told the

camera, it was of her own making. "Richard, myself and Zoe made an agreement, the day we voted off Sarah, and we decided to stick with that. But I think that was too early because people got bored and you feel like the game's too predictable because you're in a threesome and you can trust each other. Then I decided to stir it up. I said to Richard, 'Let's stab Zoe in the back' for no other reason than you think it's so predictable. Then it comes back and bites you on the bum. I think I'm probably in the firing line, if not at the next Tribal Council then certainly the one after."

But Jackie had an ace tucked up her sleeve in the form of Charlotte, who was willing to enter an alliance with Jackie and Richard. Richard had decided that the power was going to Zoe's head. "She's coming out with statements like, 'Don't worry, I've poisoned Jackie's path through to Eve and I've poisoned her path through to Mick, she's stuck, she's on her own.' It's just this complete power trip, 'I won the game, I control the game, I'm this, that and the other.' And it's just too obvious. It's standing out like a sore thumb for me … Charlotte could turn it all on its head. We can't make this work without Charlotte. I'm sticking with Jackie because there's a certain part of me that wants to be honest – that I made an alliance on day one and promised to stick to it. I nearly got sent off the game a while back, after my bust up with Sarah and Eve, and Jackie went away and did her work and made it safe. She's not just here because of me, she's here because of Jackie; she's played her part and made herself popular with people. At the moment it seems to be turning a bit sour for her but this is the part of the game now where the volume is full on, the heat is really turned up and anything could happen."

For Richard and Jackie's plan to work Zoe had to be prevented from winning immunity the next day. The challenge was Survivor Rescue. Someone was stranded at sea. On the presenter's signal the survivors had to construct a raft from materials found on the beach, paddle out to the poor unfortunate drowning at sea, pull them on to the raft and paddle back. The first one back won immunity. In this case it was Eve, who had long been threatening to win a challenge. Richard did terribly for a change, but was given a huge surprise when Mark Austin called him over to unmask the person in the wetsuit he had attempted to save. For the others it had been locals or members of the production crew. For Richard it was his brother James. When Richard had won the Reward Challenge the previous morning, despite his handing the first part of the prize to Charlotte, James had been put on the first plane to Kota Kinabalu. After arriving he was taken to the island and dressed up as a frogman. The pair spent the evening on the sand spit, with a cold beer and a cigar, talking of home. They were forbidden from discussing anything that had taken place on the island in the previous thirty-three days. That was not a worry, the game had become so intense it was a sweet release to talk about anything else.

But back on the island the mind games struck up once more. Zoe confronted Richard about whether he was in an alliance with Charlotte and Jackie, which he denied. He told her they were going ahead, as planned. Charlotte was the one to be voted off. The air was so thick with intrigue that even Richard, a psychiatrist, was wracked with paranoia. "I just get this uncomfortable feeling about the way that Eve is being nastier than usual towards the two girls, Zoe's gone quiet, and even Mick seems to be talking to me less, and talking less to the two girls." That morning he, Jackie and Charlotte were seen in a tight huddle while Zoe, Eve and Mick were in a tight huddle of their own. He was still pretending to Zoe that it was himself, Zoe and Mick that were going forward. But, he added, he, Jackie and Charlotte were having fun as an alliance, which was preferable to the whispering that was going on before. He realised that all this backstabbing and plotting was not making people popular, but added: "At the end of this game, I don't think people will be voting for who they like, I think they will be voting for who they least dislike."

As if the atmosphere was not distrustful and malevolent enough as it stood, accusations were being made that Eve, Mick and Zoe had been hiding rice for them all to eat later, having got rid of the others. Jackie and Charlotte believed they had buried it somewhere on the beach. Food was running low, and had seemingly got even lower according to Jackie and Charlotte. Weight was falling off everybody and tempers were becoming increasingly frayed. Eve blamed the lack of rice on Charlotte cooking too much the previous day. "It's getting to the stage where we'll be counting grains of rice soon," Charlotte told the camera, only half-jokingly.

That Tribal Council was yet another dramatic one. Pete had joined James and Andy on the jury and the hidden messages were become increasingly convoluted. Expecting Charlotte to be voted off, they had printed up three Helang T-shirts which spelled REVENGE if people sat in the correct order. "R" on one shirt, "EVE" on another and "NGE" on the third. A biblical reference had also been placed on Pete's shirt, Deuteronomy 32:34: "For the day of their downfall is near, their doom is fast approaching." Unfortunately, no one was able to decipher the message because the bible had been taken away after it had been thrown at Richard in Pete's fake outburst of anger: it had been Pete's luxury item and the rules stated that contestants must take all their belongings with them when they left the island.

Once the Council got underway, Zoe, to her immense shock and surprise, was voted off. She garnered three votes, as did Charlotte. However, as Richard and Jackie were aware, Zoe had five votes previously, whereas Charlotte was collecting her first votes of the whole game. A feeling of unease had descended on her that afternoon as she contemplated her voting, but she dismissed it as paranoia. Zoe made her way to the confessional after being ejected, stunned at what had just happened.

"I think possibly Jackie and Richard pulled a fast one, good on them. Yeah, I'd have done the same. So I think it was those two. I thought I was invincible too. I had a moment of paranoia whilst relaxing on my hammock earlier today when it suddenly dawned on me that if Charlotte and Jackie and Richard got together they could vote me off because of my vote history. But I put it down to paranoia. I didn't even pack my whole kit – that's how much I put it down to paranoia. So it all went pear-shaped but good on them, they got one over on me. I trusted Richard, and I guess you should trust no one, but I just felt you had to have somebody, somewhere, within the group, in whom you could put your trust and l was horribly wrong. He plays a good game. I thought I played a good game. I've done all right up until now. I was in the last six without having any sporting ability whatsoever so that's an achievement in itself, I think.

"Well, I guess Jackie betrayed me as well. She's a slippery little snake that one and, yes, she played a better game than me. I thought I had one over on her but obviously not. They did it very, very well and that's the nature of the game and they deserve to go further. I really did think Charlotte was out tonight. Possibly because everybody's had a ringing in their ears since she joined the camp and the incessant talk of chocolate bars is getting a bit dull and I thought that would be enough to get rid of her. But obviously not. Bless Mick, please be gentle with him. I love Mick and he doesn't have much of a clue what's going on most of the time. I presume this is correct, I presume Mick hasn't betrayed me. So keep going Mick, it'll be all right. I've got a beer waiting for you at the other end, mate. Eve will have had the wool pulled over her eyes twice in one game, which is never a nice feeling unless you are particularly into jumpers. I think she'll be feeling very vulnerable, not a nice feeling. I wouldn't like to be in her shoes. I would rather be here than there, let's put it that way. But Eve is an incredibly strong woman, mentally and physically, and she has the potential to win immunities and get through this thing, so fingers crossed for Eve at this point. I got way too confident. She came, she saw, she fell off the log. That would probably be my epitaph."

Now with hindsight she pins most of the blame on Richard and believes that it was a major mistake for him to double-cross her in the way he did in favour of Jackie and Charlotte. In Zoe's opinion, his chances of winning evaporated the moment he turned against her. "I asked Richard whether he was in with them and he denied it. I thought 'Surely he won't be that stupid to go with two girls who have bonded that closely. Why on earth would either take him with them to the final.' I thought it could happen but I thought he would be too intelligent to go with those two. That wouldn't have happened with myself, Jackie and him because he knew what I felt about Jackie. Jackie and I were together for convenience in an alliance. She is one of these people who portrays herself as a victim and then gets pissed off when people treat her as a victim. She sees herself as weak and portrays herself as weak. She's a passive-aggressive, which is the worst sort of aggressive you can get. I just have a problem with people like that. It was a very silly move by Richard. He knew what I felt about Jackie, presumably he's an intelligent man but not to have seen how they were behaving together and the best he could do was reach the final three was an act of gross stupidity. He had to win immunity every time. I had already said to him that if it got down to two then I would rather lose against him then win against Jackie. I meant that and still do. I can't believe he did it. It was karma what happened to him I suppose. I was like 'Ner ner ner ner ner' when he lost that Immunity Challenge.

"When he came back [after being voted off] he asked me how many alliances I was in, because he thought I was in another one with Eve and Michael. I said 'Just one, the one with you.' He said, 'Oh s**t.' I said, 'I told you I was in one and I told you what I had done. I had to trust you because if you don't talk honestly with at least one person, then it's all chaos.' His answer was, 'Yes Zoe, but when I asked you about it you looked away. You didn't look me in the eye.' I was astounded. I said, 'For God's sake, Richard, the sun was in my eyes. I hope you don't base your f***ing psychiatry on that mate.' "

Hell hath no fury like Eve scorned ... again

The walk back from Tribal Council degenerated into a "catfight" between Jackie, Charlotte and Eve. All three were "screaming their heads off" according to Richard. Jackie told Eve that "It's taken you thirty years to grow up," while Eve responded by telling her, "This is a big people's game." The men kept well out of it.

Back at the camp Mick was magnanimous about what had occurred. He went up to Charlotte, Jackie and Richard and said, "Look guys, well played. You've done it really well. We didn't see that coming and obviously there were two alliances. I got in on the wrong one." For him and Eve the signs were ominous; they would have to win immunities from now on. Mick felt, however, that there was an outside chance of trying to work his way back into a strong alliance. Eve, however, was furious and there was no way she could countenance even contemplating forming an alliance with any one of Richard, Jackie or Charlotte. She could barely bring herself to speak to them, as she told the cameras on the morning of day thirty-five.

"I feel quite vulnerable now within the tribe. I'm disappointed for Zoe and partly for myself as I get on well with Zoe. She was a victim of the game in that someone lied outright and to her face, having gained her trust. I know that it was Richard and that's why I'm not surprised. The very first day I met Richard I was sceptical about him and that scepticism was borne out when he turned tail on Sarah …. The disappointment is that I'm in a tribe with four other people, three of which I can't stand; Richard because I just don't trust him, he's a complete snake; Charlotte I just don't have the time of day for … she's greedy, underhand, selfish and vain. She's everything I don't like in a person. I've never liked Jackie. I've pussyfooted around her for five weeks trying to make her feel nice so that she feels confident and quite frankly I'm sick to death of it. It's a game of snakes and ladders and at the moment I feel like I've reached the top row of the board and between me and winning are three snakes."

She vowed from then on to try and win every remaining Immunity Challenge but she knew that that was unlikely to happen. She wanted to enjoy her last three days on the island and knew she would go before Mick because of the hatred

Jackie and Charlotte held for her. "I feel very sorry for Mick because he's got to stay on this ruddy island with three people he just can't trust knowing that if he doesn't win immunity then he will be voted off. The only grievance I have about the whole game is that there is a high probability that the last two are going to be two people that I cannot stand and it'll irk me to have to give either of them one million pounds. But I will make sure I say that."

Things were to get increasingly petty. Eve hid the tomato ketchup – which had become a popular way of flavouring rice – in her bag to stop others using it, but it was found and a row developed. It increased the suspicion that she was involved in hiding rice. That day's Reward Challenge was interesting in more ways than one. First, because of the complete breakdown in communications between Eve and the alliance that had formed to get rid of Zoe. Secondly, the game involved the five survivors looking at themselves in the mirror for the first time since arriving on the island. They had to guess how much weight they had lost, and whoever guessed the most accurately was to win the reward.

Charlotte used the opportunity to wind up Eve even further. Given the mirror, she began to contemplate her reflection at length. Such vanity was anathema to Eve and she began to tell Charlotte how "pathetic" she was being. That just made Charlotte go even further. "I started becoming overly girly because I knew it was driving her mad. I remember when they brought out the mirror for one of the challenges. I was saying 'Look at my hair, it's blonde.' She was like, 'Why don't you just tell them your weight and get out of the mirror?' I said, 'No, I want to look at my hair first. Oh, look how blonde it is.' I could just see her there seething. I laughed to myself. Whenever she was around I was asking people whether my eyelashes were alright, or how my eyebrows looked. And she couldn't handle it, she kept saying, 'Why are you bothering to pluck your eyebrows, why are you doing this that and the other.' It was hilarious."

Both Richard and Mick had lost twenty-nine pounds in their time on the island. Richard had been 194 pounds on arrival, Mick 191. Jackie had also lost a fair amount, around a stone and a half, falling from 148 pounds to 131. She was thrilled. "We thought perhaps it would be one of those arcade mirrors that make you look completely different. It was really strange looking in the mirror after nearly seven weeks of being away. I think the first thing that struck me was that I had a bit of a waist again and the second thing was how scanky my legs are with all these mosquito bites everywhere." Since leaving the island, she has managed to remain at the weight she was when she arrived back in England. Charlotte and Eve had lost less; both lost 11 pounds, Charlotte falling from 152 pounds, Eve from 131. Jackie came within two pounds of guessing correctly, but Eve was closer, getting within one pound of her weight. Eve's prize was a huge chocolate cake. For the time being a ceasefire was called. Hostilities ceased as Eve shared the cake around the rest of the tribe at tea that evening, giving everyone a much required energy boost. It was a only temporary truce, though. Normal service was resumed the next morning for what would be an extremely important – not to say eventful – Immunity Challenge.

Week 6

The final push

EVE'S AIM WAS to win immunity. That would mean the end of Mick, leaving her alone with her three nemeses, but she was determined to try her hardest to "steal" the million away from them. Momentum was with her – she had won the last two challenges – and the chocolate cake had given her strength. She knew that Jackie, Richard and Charlotte would all be gunning for her but she was confident, whatever the challenge was, of defeating the two women and Mick. The problem was Richard and his competitiveness. Her heart sank when she heard what the challenge was going to be. In the heat of the midday sun, the five had to stand on upended logs and place one hand on a large tree trunk embedded in the sand. Every fifteen minutes, they were required to change positions. The person who kept a hand on there for the longest would win immunity. Eve knew this was a test of endurance and she knew that Richard had lasted twenty-three hours standing on a log. She would have to dig awfully deep to remain on the island after this one.

The contestants took their place on their stands shortly before dawn and set themselves for the long haul. Controversy struck within the first hour – an incident that would end all hope Eve had of winning the challenge. Charlotte's period had started that day and after forty-five minutes or so she asked whether she would be allowed to take her hand off the trunk and get down in order to put in a tampon. The programme organisers said that would not be a problem as long as it gained the assent of all the other contestants, as technically it was a breach of the rules. Mick, Jackie and Richard all gave their approval to Charlotte's request. Eve, however, did not. Despite the protestations of the others she stuck to her decision and Charlotte was forced to insert the tampon with one hand while keeping her other hand on the trunk, her modesty covered by Richard standing next to her and holding a sarong in front of her.

Eve's decision caused a huge row. Richard was appalled and, such is his manner, took up Charlotte's fight on her behalf, determining there and then to keep his hand on the trunk with the sole purpose of defeating and humiliating Eve. Mick was also appalled by Eve, and he was the one ally she had left on the island. The other two women, who felt Eve had disgraced herself, were just as angry. "Seeing both sides of it, the tampon incident, I thought it was evil and inhumane and what I would expect of Eve," says Jackie. "It was just pathetic. What advantage would Charlotte have by jumping in the water for two minutes? She would still have to get back on her stand. It was stupid and just made Richard more determined to beat Eve."

Complaints of her being "inhumane" and "evil" are dismissed by Eve, who claims she was just sticking up for her principles. "If you needed a wee or anything else you had to go on the log. About half an hour in to it, Charlotte said she had her period. Everyone else said, 'It's OK, you get off and sort yourself out and come back on.' I thought, 'Hang on that's not rules. If she gets off, that's it, she's off for good. She's given up.' Why should women have special treatment? I know I'm going to get horrific stick from people for this because Rich called me 'inhumane' for making her stand there. I would never expect any special treatment for being a woman. To put it very bluntly, it's only blood. If I had cut my hand then they would not have let me get off the log because of that. So why should she be allowed to get off because she had a period, which she knew she had anyway? I just felt that that's the rules, you put up with it. If you're expected to perform all your other bodily functions on a log in front of five other people and a load of camera crews then isn't that more degrading than getting your period?"

But Eve admits that it spurred Richard on for the rest of the challenge. Charlotte and Mick eventually got down after a few hours, while Jackie made it to thirteen and a half hours, before deciding to get down as night fell and a storm closed in. As the rains came Eve curled herself up into a ball as protection against the horrendous weather. Richard, by his own admission, made himself as big as he possibly could to try and intimidate Eve into giving up. Within five minutes of Jackie going, Eve jumped off. Jackie thinks Eve did that because all she was interested in was beating her. Eve denies this but Jackie is sticking to the story "because it sounds great". Eve says the reason she called it a day was because of the terrible weather.

"Mick left, Charlotte left, Jackie left after about thirteen hours because she knew I wouldn't get off the log until she got down. Then the rain started, it was me and Richard. I knew he'd done twenty-three hours on another log challenge but I knew he had to get off and his legs went numb from the knees down. I thought I could last longer than that. We didn't speak at all. Then the wind and rain started and it was torrential. The sun had only just gone down and I knew it was ten hours until daylight and twelve hours until I could benefit from the warmth of the sun. I knew I could easily bet on five hours of torrential rain. I thought I would just collapse, so my logic said get off and I did."

The antipathy did not end there, however. For the next twenty-four hours no one spoke to Eve – she had become a pariah. There was no need for discussions about who was to be voted off on the evening of day thirty-seven; Eve was going and she knew it. On her last afternoon she claims that she needed to take some of the remaining tampons because she would be needing them over the forthcoming day or two. So she took some from the supplies in the camp. Her actions were misread. "They didn't speak to me for a day and walking to Tribal Council they wouldn't even walk with me. The only time they spoke to me the day of Tribal Council was two instances, not related: [there was] the tampon incident and the next day, there were loads of tampons in a medical box which I needed in a couple of days. They're only going to get thrown away, so I put them in my bag, thinking that Charlotte did not use that particular brand and knowing Jackie had already said 'I couldn't cope with having my period on the island,' and had taken the pill to avoid it. So it seemed OK to take these tampons because no one else was going to use them. Jackie saw me and kicked up a fuss about it so I said I would put them back. So I did. Then I walked off and when I came back I knew someone had gone through my bag. Jackie had taken the tampons out of my bag and she related the two incidents when they weren't related at all."

Not for the first time, Jackie and Charlotte's views differ

wildly from Eve's. According to Charlotte, "Jackie walked into the camp and saw Eve taking every single usable tampon from the camp and putting them in her bag. Jackie said 'What are you doing?' and she said she was taking a few because she might need them later. Even though she was staying in a hotel that night. It was very malicious of her. She also took her tomato ketchup as well, which was a bit petty. But by then Eve had lost it, she hated us and we hated her. It was good to see her go." This is a sentiment more than echoed by Jackie, who had been at loggerheads with Eve almost from the word go. "After we formed that three it was obvious that Eve was going to go next … because we hated her. I wasn't sorry to see her go – she's a witch."

The feeling is mutual. One can't imagine these particular survivors meeting up in a few years' time to reminisce and laugh about the times they spent together. Eve hates all three of them with a passion. "It wasn't until I was in my hotel room a week later and unpacked my whole kit that I found a poncho, which we had been given to sleep under. Mine had been taken out from the bottom of my bag and Richard had slashed the word 'F***ed' across it in four-inch high lettering. They did that on my last day on the island, that's what it was like. They tried to cook rice and eat it without telling me, and they hid coconut so they didn't have to share it with me. A photographer came to take photos of us and they left me in bed. They refused to speak to me at all. Charlotte said one thing to me, 'Alright?' And I told her what I thought and said they were all being cowardly and she agreed. I was glad to leave because I was sick of them, absolutely sick of the three of them. A pathetic bunch of people. Mick I hold no grudge against and afterwards we cleared the air and said whatever happened on the island happened there and it was forgotten about. But those three, there is no love lost. I look upon the three of them as you would look upon something nasty you just trod in, and I wiped them off my shoe as soon as I could."

Tribal Council was a tense affair that evening, not because the result was in any doubt, simply because the loathing between Eve and the others was blatantly obvious. The recriminations were long and loud. Mick had his say on Eve first: "I thought Eve's behaviour to Charlotte was inhumane. I was astounded what she did and that has been compounded today … but I'll let Jackie tell you that." Jackie did not hold back. "It was just compounded because our only supply of tampons were taken, every single last usable one of them by Eve, knowing full well that Charlotte needed them and I thought that was very selfish." Eve asked for a chance to answer the accusations before the whole scene degenerated into a kangaroo court.

"It's so pathetic," she told Mark Austin. "If you want to go into detail then I didn't think that Charlotte was using that particular brand of tampons …. I'm about to get my period so I took some and put them in my bag but admittedly have put about 10 back. Jackie did go rifling through my bag." Later she said she had made no mistakes and would go home "with my head held high". Then it was time to vote and, predictably, few of the competitors had kind words to say of her in the voting booth. "Hubble, bubble toil and trouble, Eve has gone and burst her bubble," said Charlotte. "I'm voting for Eve because she is a nasty, narrow-minded piece of work," said Jackie. Richard said, "Eve, it's how you play the game and not the winning. Unfortunately you played the game without respect for either anybody on the island or yourself." Eve voted for Jackie with the words, "I just can't stand you."

As Eve left she wished Mick luck, studiously ignoring the

others. She made her way to the confessional where she launched into a final diatribe at the expense of her now sworn enemies. "I feel very sorry for Mick being stuck on the island with those three because they are a nightmare .... Once I knew the alliance of Richard, Jackie and Charlotte had been formed I knew there was absolutely no chance for me because they are absolutely thick as thieves and they deserve each other. As the numbers have dwindled in the tribe, things have become personal because you can't get lost in larger numbers. You've got to live with these people, almost hand to mouth and you just can't escape from them .... It becomes very hard not to let it become personal because it's twenty-four hours a day with those people. With those three, I had gone too far down the line to make amends and I would have had to go against my principles. I said quite a long time ago that the person who wins the million has got to be a very devious, cunning liar and those three fit the bill quite well.

"I'm not a nasty liar, I'm not a devious person. I can play the game and I can have a few schemes and things like that but when it comes down to it I'd rather be able to hold my head up high so, you know, I can walk away from here with pride and a lot of self respect. I would be devastated if Jackie won it, on principle. I do not believe Mick will be given the opportunity to win it. I expect Richard to win it. If Richard was in the last two then I would vote for him to win. I don't trust him but at least he has been consistent over the last five weeks and he has decided his strategy and stuck to it as opposed to Jackie or Charlotte who just float with the breeze trying to win votes. I came, I saw, I learnt a lot. That would be my epitaph at the end of the game."

The pressure of the last few days, and the tension, then began to take its toll. Eve is, as Richard described her, a "tough cookie". Perhaps too tough, but the backbiting and sniping of the past few days had got to her and her thoughts were already beginning to turn to home and her boyfriend, Sean. She started to break down as she sent a message to him. "Not a day has passed when I haven't asked him for support, guidance, advice, strength, fitness and he's never, ever let me down and I love you so much ..." The interview ended there, as did Eve Holding's tempestuous stay on Pulau Tiga.

With hindsight, her feelings have not mellowed at all towards those she dislikes, but she can look back at the experience and see it positively, for all its traumas and ups and downs. "I played a straight game, I saw it very black and white, yet grey won. We did new things all the time that I'd never done, like eating bugs, which tasted like Stilton. Rafting and fishing, lashing ropes, little things like that I learned. I also learned that ironing face cloths wasn't normal. I do that. I iron everything. I didn't find out until I got to the island. I realised my need for order isn't normal either, because people don't need that degree of order. I believe things have their place; if you put things back then you know when something is missing is my view. But now I know that's my military background – no one else felt like that. People opening sun cream when the last bottle wasn't finished also wound me up. That way you know that you need some more, rather than having old bottles strewn everywhere, but everyone thought I was weird when I said that."

"I fooled a psychiatrist ..."

It is fair to say that with Eve gone the atmosphere on the beach improved. The preceding week, from the time that Pete was voted off, had been one filled with tension, hostility and distrust. Little had been seen of anybody's good side.

But now that many of the running personal clashes within Sekutu had come to an end the whole mood shifted. The next morning everyone was relaxed and upbeat. All four were friends, on the surface at least, and had respect for each other. It was evidence that life on Pulau Tiga, even at this late stage in the game, could occasionally be light-hearted and laid-back – every now and then it could even be fun. People could get on. The four remaining contestants sat around and talked, went for walks and fished, and enjoyed each other's company. From that day, number thirty-eight, the game changed. There were no more Reward Challenges; instead the next two days featured an Immunity Challenge. On the final evening, the two remaining contestants would face the jury, giving opening and closing speeches to the jury, and facing a series of questions from each juror before the vote which would decide who deserved the million pounds the most.

So, Mick knew that he had to win immunity because there was no way he could break the threesome ranged against him. Despite that, Charlotte was still worried that her popularity with certain sections of the jury would count against her and that Richard might turn against her and side with Mick, so she was intent on winning immunity also. "I got the feeling at that point that Rich wanted to get rid of me. We all wanted to get rid of Eve. But I think Richard wanted rid of me when we got down to the last four. Mick was saying, 'I know I'm going to be the next off,' and Rich was saying, 'You never know, you never know.' He was trying to get me to think Jackie was going to vote against me, and I knew there was no way that was going to happen. But I made sure he knew that I knew Jackie was not going to vote for me so that if anyone voted for me, it was going to be him and I would make sure that he didn't get my vote on the jury. And also I had James and Andy to back me up. And I knew about the Pete incident; I knew Richard wanted rid of him even though they liked each other, because he was still a threat to him. Rich wanted the million quid. He knew there was no way he could vote for me without jeopardising his jury votes. So he knew he had to win the final Immunity Challenge."

Richard toyed with the idea of allying himself with Mick, but rejected it. He had a lot of respect for Mick and the way that he had played the game. At one point he became concerned for Mick's physical and mental wellbeing and approached a member of the production staff to express his concern. Mick insists it was all part of his act and that Richard fell for it. "I'm very proud that I fooled a psychiatrist with my tactic," he declared. What he had managed to do was fly low under the radar as he wished and he got a lot further than he had thought he would. Richard's view of him, given to camera, was glowing.

"This is a guy that's extremely clever, very intelligent and understands the game. I think he has done really, really well to get this far. I've been in alliances with Mick and Mick and I have never talked about the alliances, which is different to how everyone else is. The other morning he came to me and said, 'I think you three are in cahoots together, are you wanting to go through to the end? If so, is it Eve next and then me because if so I'd just like to enjoy my rest of the time on the island. My response was, 'Yeah, Mick that's the way it is but no alliance has lasted longer than three days on this island.' " Richard was keeping his options open but he thought that the best thing to do was to keep true to Jackie and try and win immunity the next evening. If not, he prayed Jackie would win and take him through with her.

Mick needed immunity and he was given some excellent

news about the nature of the challenge. It was to be an exercise in orienteering, a sport Mick is involved with back in Kent. Learning this, he was extremely confident, especially when it was revealed to him that neither Jackie nor Charlotte knew how to use a compass. The four were sent off at intervals by Mark Austin, in a quest to find immunity talismans. Using maps and compasses, they had to navigate their way through uncharted jungle, finding several base points, where they must answer questions before moving on. The talismans were hidden in the crevices of the large mud volcano, from which the island had been formed more than 100 years before.

Alas, Mick's downfall came not from failing to find his way – though he had problems there – but in interpreting the clues dotted across the island. "It started with a long sprint down the beach and I felt really good and I thought 'This is mine'. But I blew it in two ways. On the second section, the directions were across two fallen logs and then turn east. I did not spot the second log; the first one was obvious. I came past Charlotte running out of the jungle and I assumed she had got lost because they did not know how to use a compass properly. I thought 'I've got to go straight on'. Then I said to her 'Have you been to the first checkpoint?' and I realised what I had bloody done. I had not turned right, assuming she was lost, and got myself lost. So I lost a bit of time there but it didn't matter because I still had plenty of power to sprint and rather than following the paths, I 'straightlined' it through the jungle and got to the volcano. I picked the clue up there and that was where I made my big mistake. It said, 'Head sixty degrees for the number of days there are in Christmas. So I went for the number of days in the advent calendar, twenty-five, when of course it was twelve. Once I did twenty-five steps the wrong way I had had it."

Charlotte also had problems with the clue about taking as many steps as there are in John Buchan's famous novel. She had never heard of *The Thirty-Nine Steps* and joked at her own expense that she would have been all right had it been a Jackie Collins novel. Richard was the winner – he described it as a half-hour of some of the roughest terrain he had run through – with Jackie coming in second, an achievement she is extremely proud of. By her own admission the challenges were not her forte and her lack of physical strength was one of the reasons people believed she was not someone who deserved to get as far as she did. But, even under the harsh regime on the island, the lack of food and sleep it afforded, she got stronger and fitter and improved her finishing positions as the game progressed.

"To begin with, the orienteering filled me with fear. Here is someone who is completely out of their depth on the island, that gets worn out after only fifty yards of running. We started out in the water so our boots were about a kilo heavier. It was just so difficult but I had such a fantastic sense of achievement at the end of that. I did a brilliant, brilliant time. It was by far the best challenge that I competed in and I was only a couple of minutes behind Rich. I just think it was a massive accomplishment, especially to finish when Mick didn't and it is his sport." She is now threatening to take it up as a hobby and a way to maintain her newly-found shape.

After the drama of recent Tribal Councils and the bitterness, that evening's was a slice of light relief in comparison. Mick had prepared himself for leaving and there existed no hard feelings between him and any of the others. Charlotte spoke about how she spent the whole orienteering challenge running around like a headless chicken, "and I've seen a few of those since I've been here," she added. She said the four of them had enjoyed a good day in each other's company. As the vote started the tributes to Mick began to flow in the booth. "You've played an absolutely superb game, you've had me foxed a couple of times but unfortunately you fell in with a bad crowd," said Richard. "I'm voting for Mick," said Charlotte. "He's a really fabulous bloke. But if his sausages can't save him now, nothing can." Jackie, who had enjoyed an excellent relationship with Mick despite the odd blip was the most fulsome. "I knew it would be a sad day for young and old when Mick got voted off the island but unfortunately that day has come." Rather than anger anyone, or leave a bad taste in someone's mouth, Jackie had told Mick he could vote for her and she would not mind. Jackie liked Mick because of his lack of ego and his easygoing manner. The pair had shared some interesting moments, notably when Mick suffered from termites burrowing into his backside as a result of sitting on tree trunks. To combat the bugs, the only treatment was to pour kerosene on the affected area. One of Jackie's jobs was to smear kerosene on Mick's bum, an experience she will surely never forget.

Austin read out the votes and Mick's time was up. He admits to having a slight lump in the back of his throat as he made a closing speech to the three remaining contestants. "I saw this coming but you've played such a blinding game that there was no way out for me and I congratulate you on that and I wish each and every one of you the best of luck because you all deserve to be winner." He then kissed both Jackie and Charlotte and shook Richard's hand. According to Mick, as he made his speech he thought he heard a male voice on the jury, he does not know whose, say "Cheap".

In his confessional he said that comment disappointed him. "It's sad because it wasn't a cheap act, it was a genuine act from the heart, simple as that." Mick's views of the three left in the game differed hugely from those submitted by Zoe and Eve. "Richard has been quiet, steady and he's been quite honest throughout. I can't say he's been devious, I don't believe he has, he's just been meticulous and clever in the way he's played the game. Jackie was not a threat to me physically but she was probably light years ahead of me mentally and that's proved to be 100 per cent right. She again assessed the situations and played them extremely well. Charlotte I could have cheerfully killed when we first met her because she's so loud. But I've mellowed to her completely. She has played the game very much the same as Jackie, very close but very honest. It would be a hell of a choice to decide between the two of them as to who is going to be the ultimate survivor." Then he went, his epitaph being, 'I blew it'. He can console himself that he was one of the few survivors to leave with their reputations enhanced. Given the personalities involved, that is some achievement. The whereabouts of the fourth sausage still remain a mystery, however.

The smoking gun

The next day, the penultimate one of the whole game, was very tense and subdued. All the main protagonists knew that the upcoming Immunity Challenge was the most important one they had yet faced. The permutations and questions were endless; if Jackie won who would she take through with her? How would Charlotte fare if there was a quiz about their fellow contestants on the island? Had she been quiet enough to take in anything that was said to her? Had Richard spent too much time talking about himself, as some of the others contend, and not found out anything about anyone else? For the most part all three kept their distance from each other, the million pounds playing on their minds.

Richard claimed to camera that it was not his motivation. In fact, he said he would prefer to split it three ways. "I'd rather do that than run the gauntlet and come away with nothing. I think a million pounds is an obscene amount of money – as is a third of a million pounds actually. If you were to ask me now, even if it was a physical challenge, I would still split the money and run. If you were to accuse me of being a liar for not being motivated by a million pounds then I would stand true. I didn't come here to win a million, I came here for the experience and it's the experience that has moved me the most. A million pounds will change my life, it will change my life beyond recognition. But if I walk away without that million pounds and I've spent the full forty days on the beach then I'll be happy. I'll have achieved what I wanted and I think it's more important to achieve your goals than it is to get a million pounds." All he wanted to do he claimed, and still does now, was to see the sunrise on that fortieth day on Pulau Tiga.

A major blow to achieving his goal lay in store for Richard. Ever since Pete's dismissal from the island, Charlotte had been saving the fact she thought could sway Jackie; a "smoking gun" that could secure her a place in the final even if Jackie won immunity. She knew that Richard had told Pete he was leaving. For more than a week she had bitten her tongue. "That penultimate day was a weird one. Everyone was quite melancholy, thinking their own things. No one discussed who was going to vote for who. I knew by then that Rich and Jackie had been in an alliance and I definitely think she would have taken Richard through with her. That afternoon I left it very late to tell Jackie, because I did not want her to tell Richard, in case he won the immunity and there was still a slight chance he might take me. But I didn't want her to tell Richard because he would be really annoyed I told her, and it could affect his vote. I left it to the very, very last moment. I said to Jackie, 'Look, don't tell Rich that you know because it will make him all the more determined in the next challenge.' And I told her. At first she said she would be taking me through but that she would be speaking to Richard after the challenge. Later on, Jackie said she was not sure who she was going to take through, that she couldn't make up her mind because obviously I had two guaranteed votes on the jury. I knew then I really had to win that challenge."

Charlotte told Jackie while the pair were in the sea, only a couple of hours before Tribal Council, which would be the venue for the final challenge. Jackie was shocked. Charlotte revealed how Richard had managed to "kill two birds with one stone". Firstly, by getting rid of Pete, a strong competitor, and secondly, he was able to twist it so he looked like a good guy. It dawned on Jackie that the bible-throwing episode had all been an act and when Richard had been wondering whether Pete had forgiven him, he had been pretending all along. Charlotte told Jackie that she would take her through to the final with her because Richard's popularity with the jury, or at least with certain members of the jury, was high. Jackie then confessed to Charlotte that they had formed an agreement on day one and stuck to it ever since. It was news to Charlotte. Jackie finished by saying, "He has sealed his fate now," and the pair went for a cup of tea made with the tea set won on the second day by Ular, vowing not to tell Richard until after the challenge. At that stage they did not know there would be no "after the challenge".

Knowing that Richard had lied outright to her about Pete still irks Jackie now. "When I found out about it all from Charlotte I was a bit annoyed really. I know you can't trust anyone, but Richard and I had worked quite well together throughout the whole time and he said he wouldn't. I said 'Look, if you're going to tell Pete, fine, do it, but tell me as well because I don't want to look bad.' I am bad, but I don't want to look it. But he went ahead and told him anyway and I think that's a bit of a shame."

Charlotte was happy that she had put doubts in Jackie's mind and let her mull it over. Of all the three, she was the most delighted to be there because little more than a week earlier she had been convinced she was going home. Yet here she was in with a very real chance of reaching the final two and a prize of a million pounds. It was an unusual position to be in, she declared. She had worked out that Richard had influence with a number of the jury. Pete would definitely vote for him, as would Eve, though not with a great deal of enthusiasm. If Jackie was Richard's opposition then Andy and James would vote for him because they felt Jackie was undeserving, so that would be victory. For that reason, she was hoping Jackie would take her through with her if she won the quiz. Then she outlined why she believed she had gone so far in the game.

"Telling Jackie that is the first obviously pro-active thing I've done in this game," she said. "Throughout the whole game I've been dropping subtle little comments. All it needs is one little word and you'd be amazed how people's minds start racing. People don't need to be told a full sentence or given reasons to go on – if you drop in a little word people will start thinking and worrying far more and I know that because I'm exactly the same. That's how I've played the game, just dropping a word here and there; nothing conniving, nothing too sly. I've never caused any trouble … I've tried to keep as many friends as possible and do it that way and also been aware who the people are who are plotting, who the people are that are forming alliances, what alliances those are and which alliances to become part of.

"I've always been more aware of what's going on and I've always been listening and keeping my ears open because that is extremely important. You don't have to be a major player but you do have to know what is going on around you. For example, yesterday Richard was trying to get me to believe that Jackie was very close to Mick and maybe wanted to vote me off. So I made sure that I was around Jackie all the time. Richard, I knew, trusted Jackie and I think his plan was to vote for me himself and get rid of me because he knew what I knew about Pete and he felt that I would be a good jury member and vote for him. By just hanging around and being in the area all the time I made him realise that I knew Jackie would not vote for me." She was proud that she outlasted all the other members of Helang and most of the Ular tribe when she had been written off. Her success was down to her persistence and her ability to get on with the right people, she said.

Fallen comrade

Richard was praying for a physical challenge but his entreaties were to go unanswered. The challenge was to be a quiz on the thirteen other contestants who had been on the island to see how closely the remaining three had paid attention to others and to the events that had taken place. The fact that the challenge was to take place at Tribal Council offered Richard a dilemma; for every Tribal Council he had "muddied up", but had never done so for a challenge. Not wanting to break his routine he decided not to cover himself with mud, and as there was no time for him to rush off to the mud volcano and perform the ritual after the quiz, it meant that for the first time Richard arrived at the Tribal Council without his mask. The production crew had turned out in force for this climactic moment – Richard was the hot favourite to win and had been since merger – but a gasp of amazement spread around those watching as they realised Richard was "mudless". Could it be some kind of omen? Did Richard know something?

The three, looking very nervous and uncertain, made their way to their seats. Mark Austin explained to them about the quiz, devised by Austin himself, Nigel Lythgoe and programme executive Ed Forsdick. "Basically it's what you've learnt over the past thirty-nine days about your fellow survivors, about life on the island and the little things that perhaps passed you by and which may now mean the difference between a million pounds or nothing. I've got ten questions here and you'll get a point for each question that you answer correctly. You'll write the answer on the paper provided and then I'll ask you to show it to me after thirty seconds. Quite simply the person who gets the most points after those ten questions wins the immunity amulet. If there is a tie there will be sudden-death questions. After the quiz we will go directly on to the vote. Is that understood?" The three nodded solemnly and Austin began.

The following is a complete transcript of the quiz:

1 **Who were the two survivors hanging from the tree in the Parachute Rescue Challenge?**
Charlotte, Jayne and Eve is correct – one point. Jackie, Adrian and Eve is incorrect. Richard, Jayne and Eve is correct – one point.

2 **What were the two final words formed on the raft when you dived for the letters in the ABC of survival? You must give me both words.**
Richard, you are halfway there; "jury" was one of them. "Cleans" is the other. No points for anybody.

3 What is Zoe's partner called?

They are all correct. Sindy is the right answer.

4 What does Sekutu mean in English?

Merge, coming together, join/merge are all correct. One point each.

5 How long did James stay underwater to win the Reward Challenge?

Charlotte, 1:49 is wrong. Jackie, 1:56 is wrong. Richard, 1:54 is wrong. It was, in fact, 1:52.

6 What bad news from home did Mick receive on the island?

All various accounts of the same story, the right story. A heron had eaten all his fish. You all get one point.

7 What is the Malay name for the island delicacy you all ate on day five? If you can't spell it properly, I'll forgive you. It's what it sounds like.

Charlotte, *bootam* is wrong. Jackie, *bootak* is wrong. Richard, *bootu* is wrong. It is *bootah. Nil points!*

8 How many members of Sekutu, and I emphasise Sekutu, brought toothbrushes as their luxury item?

Charlotte, four is correct. Jackie, four is correct. Richard, two is incorrect. Two questions to go: Richard you have four points; Charlotte you have five points; Jackie you have four points.

9 In the island quiz, what did Andy think termites were commonly called?

Charlotte, white ants is wrong. Jackie, fire ants is right. Richard, red ants is wrong. One question to go; Richard, you have four points. Charlotte you have five points. Jackie you have five points. The last question:

10 Name the two survivors who cut free the rafts on day one?

Charlotte, Simon is wrong. Jackie, Nick and Andy is wrong. Richard, Nick and Andy is wrong. The answer is Nick and JJ. So, Charlotte you have five points; Jackie you have five points; Richard you have four. So, we move to sudden death. Just the two girls.

11 Which two survivors ran the first stage of the Assault Course?

Simon and Mick is correct.

12 In order, name the first two survivors to come off the log and into the sea?

Zoe and James is correct.

13 Which football team does Pete support?

Manchester City is correct.

14 How many children does James have?

Five is correct. We need to consult …. We're running out of questions.

Charlotte and Jackie had done much better than expected and there was only one question left for Austin to ask. With that in mind, he halted the proceedings and went off to discuss more questions with Forsdick and Lythgoe. As the three huddled together off to the side of the set, Richard looked into space forlornly. His chance seemed to have gone. His last hope lay in Jackie winning the quiz and taking him through with her. Should Charlotte win, then his hopes of seeing that precious last sunrise had disappeared. The next two minutes were crucial. Running out of questions, and the fifteen-minute delay that ensued, only served to add to the drama. Eventually, armed with a fresh set of questions, Austin was ready to resume:

15 Who was the seventh person voted off the island?

Both correct, it was Simon.

16 On the day we last weighed you, how much weight had Richard lost?

Charlotte, twenty-nine pounds is correct. Jackie, twenty-six is wrong. Charlotte, this immunity amulet belongs to you. We should move to the vote.

Richard's face fell as he began to accept that he would not be realising his goal. Charlotte looked across at him and mouthed an apologetic "Sorry". But it was scant consolation. Finishing third was neither here nor there in his opinion. Richard's first thought was that Jackie had thrown the last question because she did not want to have the quandary of whether to take Charlotte or Richard through with her to the final two. Initially, he was convinced that was what she had done. Now, however, he has altered that view. He believes that if she had decided to throw it then she would have done so a lot sooner. Charlotte, however, disagrees.

"I personally think she threw that last question because if anyone knows about weight then Jackie does," she insists. "She did nothing but go on about it the whole time she was on the island. She loved the fact that she had lost weight. She made a bad mistake about blowing it on that question. I suppose it could have been the pressure, but that was something we had talked about so much, because Richard and Mick were really concerned that they had lost twenty-nine pounds and it's an awful lot of weight to lose. It was something we discussed, and only a few of us were weighed, and I just found it strange. I thought she'd thrown it, but I didn't care. After I had voted, I turned to Richard and said 'Sorry'. I wasn't sorry. I was in a way because we had all done so well to get that far. But that's the game, someone's got to go. I don't know whether I would have won it with Richard but I took Jackie because I thought

I had a better chance, having had conversations with Eve, and knowing what Andy and James thought of Jackie."

Jackie is adamant that she genuinely could not remember how much weight either Mick or Richard had lost. "I didn't throw it. I know he thinks that and Charlotte thinks I threw it. If I wanted to throw it I would have done it a lot sooner. Also, when I fell behind and Rich and Charlotte were ahead in the quiz, I was thinking to myself that I had to get them right. I managed to get back in it and it was between Charlotte and me. I definitely, definitely didn't throw it." The other question is: had she won the quiz, would she have taken Richard through to the final two with her, or would it have been Charlotte?

"I did want to win that final immunity. There are two ways of looking at it: all the way through the game I got better and I have also maintained that I was an average sort of person and I came in average. For instance, if there were ten people in a challenge, I might come fifth, then further on in the game I was coming in second and third, though there were less people in the game, but I was maintaining my average position. In the last few challenges I had come in fifth, fourth, third and then second in the orienteering. It would have been fantastic to have won that final challenge. But it meant I would have had to make that final decision between Charlotte and Rich. That decision really was worth a million pounds. If I had been up against Rich then I don't think I would have had a chance, but with Charlotte I had a chance – maybe not a great one but it was still a chance. To this day I don't know how I would have voted."

The voting went according to expectations. Richard went up first and voted for Jackie, simply because there was no one else left to vote for. He wished Jackie luck. The person he forged an alliance with in order to see him through the game had pipped him at the final challenge. He could see the irony. Jackie voted for Richard, again because there was no alternative. Charlotte, unsurprisingly, voted for Richard as a "stronger competitor". That was it; Richard's time on the island was up and his fire was extinguished. He is still bitter that he lost out on the chance to reach the final two on a quiz. He feels it is not a worthy way to decide a winner. "Quizzes are girls' things. They know stuff about each other. Men know nothing. I was tempted to write on a pad, 'Is this the true test of the ultimate survivor.' So yes, they were a threat but as soon as I realised it was going to be a 'girly' quiz then they became an even bigger threat. I knew I was going to lose, call it intuition." Richard protests too much, however. As a *Survivor* expert who had researched other countries' productions he knew this challenge might lie ahead and he should have listened accordingly. Charlotte won by keeping her ears open, even when people believed she was too busy talking to listen. She thanks her police training for the skills to win that challenge.

"As a police officer you have to pick up things all the time and look at what is going on. Even in my own time when I'm driving my car I'm looking at what is going on, what people are doing, are they acting suspiciously, weighing up the whole situation. Certainly, I'd picked up on different things on the island and they stay in my mind, because I'm trained to remember things, like number plates, people's faces, what's happened. We're all into intelligence-led policing and that's all about knowing and learning everything about a person that you possibly can. So when things have gone on, that helped, particularly with that final challenge. With some of the answers, I couldn't believe that I couldn't remember them.

But that was because of the nerves, and the pressure of the situation. I mean, when they said the answers, I was like, 'Of course.' " Being a police officer also means having to stand up in court and answer questions under intense pressure, another experience that stood her in good stead for the quiz.

Richard left, not saying a word or even looking at the two that he left behind. So, what was Jackie's view when she saw her main ally leave the game he had tried so hard to win. Was she sorry to see him go? "No, I didn't like him. I couldn't stand the guy. I always knew there was an element about him that I just couldn't quite bond with. I can remember saying early on in the game that I wasn't sure about Richard, that I thought he might be a bit of a dodgy boiler. When Nick was saying I don't think he was a doctor, I knew there was something there but I couldn't quite put my finger on it. And I think he was really odd at council as well – he just looked like a nutter. When he muddied up for Council he went really quiet and never spoke to anyone for a whole day preceding Council. He's a bit moody and I don't feel comfortable around moody people. I don't think I felt guilty at the time, I certainly don't now. Guilt for what? Guilt for not winning the quiz? I doubt it. I would have to have been guilty for the whole time I was on the island because I didn't win anything."

As Richard made his way to the confessional, members of the production crew gathered around a walkie-talkie in the compound to hear his final words. His ejection had come as a tremendous shock to many who were convinced he would win and felt his effort, particularly in the challenges, meant he deserved to. The group sat in silence as his disembodied voice crackled down the line, as candles guttered in the darkness. It was like a wartime scene, people gathering around the wireless to hear the latest news from the front. Despite his bitter disappointment, Richard approached the situation with dignity. His full confessional is reprinted here:

"I'm disappointed, but at the end of the day I played a good hard game and lost at the last hurdle so I guess I should be pleased with that. I think Charlotte voted against me because we've had conversations where she said that she's sort of jealous of the immunities that I won and the performance that I've put in. She feels that I'd be very popular with the jury so I guess that she's watching her own back really and voting for me. I don't blame her for that one bit.

"Yeah, I think it's quite ironic that Jackie and I have been in cahoots for all this time right from the start and she gets a question wrong about me, but there you go. I have had a bad feeling about today since I woke up this morning. I'll never know if Jackie spoiled her answer on purpose. If she did, good luck to her, she beat me at the game. I guess Jackie wanted a fighting chance against the jury so now she's got that. It's very difficult to say who's going to win at the moment. I think Jackie would want me to try and sway the jury in her direction. I've really enjoyed the company of Charlotte so I guess I'll just get a feel for how the jury are thinking and then make a decision from there really. No, I'm not looking forward to being on the jury. I never wanted to be there.

"I have no regrets about not voting Charlotte off at an earlier time. At the end of the day, there would always have been three of us in that quiz and I'm not a quiz person. It wasn't for me you know – I would have liked a chance to go down kicking and screaming and fighting. So, whoever the third person had been, I think the same outcome would have happened. I don't think I'm a more deserving winner than either Jackie or Charlotte. I came third. I didn't win, so they are more deserving than I am.

"The feeling I have in my stomach is that I still yearn for that last sunrise but I'm not going to see it so I guess there is just a little loss there, but I had a great time. In my heart I believed Jackie would have picked me if she had won the quiz. My epitaph for the island would be, 'I missed my last sunrise'.

"I had a bad feeling about today. When we were leaving camp I looked back for what I believed was going to be the last time and then when I realised the challenge was going to be at Tribal Council there was no way I was going to break the cycle that I've got myself into, which is really following what I believe; spirit, gut instinct, whatever you want to call it. I don't put mud on my face for challenges and I do put mud on my face for Council. I suppose whichever way you look at it I was either going to be muddied up for a challenge or have no mud for a Tribal Council. I went with my gut instinct and now I can hopefully enjoy a nice cold lager and not have mud in my head.

"Jackie is ... she's a good laugh. She enjoys fun and she enjoys banter. She's quite sharp-witted. I think she is one of life's genuine people. Charlotte is loud and out there but has a great time and makes no apologies for who she is and ... I don't ever think she should do. She's a really nice person and I wish the best of luck to both of them."

Richard feels his strategy was the correct one and what scuppered his chances was the quiz, which he was never going to win. Others, like Zoe and Mick, feel his strategy left something to be desired because it meant him having to win all the challenges. Whatever, he left on a boat for the mainland that evening, drained physically and mentally, having given the game his absolute all. That night was long and liquid and he had little time to recover from what was an incredibly intense experience for him before he had to return to the island the next day to join the jury. As the boat bringing him to the shore neared, the six jury members all ran into the sea and stood on a log, a gesture to welcome him back to the island. Andy explains: "We knew that of all the jury members, Richard would have the toughest time. He seemed to be utterly focused on winning in a way that other people did not seem to be. We knew that it must have been a huge shock to him to have not made the final. Also, to have the dislocation of leaving the island and coming straight back would be very difficult. It was less than twenty-four hours since he had been in the game. Because of his intense nature we just knew he would be suffering. We wanted him to have a visual idea that we were welcoming him into our group. When everyone came off we gave them a big hug because it was a kind of way of saying that all the voting, and everything else that happened on the island, was forgiven. We wanted to make an impact on him because we thought he might be worried, because he had voted us all off. When he arrived, he saw us and just burst into tears."

Richard now sees it as a consolation that he had a chance to meet the jury and clear the slate. "I got to join the jury on the final day and make peace with people who I had just systematically voted off. Without exception, there wasn't a single person on that jury that I did not want to vote off. They had to go if they stood in my way, and unfortunately for them most of them did."

Richard, out of everyone, played the game to its fullest, being as effective in the challenges as he was in forging and breaking alliances. Whether the character he played on the island was his true self is another matter. He admits he immersed himself in the experience but doubts whether anyone could be their true self given the unique conditions. On his application form when asked what sort of person would win the game, he wrote "pragmatic sociopath". When asked to describe himself, he said "sociopathic". His strategy, if that is what it was, got him very far and while losing was a bitter experience, it did not take him long to recover from the disappointment. Despite losing twenty-nine pounds in weight, a week after the game finished he ran a marathon in Rotterdam – and completed it, a testament to his strength and resolve.

The last day

As Richard was being taken over to Kota Kinabalu, Jackie and Charlotte were making their way back to the beach in a state of shock, trying to comprehend their achievement. It was too much for Charlotte and she burst into tears. "As we walked back, we said nothing on the way back to the beach," she says. "It was really strange. As we came out of the Tribal Council, I was overwhelmed. I was in tears. I thought it was brilliant, because I was down to the final two. A minute ago I had been ready to be kicked off. It was incomprehensible. Two weeks before I was thinking, 'How long left' and scratching out the number of days remaining on a pack of malaria tablets. I walked back ahead of Jackie and you could tell there were so many thoughts going through each of our heads. We were just silent."

The silence did not last for very long. As they neared the opening just before the beach, it dawned on the two of them that it was just them, no one else. They had survived. "When we got to the final part of the jungle just before the beach we just looked at each other and started jumping around and screaming," Charlotte recollects. "We ran to the beach like a couple of kids. It was like a party night for the girls. We were running on pure adrenaline. We burnt everything. We created this humongous bonfire and burnt all the bamboo.

We were singing, lightning was flashing in the sky. We went to bed and just told each other the stories of our families, and got on very well. I just kept thinking, 'I'm so glad I'm here with Jackie and not with Richard. That would just have been a nightmare.' Instead, it was a really good girly night out on Pulau Tiga." Charlotte said she was worried about having to perform speeches to the jury next day but Jackie reassured her, telling her she would help her with it, an astonishing gesture considering that there was a million pounds at stake.

As it was, they did not have chance to help each other with their speeches the next day. In the morning, after getting up to see the last sunrise as Richard had instructed them to do, they went out to catch stingrays and then they were interviewed all afternoon about the previous forty days, their thoughts and feelings on all that had gone on and their opinions of the other survivors. As they admitted, it all seemed so long ago when they had arrived on the island – Jackie struggling to stop herself being sick, Charlotte fuming after being handed a dressing down by Jayne. Since that time, both had seen times when they thought they were going home – times when they *wanted* to go home, desperately so in Charlotte's case. They had weathered storms, literal and metaphorical. They had seen off people who hated them, people who looked down upon them. They had survived rats, snakes and insects galore. Not to mention the endless hunger, alleviated only by the occasional treat. It had been a bewildering but wonderful experience.

About forty minutes or so before they were to leave for the final Tribal Council, they started to write their speeches for the evening. Jackie said she did not even consider including anything that would put Charlotte down; she wanted to be positive not negative. The two had not consulted but Charlotte had the same idea. She wanted to say something that would sway the jury towards her without "slagging" Jackie off. The pair of them had become good friends, something they hoped would be the same when Tribal Council that evening had finished. That night was the only time that Jackie ever left for Tribal Council with all her belongings on her. She had always known exactly how the vote was going and been confident she would be staying. It still amazes Charlotte how blasé Jackie could be about Tribal Council. As they departed the beach for that final time, they had one last look back at the shelter "Goodbye hut," said Charlotte. Then they disappeared into the dark, looming jungle for the final time.

Seven angry men (and women)

Charlotte and Jackie were not the only two with butterflies in their stomachs; the jury members who would have to quiz them on their conduct on the island and how they would spend the prize money should they be fortunate enough to win had a few fluttering around inside them too. Mark Austin greeted the finalists and the jurors as they filed in to the Tribal Council building for the final time. Then it was time for the opening speeches to be made, which would be followed by questions from each jury member and then finally the two women could offer a closing summary in which they had the chance to assuage any doubts lingering in the juror's minds. Jackie went first. Public speaking is not something she has great experience of, she admits, but she overcame her early nerves. Her aim was to dispel the view that because she had not stood out in the physical side of the game, though she had improved her efforts in that respect, she should be overlooked for the top prize. Instead, her claim was that by playing the political side extremely well, and tenaciously fighting for her survival, she was a deserving winner. Here is her speech in full, though edited for readability:

"When I got up this morning to watch the final sunrise, I started to think about the words I could use to try and convince you to award me the worthy winner of one million pounds. It is an impossible task. What will I try to do for those of you who don't know me as well as the others? I will try to let you in on the strategy I have used, both in playing the game and voting. It may help you understand my actions on the island a little better. First of all my strategy when I landed on the island was to fly under the radar, to make a strong alliance that I could stick to until the end and to make it to the merger. Now all of those things I have managed to do to a certain extent, but it wasn't quite as simple as that. My alliance strategy had to change as the game changed and the situations changed. There were two types of alliance that I made; there were ones, such as the ones when I voted off the former Helang members, where I went along with the group and a majority, as I also did, unfortunately, in Pete's case. The second type were alliances of self-preservation. It was about staying one step ahead of the game. Perhaps I made an alliance after I heard it through the grapevine that people had changed their opinion of me; they wanted me off the island and I had to do something to rectify that situation, regardless of any alliance I had made and that is when the plotting really started. I had to save my own skin and I had to work on other people and other friends that I had made to try and turn that situation around.

"That is an example of where I have got today and how I have got here today," she continued. "It is a case of staying one step ahead of the game and saving my own skin. Now, I have saved myself more times than I could probably count. From the day I landed on the island, I have been under attack. I was due to be the first person to leave and managed to swing that around with the help of other people with whom I made an alliance. I was living on borrowed time from there on in. I am glad to say that I did make a strong alliance, which stood me in good stead to get me into the final three.

"That has briefly touched upon my strategy for the game and my voting strategy. I also wanted to touch on the point that I think a lot of you have already made the decision on who actually deserves to win. There are so many criteria and I hope you are not just basing your decision on who has the most strength. I am not the best person to be blowing my own trumpet. I have a self-deprecating manner, and a lot of people tend to believe what I am putting out rather than what I actually achieve. The fact of the matter is that I know I can achieve a lot and when I was on the island it wasn't a case of maintaining my fitness so I could do these challenges, it was a case of improving my fitness so that I continually got better and better. Not only at the challenges, but at staying one step ahead and securing my position on the island. And for those of you who were around at the later stages of the game you will see that I did improve my performance in those challenges, and there are some performances that I am completely proud of. Although I didn't win, I have far exceeded my own personal targets. Some people find it easy to do strength things, others don't. I don't. I gave it 100 per cent. The only thing is how do you decide who wins it? Is it a case of strength, or is it a case of the person who plays the game well, and secures their position many times over to get into the final two. Those were the words I chose."

With that she sat down and Charlotte approached the ladies and gentlemen of the jury. In contrast to Jackie, Charlotte wanted to emphasise her all-round attributes, that she was able to play the game and contribute and compete in the physical challenges, as opposed to Jackie whose main successes came in the political sphere only. She also wanted to outline how much she had learned on the island.

"When I first came to this island," she began, "I wanted to have a life-changing experience and everything I have gained from the minute that I got here has far exceeded that. All the time I have learnt how to live on this island, learning how to get on with different individuals and learning to survive, which is what this show is all about. I never expected to be in this position. I just find it incredible. I have always wanted to work hard ever since I got here, because I feel that no one deserves to get somewhere for no reason and you never get anything from life unless you put in 100 per cent all the time. No matter when I was feeling down or when I was feeling happy, I always put in 100 per cent because I knew I would never forgive myself unless I had done that.

"I did that when I was with the Helang tribe. I always went for every single challenge to help them. I always tried my best, even when I was worried about going into the swimming challenges and having to dive. I thought, well, I am going to do it anyway. There was no way I wanted to be carried into the merger. I wanted to be part of the people who got us through to the merger. As you could see, we had to vote off four of our members and as you can see I made the final four and there must have been reasons for that. It must have been all the hard work and everything that I achieved in helping my tribe.

"I have tried to use my personality a lot since coming to the island. I feel that I have got quite a bubbly personality, although it probably annoys people at times. But I have always felt that I want to try and make as many friends as possible and make people's lives happy, because the whole island experience is something fantastic in itself and is something that we have all won while being here, no matter what happens today. There have been many, many personal goals that I wanted to reach and often team challenges were so frightening. I know Zoe and myself were worried about the assault course because it is not just yourself that you are looking out for at that time, it is the whole team. There is so much pressure but it was in those that I put in the maximum effort, which I did all throughout the individual challenges as well.

"The strategy I used was to just try and be myself and take it as well as it comes. I have tried to get on with as many people as possible, be happy and keep spirits high so that people want me around the camp. I wanted just to try and get as many people from my tribe to merger as possible. That leads me to the merger; I mean, we arrived there and we were sitting ducks waiting to be shot. For that reason, I feel that my most incredible achievement is that nobody shot me. Was I forgotten about? I doubt it. I'm a bit loud. It is incredible that I managed to come from nothing and get to the final two when there was a time two weeks ago when I was just waiting to leave the island. But even when I was waiting to be voted off, because I thought that was the strategy that was going on at the time, I still put everything I had into getting on with everybody from the different tribes. I still carried on going out to fish. I was always going to try my hardest and I've always put in maximum effort, no matter what I have done. I want you to look at us individually today. Obviously there are more members of the previous tribe [Ular], but I want you to look at which individual members helped my tribe get through. I feel that I have helped 100 per cent and have always given every single last bit of energy in every single challenge. Even when I haven't won them, I've been thrilled that I gave the maximum effort possible.

"I just wanted to mention one thing to Richard and that is, I felt terrible about what I had to do yesterday. You were so nice to me, you gave me that reward and if I had chosen you to come through with me you would have probably committed me to the mental home because I know you probably deserve to win this more than I do. If I had chosen you I would have played the game extremely badly and I am sure you wouldn't have chosen me either. I just let you know that that's the reason I picked Jackie." Richard thanked her. "I just want you to look at me and try and remember as many things as you can. Not just incidents, but loads of different qualities in yourself that I have got in myself and that would make you deserve to win then. I hope you can look at me and see the qualities that I have brought to this show, brought to the island and see how hard I have worked every single step of the way."

Then it was the time for the jury to question the two, in the order members had been voted from the island. Andy rose first, and told them it was a pleasure to speak to them rather than being forced to communicate via T-shirts and covert nods and winks. His first question was how would they cope with winning a million. Jackie's answer was that she knew from personal experience that money did not bring happiness. As someone brought up to respect her family, and money, and wedded to hard work, the money would not change her, she claimed. She would spend it wisely. Unsurprisingly, it was a view shared by Charlotte. "Quality of life is what you achieve yourself and if the money can help you do that, and help make your family happier and more comfortable, then that is where the money becomes an issue."

Andy's second question was again about the effects of the money. His concern was that the person winning the money would squander it and not use it in a beneficial way. So he asked how the money would change the course of their lives over the next twelve months. Charlotte acknowledged that her life would be changed. She would use it to pay off her mortgage, set up her own business and give some to her family, she said. As a result, she would change for the better. If she did not win it then the whole experience would change her life because she had changed as a person and gained new insights. In her response, Jackie mentioned that she was due to begin a new job the following month as an airline purchaser and whatever the outcome of the vote it was her intention to keep that job. One thing she might lavish the money on, though her boyfriend Martin might be alarmed, was a big wedding. "It would make things a bit easier for me to go ahead and make a family," she said.

James was the next juror to the stand and he was focused on finding out what the contestants had learned about themselves over the course of forty days. Charlotte answered that she had always feared spending time on her own but she was far now more comfortable with her own company. She had discovered her independence. James tweaked the question slightly for Jackie, asking what she had learned from aspects of other people's personalities. "I am not sure I have seen real personalities," she pointed out presciently. "I may have seen shadowed personalities ... I have certainly learned that there people who are going to wind you up no matter how pleasant you think you are being." James was more pointed in his response, accusing Jackie of not learning anything positive from the fifteen people she had been marooned with. Jackie dealt with it admirably, however. "I have learnt that people from all different walks of life can get on together and survive in that sort of environment and under extreme hardships, and I have experienced great encouragement from people and acts of kindness and strength." In among all the bitterness, bitchiness and backbiting that characterised island life it was rare to hear positive sentiments like that comment of Jackie's. Asked what aspect of her personality had helped her most, she singled out her determination in the face of adversity.

James thanked them both before giving way to Pete, who congratulated the finalists on "playing a blinder". Thinking of his own refusal to compromise his principles for the game, Pete asked what compromises the two women had made and whether they were worth a million pounds. For Charlotte it was voting for James in the final Helang Tribal Council when Adrian was eventually chosen. "I can see that Adrian was the person who should have gone because he had not been working hard. He had been staying out of challenges when really he could have been assisting with them and James gave 100 per cent all the time. He might not have succeeded in one certain challenge but he was always there and willing to put himself forward and voting for him was something that I certainly regret. In hindsight, I would certainly now look beyond people's personalities, what you initially see, and look deeper into the whole picture that counts." James cites this as evidence of Charlotte's growing maturity on the island and how her shallow outlook altered as time passed. She recognised her loyalty to "Lazy Ade" was ill-advised.

Ironically, when her turn to answer arrived Jackie said her biggest compromise involved getting rid of Pete himself. Both Charlotte, in the replies like the one she gave above, and Jackie refute claims they were shamelessly trying to shore up their vote (though that must have played some part) in their answers. Jackie told Pete that she regretted that she did not keep her word to him but added, "it is worth a million pounds". "I knew I would have to stitch up a mate once here, and you were the mate that was stitched up I'm afraid," she said. Pete's follow-up question was in a similar vein, asking which person each woman felt she had stepped on the most and, therefore, dreaded the most.

"I felt that I stood on Richard's toes the most," replied Charlotte. Again, this could have been a ploy to turn Richard away from Jackie, whom many would expect him to vote for, given their past. Jackie claimed there were two ways of stamping on people's toes; jumping up and down with both feet, and giving them a little tap. "I guess with you Pete, I jumped up and down with both feet, while with Zoe and Eve I could say I gave them a bit of a tap, but, in my defence, it was solely to save my own skin."

Zoe was up next and made an interesting point. "I felt that perhaps us girlies were quite good at the old lying and manipulating side of the game and, well, you don't get what you want for Christmas without a manipulation," she said. It seems that most of the intrigue came from the females, Richard excepted, and with it most of the bitterness. Earlier in the game, Jackie had made the same point to camera. She suggested women were more cunning than men and possessed a far superior talent for deviousness. "Many of the boys see this as a 'strong man' competition, and maybe we all did in our hearts, because we have been voting off strong males. But they don't understand, some of them at least, that there is far more to this game than being a beefcake."

Zoe then launched into a spirited defence of herself following the allegations put to camera by Charlotte and Jackie – and Richard – that she was involved in stealing rice. Either Eve or Mick must have told her of the accusations. "Myself and halitosis have been very close friends over the past few months, but to be branded a liar and a thief after my departure has left a nasty taste in my mouth." She asked how the story had arisen.

"It was the following day [after Zoe's departure] and Richard said to me that the rice had gone down drastically and when we checked the bag it had about six to eight bowls in it. I was told six to eight bowls were missing and gossip started from there," said Charlotte. Jackie backed her up and said Zoe had not been branded a liar or a thief, it was just their impression it had gone down and the rumours started from there. Satisfied, Zoe then asked her next question, about whether, given their separate admissions at one time that they wanted to go home, either of them deserved the accolade 'Ultimate Survivor'. Jackie said she did because, she claimed, wanting to go home never meant she stopped trying, she was just being honest about how tough it was. " I could have held my hands up and said OK, people are going to vote against me so I'll go gracefully. But I didn't. I had that fighting spirit …. If you could tell me that all of the jury members didn't want to go home at one point then I would be very surprised by that." In her reply, Charlotte was equally spirited. "I don't feel ashamed that I showed my feelings … but the sheer fact that I pulled myself out of it encourages me and gives me strength."

As Zoe sat down Eve took the floor for what promised to be an interesting exchange. The gallery – the watching crew – edged forward: they wanted a ringside seat for this one. Through gritted teeth, Eve congratulated the pair of them and admitted they had played a better game than hers. "But," she added, looking at Jackie, "I would be very interested to know why you think I hate you so much." When Jackie replied that it was down to the way Eve spoke to her, her response was: "Do you think that is in fact my personality, or do you perhaps think that is a role I was playing for the game?" Jackie did not think much of that, however. "I think that was you," she said, before adding, perhaps to mollify Eve, that "I never behaved great around you. Maybe that is something we can discuss off this island." Eve asked Charlotte if there was anything she had done that deserved her vote in particular. Charlotte could not dredge up a specific incident as Eve required, but pointed to her industry in Sekutu to appeal to Eve's hard-working nature. This was one vote whose destination neither Jackie nor Charlotte could predict.

Fifty minutes of questioning had passed when Mick took his turn at the lectern. He apologised in advance for his "probing questions," before asking Jackie what qualities she possessed that would persuade him to vote for her, considering the fact she had not been successful in the challenges. Knowing that if Mick did not vote for her then no one would, she felt confident enough to contradict him. She felt she had done well in the challenges, improving all the while, and had always tried her best. Mick's next question was, "Throughout the contest I have heard you variously described as a cross between a leech and a limpet. Is that your perception of yourself? And if it isn't, what is your concept of yourself for the contest." It was as if Mick, as Jackie's friend, was giving her a chance to hit back at what her detractors had been saying. Denying being a leech or a limpet, she said she was someone who persevered and as a result had far exceeded her personal goals.

Mick then turned his attentions to Charlotte, asking if, at twenty-five, she was too young to handle the pressure of £1 million, considering he felt she was "less mature" than her years. Charlotte disagreed strongly but accepted that other people as a result of her "bubbly" personality sometimes took this view. "In the police force, however, you have to deal with many, many different situations and scenarios and these can be extremely serious. I have seen many sights, " she added, "that would shock people who have stood here today. But I have had to cope with those situations and have had to deal with them …. For that reason I feel that I am definitely mature enough to experience winning a million pounds and learn how to cope with it …. And because I seem always to have a good time and enjoy fun does not mean there isn't a sensible side to me." Mick hit back by saying that he had heard her described on the island as alternately greedy, underhand

and deceitful. Charlotte once again defended herself.

"That is certainly not my perception of myself, although I can see where each of those terms have come from and it might be a single incident and it might be a series of incidents. There have been things which have happened on the island that I have been proud of, and there have also been situations where I have acted and not been proud of myself, and I can only apologise for the times when I have behaved like that, and it is only myself that I have upset and offended .... I can understand where each one of the words which you just said have come from and I can probably remember the situations, but those were in extreme circumstances and certainly not my personality." After hearing that answer, Mick resumed his seat.

"Congratulations ladies of Sekutu – have you heard the story of the sparrow and the eagle. Wrong answer. I have a million questions running around my mind. Did you get up and watch the sunrise this morning?" Richard was asking the questions and his behaviour was enigmatic. The pair said they had watched it and Richard asked Charlotte why. "It was the last words you said on the island and I thought it was the least I could do," she replied. He asked what she saw above it and, puzzled, she said orange and yellow lights. "There is a bright white light above the sunrise, did you spot that?" Neither of them had

He then confessed to being a psychiatrist and accused both of them of stigmatising people with mental illness on the island and asked, having done that, how could they win his vote. Baffled, they denied saying anything but apologised if they had. Charlotte says that Richard scared her that evening with his questioning. "He was very frightening," she says, "especially when he said he was a psychiatrist. He turned around, and he looked like he should have had a cloak, like Count Dracula or something."

Richard then turned tack, asking Jackie how much weight he had lost, indicating that he believed her wrong answer of the previous night was not an error. She said she now knew, as a result of the previous night, that it was 29 pounds. If he had been enigmatic before, he became positively obscure in what he said next. "The eagle said he could fly higher than the sparrow and the sparrow tucked underneath the eagle's wing, and when the eagle had almost reached the sun and was exhausted, the eagle had to stop and the sparrow flew that little bit higher." He then murmured something about blackmail, before thanking Charlotte for her thanks. Then he ended with a flourish. "I covet your position, I covet the sunrise that you saw. I have spoken with the jury. You are both very, very scared of the jury. You should be," he said before thanking them once more. The short time since he had left the island had obviously been difficult for Richard and he was tired and emotional as a result. It certainly made for interesting theatre.

His interesting parable about the sparrow and the eagle was obviously a coded reference to the relationship he and Jackie had on the island. He now claims all he was doing was trying to wind things up, make Jackie feel she could not take his vote for granted. "That last Tribal Council," he says, "it was never about the questions we were asking, they weren't going to change anything. I thought, 'Sod it, I'm going to have a laugh.' " His approach upset Jackie, however. "I was really angry about that eagle and sparrow thing. I struggled the whole time I was on the island and, yes, maybe I did have an alliance with him but there was nothing to suggest why I should trust him more than I trusted Nick or anybody else. It was a case of putting my eggs in one basket. I thought it was really out of order. It was almost like he's done all the hard work and at the end he's lost and I've sneaked through to the final. I disagreed with that at the time and I disagree with it now."

After Richard sat down, it was time for the pair to make their closing speeches, addressing the doubts and questions raised by the jury. "After listening to your questions tonight," Jackie told the jury, "I realise that the answers we give tonight will go a very long way towards helping you make the decision you will make tonight." She went on to pay tribute to Charlotte, from whom she said she had learned a great deal. "In the face of adversity, and the constant nagging, criticism and badgering, the way she handles it is superb. I would like to think that in the face of that sort of adversity in the future I could just turn the other cheek and roll away from it without snapping back."

In her closing speech, Charlotte urged the jury to step away from their tribal perspectives and think individually. She repeated her mantra about being hard-working and giving her all in every challenge. "Look at qualities," she urged, "which you feel would cause you to win £1 million pounds and make a decision that you can be proud of in many years to come and not based on just a whim, but based on the whole picture. It is every day spent on this island that counts as to who should be the one and only survivor." The speeches then ended. Churchill might not have to worry about his place in history as a leading orator being usurped by either Jackie or Charlotte, but both had managed to put across their argument eloquently enough. Whether it made much difference, only time would tell. Just prior to the votes being cast, the set was cleared so that the only people that remained were the contestants, jurors, and three senior members of staff: Peter

Johnston, the Technical Director, who filmed the votes being placed, series producer and director Nigel Lythgoe and Planet 24 Managing Director Mary Durkan. They were the only three who knew the outcome of the vote until its announcement in late July.

Once the voting had finished the jury departed and Jackie and Charlotte were led to a waiting boat. Finally, after forty days, they were leaving the island. In the boat, together with psychologist Stephen Flett, but slightly more appetising, was some food and beer. Quickly, they cracked open the beer and toasted each other, still amazed by what was happening. After a hearty swig, they turned their attention to the box of food. What could it be, they wondered? Chips, pizza, curry? Charlotte opened it and immediately groaned. It was rice, albeit with chicken. They poured the rice overboard – they had after all been eating little else for the past six weeks – as the boat headed for the mainland. As soon as she arrived at the hotel Charlotte strode up to the bar and ordered a double Bailey's and five packs of cigarettes. They made her feel sick.

They spent a week in Kota Kinabalu, enjoying each other's company in rather more salubrious surroundings. They never talked about the money even though it was never far from their minds. As both say, talking about it and who won could drive you mad, so they determined just to enjoy themselves as much as they could. Anyway, they were more interested in having their legs waxed, having a facial, going to the bar. To any other holidaymaker seeing them lounging and laughing around the pool, they would have seemed just like two young women enjoying a winter break together. There were no outward signs that within three months one of them would be a millionaire, while the other would get nothing.

The Ultimate Survivor

O N WEDNESDAY 25 July at Pinewood Studios all was finally revealed. Mick, it emerged, stole the rice, hiding it in his pockets for much of the time, his reasoning being that he hoped to spread suspicion and division among his fellow competitors. The ploy worked, albeit to little eventual advantage for Mick, with Eve in particular bearing the brunt of much of the resulting backlash. The retired policeman also admitted, unprompted, to tampering with the fishing lines for a similar reason. But the real issue – who won the million pounds – was also settled and in that respect Charlotte came out a crushing, unanimous winner, to the surprise of many. Her stance at the final Tribal Council had been much less confrontational than the one chosen by Jackie, whose honesty emerged in several feisty responses to the juror's questions. However, it seems unlikely that what took place there changed many minds. All had decided – and they insist it was not a collective decision – that Charlotte was the more deserving winner.

Prior to the vote being revealed discussions centred around

the "floating voters", identified as Pete, Zoe and Eve. Andy and James were Charlotte certainties, Richard and Mick a sure vote for Jackie, the consensus said. As it turned out, Pete voted for Charlotte, as did Zoe, and Charlotte had gained the four votes required for victory. As she celebrated, the remaining votes all went her way, offering Jackie little consolation. Eve's dislike of Jackie prevented her voting for her, while Mick and Richard decided Charlotte's efforts were more decisive than their friendship with Jackie. The Welsh policewoman had earned the respect, if not the affection, of many jury members by surviving when all seemed lost. As Pete put it, when the ex-Helang members were being purged from Sekutu, "the fat lady was clearing her throat, but she never got to sing." Charlotte hung in there, displaying guts, determination and an instinct for survival when many would have given up. For that, and her athletic ability in the challenges, all seven jury members decided she deserved the accolade, "Ultimate Survivor".

After the show, Charlotte was whisked off to meet the world's press, while Jackie and the other fourteen survivors went to a party to celebrate the end of the series. Though many personal rivalries were still extant, the evening was an harmonious one, with all differences set aside. Despite the shock of the result, Jackie bore up remarkably well under the disappointment. Her dignity and graciousness in defeat won her the respect and affection of many present. Asked to contribute a small speech to the party, she said only four words, "Thank you and goodnight." Her humour was still intact at least. That said, she did not try to hide her disappointment at the vote, which she described as the "worst-case scenario". She also felt let down by James's ill-considered comment that she was a "leech who grew fat on the misfortune of others". James holds his hands up now and says perhaps he went too far, but the pressure of the game and its unique atmosphere did occasionally cause people to lose perspective.

For Charlotte, it was, as she kept repeating during a high-octane round of interviews, "like a dream". She was genuinely surprised to win the money and to win so convincingly made the victory seem even more surreal. In her dressing room afterwards, sucking deeply on a string of cigarettes to calm her frayed nerves, she talked exclusively for this book about the whole experience.

When we spoke last it was before the programme aired. What has it been like over the past couple of months, not only waiting to see if you won the million, but also to watch yourself on TV and all the tabloid press that went with it?

At first I thought surviving after *Survivor* was going to be harder than surviving on the island. But things have got a lot better. At the start there were some horrendous reports stemming from people like JJ and they were so nasty. I find that quite incredible because on the island JJ and I got on quite well, I think. She just showed extreme bitterness which let herself down a bit. Even though Eve, Zoe and myself all had our moments of screaming and arguing with each other, when they got back home with the people they love, they came on the *Survivor Unseen* show and showed their true personalities, which were not like some of the nasty things they said on the island. Hopefully, I have done the same. I haven't been all roses while on the island but I have come back and people have, hopefully, seen the real me.

What do you say now to those people who were quick to pass judgement on you?

I would say, "It's amazing how far you get being fluffy and useless."

Who was the person that you were least looking forward to being reunited with this evening?

JJ definitely. It has to be. I thought she was particularly nasty and vindictive. She has shown aggressive verbal behaviour towards me and some of the things she has been saying are beyond belief. She lives near me and she has been saying some awful things. I kept thinking, "It's only a game." If I had not won tonight I would still have seen it as a game. Mark, my husband, and I had decided it was up to fate. JJ got voted out and she has no one to blame but herself. She didn't have a clue that was coming and she was so intent on her own opinions that she had no idea what anyone else was thinking. Her listening skills were terrible and certainly need to improve if she ever wants to go in for a show like this again.

Were you surprised by the 7-0 vote in your favour?

Yes. Mark had to tell me because by the fourth vote I had won and I did not realise what was going on from then on, because I was so shocked. Mick's vote was the biggest surprise. He and Jackie really, really got on well but what it showed me was that people did look at the decision objectively. It was not about whom you really liked and whom you got on with the best, or about tribal loyalties. They looked at us as individuals and I am really pleased they did that.

What do you think was the secret of your success?

Determination, I would say. I was always determined to get to the end and win. I had some bad days, as everyone saw. But I pulled myself out of that and showed determination. The turning point was seeing that video from home, which gave me a hell of a lot of strength. On that island, you did not have anyone else. Seeing Mark and my Mum pitched me straight back into reality and I was able to snap myself out of that depression. I was back in the game then, I was chatting to Jackie and to Richard. It wasn't just surface chat, we really got on well and I realised I was there for a purpose, they didn't just feel sorry for me.

Is there anything you would like to say to Jackie?
Jackie, I think you are fantastic. You deserve it just as much as me. We are both winners because we both made the final. You are a truly great person and I really, really hope that we will be friends for a very long time.

On the show that was filmed before you went on the island, Meet the Survivors, *you said that if you won then you would spend the money on flash cars and diamonds. At the last Tribal Council, however, you mentioned that you would pay off your mortgage and help your family out. Was it the case that you played down your true intentions with the money so as not to damage your chances with the jury?*
No, not really. That's how I intend to spend the money and if there's enough left to pay for cars and diamonds then we will see. I told Mark when I got back that I got through to the final two. We started talking about sensible things and how great it would be not to have these massive lumps of money coming out of your wages every month to go on the house. If we pay off the mortgage that will give us more money in the long run. I do think sensibly about it. A million pounds is an awful lot of money. It's a fantastic amount of money and just enough to ensure Mark and I have a fantastic life and make my family as happy as I possibly can.

How has the experience on the island changed you?
I feel I have definitely become a stronger person, stronger being

on my own and more confident and more adaptable. I feel I am able to appreciate things more. It is amazing how lovely it is to clean your teeth every morning. Just the smallest little things like that I really missed. The main thing is being able to be on my own. That is something I have never been good at in my life. I have three sisters and one brother and we have always been a bit of a tribe. I'm married now as well so I am always with people and I found being on my own very difficult. At the merger, I was very isolated and I had to learn to live with that. I learnt to sit, think and enjoy my own company.

Given all the publicity and all the vitriol directed at you from some quarters, was it all worth a million pounds?
For a million pounds, yes it was. There have been some very difficult times and some things have been totally blown out of all proportion but the money will make me, my husband and my family very happy so, yes, that makes it all worthwhile.

The press was tipping you to win from the time the show went on air. Did you have any inclination that you might win, any secret tip-off or anything?
It was only what I read in the papers. I knew for a fact that the votes had been sealed. I saw it happen. Only Nigel Lythgoe knew the result and I knew there was no way he would risk telling anyone because he's the show's producer. There was a lot of speculation, which I hoped was true. The only clues I got were from watching the show and working it out like everyone else.

Which of the other contestants will you keep in touch with?
Obviously, some of us were picked because we wouldn't get on, so there are a few I won't be keeping in touch with, people like Adrian, JJ and Jayne. Jackie, of course, I will. Eve and Zoe, even

though they showed some bad traits, showed their true personalities on their *Survivor Unseen* shows. On that island there was so much pressure and it was very difficult so sometimes the nasty side of people's personalities came out. I think Andy is fantastic, like everyone else does. James is so funny, he has to be one of the funniest blokes I have ever met. He is so dry. Pete is a lovely bloke and Simon is great fun. Uzma is great as well.

When you applied for the show, you wrote this on your application form when asked why you thought you would be the "Ultimate Survivor": "Because without a shadow of doubt I would be the most strong-minded person on the island …. I would laugh in the face of danger and adversity and overcome challenges with innovative ideas and unusual tactics … for that reason, I would have to be the one and only remaining survivor." Were you always confident of winning?

I was always very confident and, Mark will confirm this, I said to him before I went, "I am going to win this." Before I went on the island a million pounds was all I was thinking of. For the first few weeks on the island, surviving was all I was thinking about. In the last few weeks, the million pounds reared its head again. I went on to win it and for no other reason than that I really, really wanted to win it. I had a fantastic experience. A better experience than I could ever imagine. But the million was all I wanted. I was away from my family and the people I love and the million pounds will help them. The experience was my own personal one but the money is for all of us.